YUGOSLAVIA'S DISINTEGRATION
AND
THE STRUGGLE FOR TRUTH

Alex N. Dragnich

EAST EUROPEAN MONOGRAPHS, BOULDER
DISTRIBUTED BY COLUMBIA UNIVERSITY PRESS, NEW YORK
1995

EAST EUROPEAN MONOGRAPHS, NO. CDXXXVI

To Adele

CONTENTS

Part III - Op-Ed Columns: Unpublished

(During the past several years, I submitted over 50 proposed op-ed columns to a number of major U.S. newspapers, usually simultaneously. The few that were published are reproduced in the preceding section. The following is a selection from among those not published, in chronological order.)

INTRODUCTION

In some three decades of academic life, I wrote a number of books and articles about Yugoslavia's history and politics. For the most part, these were scholarly research efforts motivated solely by a desire to produce objective studies. By the mid-1980s, when I was living in retirement and for all practical purposes had stopped writing about Yugoslavia, I began to notice certain developments in the Yugoslav picture that piqued my interest. Specifically, I noted that some Serbian Communists were speaking up in defense of Serbian interests. This was highly unusual, because in all of the years of the Tito dictatorship (he died in 1980) and after, the Serbian voice was never heard. Even Serbian Communists in high places were purged if they were suspected of Serbian nationalist views. In 1987-1988, I wrote the article, "The Rise and Fall of Yugoslavia: The Omen of the Upsurge of Serbian Nationalism" (published in June 1989), because it seemed to me that that was the most significant development in Yugoslavia at that time. In October, I published my first op-ed piece in the *Christian Science Monitor*.

As the signs of a possible breakup of Yugoslavia appeared on the horizon, I decided that it would be useful to write a brief history of Yugoslavia for the general reader. I did this in 1991 under the title, *Serbs and Croats: The Struggle in Yugoslavia*, published in October 1992.

At the same time, I was following the reporting of events, particularly when fighting broke out in Slovenia in the summer of 1991, and subsequently in Croatia and later in Bosnia-Herzegovina. I began to see errors in the reporting concerning Yugoslavia in general. One of the first was the oft-repeated assertion that the country had been a creation of the Treaty of Versailles. Other erroneous or unqualified assertions followed, such as "centuries-old blood feuds," "Serb-dominated Yugoslavia," "Serbian aggression," "ethnic cleansing," "Serbs conquer much of Bosnia." As time went on, I could not escape the conclusion that in more than forty years of following world developments, I was witnessing the most poorly reported -- really mis-reported -- international events that I could recall. Beginning in early 1992, I noticed a steadily increasing crescendo in the media (print and electronic) of blaming the Serbs solely for all the misdeeds in the Yugoslav tragedy. It was then that I began to write proposed op-ed pieces, some of which were published. Many more never saw the light of day. Both are included in the collection within these covers. I also wrote a number of longer articles, and they are reprinted here. In addition, I wrote many letters to editors of different newspapers and magazines.

I knew that much of what was being written was not so, to say nothing of the half-truths. I began to wonder why, and the ultimate answer to that question will have to be left to the historians. A number of my friends who were not Yugoslav experts, but who nevertheless knew something about the Balkans, asked why leaders in Britain, France, and the United States were so anti-Serb. They were particularly puzzled, because they knew that with the exception of the Greeks in the Second World War, the Serbs had been the only Balkan allies of these countries in the two world wars. Had the Serbs been on the other side, as were the Croats who, as allies of Hitler, had declared war on them as well as on the Soviet Union, these friends of mine could very well have said, "serves them right."

Knowledgeable observers asked: should not policy makers in the West, in thinking about long-range strategy, have considered that as loyal allies and the most populous people in the Balkans, the Serbs might have an important future role to play in that part of the world? Unfortunately, except on rare occasions, such words of caution were not heard in the media.

And as for the policy makers, they seemingly either (1) knew no Yugoslav or Serbian history, else they would have known that the Serbs would not be satisfied to live in Croatian- or Muslim-dominated states; or (2) the policy makers did not care; or (3) were in the pay (blackmailed?) of some one other than the government which they were chosen to serve.

Also puzzling was the fact that Western policy makers were fully in favor of self-determination for the secessionist groups, but not for the Serbs. Yet the Serbs were not doing anything different than the secessionist groups, i.e., they were seeking self-determination for their compatriots who wanted to continue living in one common state in which they had lived since 1918.

Finally, in answer to those who may believe that I am biased, I have a simple answer. Yes, I admit that I have three basic biases: one is on behalf of freedom, another is on behalf of truth, and still another is my desire to help my government in Washington avoid making mistakes in those areas of foreign affairs that I know something about. I may have sympathies for this or that cause, person, or party, but in my whole academic career -- teaching and writing -- I have sought not to let those intrude upon my objectivity. Others will have to judge to what extent I have succeeded.

PART I

THE RISE AND FALL OF YUGOSLAVIA:
THE OMEN OF THE UPSURGE OF SERBIAN NATIONALISM*

The demonstrations that rocked Yugoslavia in the autumn of 1988 can be understood only in terms of some critical historical background. First of all, it is important to note that these demonstrations have been among Serbs, the largest ethnic group making up over 40 percent of the total population (residing mainly in the republic of Serbia proper and its two autonomous provinces of Kosovo and Vojvodina, in Montenegro, and in Bosnia-Hercegovina). Secondly, it should be made clear that historically the Serbs have been the strongest supporters of the common state, support that seems to have been ebbing rapidly, with possible dire consequences for the integrity of Yugoslavia as a state. Thirdly, the demonstrations are the culmination of protests that have been building during the past six or seven years.

From the beginning of the Tito regime, the Serbs had many grievances, but these could not be expressed until after Tito's death. More precisely, the beginning of the ventilation of these grievances coincided with the violent demonstrations in 1981 by Albanians in Serbia's autonomous province of Kosovo, which led to revelations of many brutal Albanian actions against the Serbs and their Christian historical monuments in Kosovo. In brief, the news of the Albanian anti-Serb activities not only opened the floodgates of the dictatorship that had held back the airing of Serbian grievances, but in addition, greatly broadened the scope of these grievances.

The 1981 Albanian demonstrations were put down in some bloodshed and paved the way for disclosures that over the years monstrous crimes had been committed against the Serbian population of Kosovo, of which there had not been a word in the Yugoslav press. These crimes were of such a vicious and repugnant nature that the Yugoslav regime in Belgrade could not longer prevent their

* Reprinted with permission from: *East European Quarterly* 23 (June 1989), pp. 183-198.

public airing, at least in a limited way. This in turn led to the ventilation of many other grievances that the Serbs had not dared attempt
earlier. Or, to use another figure of speech, Kosovo was the straw
that "broke the camel's back."

   The ventilation of Serbian grievances that began to emerge
visibly after 1981 found Serbian intellectuals in the forefront. There
was no discernible patter or order to these complaints. Some
intellectuals concentrated on specific issues, such as Serbian wartime
activities during the Axis occupation, and the massacre of Serbs in
the Axis-supported quisling regime in the so-called Independent State
of Croatia. Others began reaching back to Comintern decisions
during the 1920s to find evidence that Yugoslav Communists were
following an anti-Serb policy early in their history. Still others
began examining the history of the formation of Communist
Yugoslavia in an effort to discover how and why Serbs were treated
as they had been.

   Before discussing the issues, however, let us take note of some
history. Yugoslavia (South Slavia or the land of the South Slavs) was
born on December 1, 1918. It represented the realization of a dream,
nourished especially by certain Serbian and Croatian political,
spiritual, and intellectual leaders. Among the best known of these
articulate dreamers were Bishop Josip Juraj Strossmayer, a Croat,
and Serbia's politician and statesman, Ilija Garashanin. Other
observers would quickly add the names of Franjo Rachki (Croat) and
Jovan Skerlich (Serb), and perhaps others.

   To all the dreamers, but especially to the South Slavs still
under Austro-Hungarian and Turkish rule who aspired to independence, their dreams were not entirely unrealistic. They had seen the
Serbs regain their independence and set up a free and democratic
political system. And they had seen tiny Montenegro, never fully
conquered by the Turks, existing as a second Serbian state, relatively
powerless but symbolically important. The dreamers outside Serbia
looked upon the Serbs as brothers, and with confidence that Serbia
would assist in their liberation. To many of these dreamers it seemed
only natural that they should even become a part of Serbia, perhaps
constituting an amorphous union of South Slavs whose precise nature
had not yet been defined.[1]

Many would argue that the creation of the new state, initially known as the Kingdom of the Serbs, Croats, and Slovenes, was premature. Be that as it may, the new state was brought into existence by practical political leaders - Prince Regent Alexander Karadjordjevich of Serbia and his Prime Minister, Nikola Pasich, and Ante Trumbich, President of the Yugoslav Committee. The creation was precipitated by World War I, in which Serbia and Montenegro suffered enormous losses. Consequently, it is understandable that the Serbs should feel that they sacrificed most in the establishment of the new state. Certainly it could not have been done without Serbia's unstinting support.

The Yugoslavia of the interwar years, which I have called the First Yugoslavia, is a chapter unto itself.[2] And while all generalizations are dangerous, I believe that it can be said that support for the new state was strongest among the Serbs and weakest among the Croats.

With the rapid collapse of Yugoslavia in 1941 under the blows of the armed might of the Axis powers, and the subsequent tragedy of genocide and civil war, the Serbs once more suffered the greatest losses.

With the creation of the Second Yugoslavia under Tito's Communist rule, the Serbs, although making up close to one half of the population and being twice as numerous as the next largest group (the Croats), were dispersed under a federal arrangement that discriminated against them in various ways. Yet they have been unable to vent their grievances, a situation that has changed considerably since Tito's death, but mainly in the past year or so.

I

What is Kosovo and why is it so important?[3] Kosovo was the cradle of the Serbian empire of the middle ages. It was the place where a defeat by the Turks in 1389 led to the enslavement of the Serbs for nearly 500 years. It is the area where the Serbs' principal religious and cultural monuments are located. It was the place that the Serbs, after gaining independence in the 19th century, planned to liberate and did so in the Balkan Wars of 1912-1913. In short, for all the Serbs, Kosovo is hallowed ground.

But the national composition of Kosovo has changed over the centuries, from being exclusively Serbian to approximately 80 percent Albanian at the present time. This came about for several reasons. After the Turkish conquest, many Serbs fled to Austria, Hungary, or elsewhere, to escape enslavement, while the Turks brought in more and more Islamized Albanians as their loyal servants. Bulgarian occupation in World War I brought many Albanians to Kosovo. At the end of the Second World War, Tito helped to bring to Kosovo at least 100,000 Albanians. Moreover, toward the end of the war, he promised the Kosovo Albanians that they would be free to join Albania after the end of the conflict if they so desired.[4]

While it can be said that Tito reneged on his promise, he did allow them to form an autonomous province within the republic of Serbia. The Kosovo Albanians, however, soon began the process of making Kosovo ethnically pure, engaging in every conceivable tactic to force the Serbs to leave Kosovo.

The Kosovo Albanians raped and pillaged. They desecrated Serbian cemeteries and Serbian religious institutions. They set Serbian barns and haystacks on fire. They cut down timber on Serbian lands, and constructed buildings on Serbian property. No method or tactic was excluded in the effort to force the Serbs to flee Kosovo. And they did so in large numbers.

Many of the injustices inflicted upon the Serbs by Albanians have in recent years been reported in the Yugoslav press. For example, the authoritative voice of Yugoslav Communists, *Borba*, reported that a working group of the Yugoslav parliament, in which the Serbs were a minority, concluded that the majority of Serbian complaints were justified, that there was illegal seizing of land, and that there was no respect for the mother-tongue (Serbo-Croatian). *Borba* also cited a whole series of incidents where Serbs were denied basic cultural and property rights.[5]

While these various crimes were being committed in Kosovo, the local authorities (Communist) looked the other way or actually conspired with the perpetrators. Protests by Serbs to Kosovo as well as to federal authorities were to no avail. Although theoretically an autonomous province of Serbia, Kosovo has been ruled as if it were a sovereign state.

Since the Albanian demonstrations in 1981, demanding the status of a republic or even outright annexation to Albania, the picture has changed a little. The Albanian persecution of Serbs has continued, but there has been an increasing public outcry by Serbs in Serbia, although the Yugoslav media have until recently given it little notice. The petitions from Kosovo Serbs (some with over 2,000 signatures) have received supporting statements from well-known Serbian intellectuals in Serbia. The Belgrade authorities have admitted that while many of the allegations in the petitions are valid, the petitions could not be accepted because they contained expressions of "Great Serbian chauvinism."

Some apologists for the Kosovo Albanians made an effort to equate Great Albanian nationalism with Great Serbian nationalism, but the Serbs ask" "How many Albanians were forced to leave Yugoslavia and go to Albania as a result of Great Serbian nationalism?"

It is interesting to note that a number of retired Yugoslav army officers, mainly colonels and generals, have used some of the harshest language in condemning what has befallen the Serbs of Kosovo. In statements sharply critical of the Yugoslav regime, "which publicizes South African terrorism while hiding from the Yugoslav public the terrorist acts of Albanians and the brutal actions of the state security organs in Kosovo-Metohija," several have resigned as party members.[6]

In short, for the Serbs as a whole the revelations about the horrifying actions against the Kosovo Serbs was the "genie" that escaped from the Yugoslav political bottle. Consequently, they began to write and at public meetings to talk about a whole series of injustices that the Serbs have endured and had not been able to talk about. To be sure, much of this has not seen the light of day in the Yugoslav media, although widely publicized abroad. Of the various topics or themes that have been "taboo" in the past, several have been able to surface publicly in Yugoslavia in the past year or two. Among these are the following: (1) an objective examination of the role of the Chetnik guerrilla movement in World War II; (2) the massacre of the Serbs in the Axis-puppet regime in Croatia; (3) the postwar scattering of Serbs over several republics; (4) a critical appraisal of charges of Serbian hegemony in the First Yugoslavia (1918-1941).

II

The Yugoslav public had to wait forty years to hear that the guerrilla movement led by Draza Mihailovich in World War II was not treasonous. Many Serbs (and others) knew the truth, but nothing positive about Mihailovich's Chetnik movement could be written. In 1985, however, the public heard from a historian, Communist party member, and person whom the regime had regarded as loyal, that much of what they had heard on the subject was false.

In a scholarly objective work, entitled *The Allies and the Yugoslav War Drama*,[7] Veslin Djuretich told the Yugoslav public that both Mihailovich's movement and Tito's Partisans were anti-fascist. By using the terms "Chetnik Commandant" and "Partisan Commandant," he put the two men on an equal footing. As a matter of fact, he points out that in some areas where the Partisans were weak, the Chetniks were the only anti-fascist force. Moreover, from the way he describes the beginning of the civil war in Yugoslavia, one can conclude that it was begun by Partisan attacks upon the Chetniks rather than the other way round, as regime accounts would have had it.

Soon after Djuretich's "bombshell" hit the bookstores, he, a member of the prestigious Serbian Academy of Sciences and Arts, was expelled from the party, and the two readers who had read his manuscript and recommended its publication received party reprimands.

Djuretich's two-volume work is far-ranging, but this is not the place for an extensive review. Its chief significance lies in that it constitutes the first open rehabilitation of the Mihailovich movement in Yugoslav historiography. While he views Mihailovich as counter-revolutionary (i.e., against the Communist revolution), he certainly does not view him as an enemy collaborator. Moreover, while Djuretich acknowledges considerable suffering during the war by all peoples of Yugoslavia, he insists that only the Serbs, *as a people*, were on nearly everyone's hit list, with untold losses in human life, to say nothing of property.[8]

Djuretich's book makes clear that the Allies decisively influenced the future of Yugoslavia. The whole strategy for international recognition of Tito's movement was led and financed by Moscow, and Tito's whole effort, military and political, was in

Moscow's global interests. On the other hand, Churchill's abandonment of Mihailovich, thinking that he would thereby outsmart Stalin, proved catastrophic for the Chetnik leader and for the Serbs, without any benefit to Churchill.

It is worth noting that early in his work Djuretich categorically rejects the thesis (long popular in Tito's Yugoslavia) of Serbian hegemony in prewar Yugoslavia.[9] This charge, he says, was borrowed by the Communists from anti-Serb parties in prewar years. The Serbian people, he says, did not reap any economic benefits as a result of prewar government policy. On the contrary, he points out that the lion's share of investment went to the more industrialized northern regions (Slovenia and Croatia), incidentally a pattern followed by Tito's Yugoslavia.

III

Another "taboo topic" was the massacre of Serbs during World War II. Although some three-quarters of a million Serbs - men, women, and children - were massacred in cold blood by the adherents of the Ustashe regime in Nazi-Fascist satellite Croatia during World War II, it was impossible to write about it for years. Even when mentioned in the press it was always the fascist elements who did the killing, with no mention of the Croats. The Tito regime made it clear that to write about the crimes of the Ustashe Croatians would undermine its "Brotherhood and Unity" theme.

Recent years have, however, seen the publication in Yugoslavia of a number of books and articles dealing with the subject. Vuk Draskovich, one of Serbia's most talented writers, has recently written two books, *Knife* and *Prayer*, about these massacres.[10] He maintains that at least 1.5 million Serbs perished there. Yet four decades later, he says, there is not a novel, drama, elegy, lament, or newspaper feature concerning the Ustashe genocide by a Croatian author. By contrast, he points to Willy Brandt, who even though he fought against the Nazis, nevertheless went to Warsaw after the war and in the name of the German people knelt at the monument to the martyrs who were killed by the Nazis. Moreover, he says: "We owe it to the dead" that the memorial plaque at the Jasenovac death camp be changed to show that in the main it was the Serbs, Jews, and Gypsies who were massacred there and that the executioners were the Ustashe.

When a Zagreb newspaper (*Vjesnik*) attacked him as a "Great Serb," Draskovich in September 1986 went on the attack. He readily admitted that he was a Great Serb, and added: "God forbid that I should be a little-Serb." He pointed out that Great Serbianism "never grew out of hate for any other people, and never led toward human downfall, collective madness, and genocide." Only the Great Serbs created Serbian culture and Serbian history. Moreover, he said that Great Serbdom always sought to defend its own, "but never to build its freedom and its fortune on someone else's lack of freedom or misfortune." In a sort of parting shot, Draskovich proclaimed: "Steadily, for four decades someone is forcing the Serbian people to admit sins which they never committed, and requesting ever new proofs that they have rehabilitated themselves." But Draskovich's rejoinders were not published in Yugoslavia, only abroad.[11]

IV

One topic that received little attention in Yugoslavia while Tito was still alive, but which has received considerable note in recent years, has been the scattering of Serbs after the Communist victory. The Tito regime avowedly decided that in order to deal with the nationalities problem a federal arrangement was needed. Tito, however, was first of all desirous of weakening the Serbs. The result was six republics and two autonomous provinces. The Croats got their republic (but with a Serbian minority), as did the Slovenes and Macedonians. The Serbs got a republic, but with two autonomous provinces within it - Kosovo (to accommodate the Albanian majority there) and Vojvodina (to accommodate the Hungarian minority there). As it turned out, Serbia had very little control over these so-called autonomous units. Moreover, to further weaken the Serbs, a separate republic of Montenegro was created, even though its people think of themselves as Serbs. Finally, a separate republic of Bosnia-Hercegovina was created, ostensibly to eliminate the competition there between the Serbs and Croats and to satisfy the large Moslem population there.

The long and the short of it is that Serbs are to be found in significant numbers in every other republic except Slovenia. The result is that 40% of all Serbs live outside the confines of "narrow Serbia," i.e., exclusive of the autonomous provinces. For the Serbs this is a terrible injustice, particularly since they are subjected to all sorts of indignities in the other republics.

Serbs in the republics of Bosnia-Hercegovina and Croatia, especially teachers, professors, and literary people, have been particularly singled out as questionable citizens. The regime actions against the Serbs in these republics, often accompanied by the flight of Serbs to Serbia, have been sharply protested by Serbian intellectuals in Belgrade. The latter see in all this, unless actions are taken to put an end to it, steps toward a "new Kosovo."

It is estimated that four to five million Serbs live outside the narrow confines of Serbia proper, the largest number being in Bosnia-Hercegovina (about 1.5 million), with the next largest number being in Vojvodina and Croatia, although significant numbers live in Montenegro, Macedonia, and of course Kosovo. Tragically, the Serbs in Serbia have come to feel that not only can they not protect their brothers in the other republics, but that in addition, they are not even in a position to protect Serbs in Serbia.

In an appeal in December 1985 to the authorities in Croatia, a leading Serbian writer (Vuk Draskovich) complained about what he called "cultural genocide" against Serbs in Croatia.[12] He pointed out that under Austria-Hungary tens of newspapers were printed in the Cyrillic alphabet in the areas where Serbs lived. He also pointed out that during World War II, the Partisans in Croatia printed an underground paper in Cyrillic. He brought out that after the war Serbs in Croatia had their organizations and newspapers. Moreover, he said, textbooks for Serbian children were printed in Cyrillic and that Cyrillic even had priority where the majority of school children were Serbian. In the period 1950 to 1980, Draskovich observed that there was a gradual elimination of all newspapers in Cyrillic as well as all cultural institutions which contained the name "Serb."

What is crucial to Draskovich is that the rights to equality which were promised by the Partisans, and for which rights the Serbs of Croatia fought, have been a shameful mockery.

Draskovich goes further, and says that today the Serbian people of Yugoslavia are further removed from the ideal of cultural and spiritual unity than in the first half of the previous century. "The Serbs are a culturally and spiritually endangered minority in Croatia and Bosnia-Hercegovina, while in Kosovo and Metohija there is an effort to exterminate them ethnically."[13]

These observations of Draskovich have not appeared in the Yugoslav media.

V

Although touched upon already, a certain aspect of the Titoist policy of reducing Serbian influence deserves special note. This is the policy calculated to get the inhabitants of Montenegro to think of themselves as Montenegrins and not Serbs. This policy went so far as to seek to deny that the greatest Serbian literary figure, Njegosh (19th century Bishop and ruler of Montenegro) was a Serb. Njegosh could not be listed in the encyclopedia or in the section on Serbian literature as a Serb. In the printing of an anthology of his works, Njegosh was censored by cutting out the words "Serb" and "Serbian" wherever they appeared. Moreover, at the time of the dedication of the new (and controversial) Njegosh mausoleum on Mount Lovchen a few years ago, only parts of his classic, *The Mountain Wreath*, that did not contain the words "Serb," "Serbian," or "Serbs" were read.

These attempts to re-write or to re-orient history had few takers except for a handful of intellectuals in Montenegro. But it was impossible for anyone to take issue with official policies. In the summer of 1986, however, a literary bombshell hit the Belgrade bookstores in the form of a book entitled *Montenegrins About Themselves*,[14] which is an answer to those, as the author maintains, who "grossly falsify history." The author is none other than Batrich Jovanovich, a Communist party member since 1940 and the holder of the Partisan Medal of 1941, meaning that he was among the first in Tito's movement. He is also a former member of the Yugoslav parliament, who has held a number of other responsible positions in Yugoslavia.

Jovanovich has read most of the historical works by Monte-negrins and has found that they always thought of themselves as Serbs, many asserting that they were the best Serbs. Jovanovich told a Belgrade interviewer that he had also read many books about Montenegrins written in French, Russian, English, German, and Italian, and all of them treat Montenegrins as Serbs, as part of the Serbian people.

VI

As is evident from much of the above, Serbian intellectuals were in the forefront of raising a whole host of questions about Serbia's position in Yugoslavia. They were virtually unanimous in concluding that Serbia was in an unequal position in the Yugoslav federation. It is of more than passing interest that this conviction is widespread among Serbian intellectuals, most of whom have been known for their support of an integral Yugoslav state, and many of whom are former members of the Communist party.

One of the things that many of them pointed to first was the historic anti-Serbian mentality of the Comintern, two of whose dogmas were Serbian hegemony and the need for the dissolution of Yugoslavia.[15] Professor Mihailo Markovich pointed out that economic statistics refute the first of these: after two decades of so-called hegemony, economically Serbia was behind Slovenia and Croatia. Moreover, he added sarcastically that in 1941 the Serbs entered into a struggle "against the regime in which they enjoyed so-called hegemony."[16]

Another Serbian writer published a document showing that in prewar Yugoslavia an anti-Serb agreement was signed by Mose Pijade on behalf of the Yugoslav Communist party and Dr. Mile Budak on behalf of the Croatian Ustashe organization, that their aims could not be realized until the backbone of Serbdom and the Orthodox Church were broken.[17]

Another thorny issue for many Serbian intellectuals is the way that the Yugoslav federation was constituted after World War II.[18] In essence, they conclude: (1) it was formed without the participation of the Serbian people, and (2) the result is severe injustices to the Serbs and to Serbia. Kosta Cavoski notes that the republic of Serbia was reduced to Serbia's pre-1912 boundaries, thus not recognizing any of her gains in the Balkan Wars or in World War I.[19] He points out that if the post-1912 boundaries or those of 1939 were used, Serbia would be immeasurably larger. Moreover, he observes that the decisions of the Partisan Second Avnoj Session provided for six units in the forthcoming federation, and only later were decisions taken to create the autonomous units of Kosovo-Metohija and Vojvodina inside the republic of Serbia, but without consulting the Serbs. He also reports that at the constituent assembly in 1946, proposals for autonomous units in other republics (e.g., Dalmatia) were rejected by top Communist party leaders.[20]

In the words of Mihailo Markovich, "The borders of the Serbian republic were so drawn that millions of Serbs remained minorities in other republics.... Serbia found itself in the absurd political position with a third of its population in other republics, divided into three parts in its own republic, deprived of any legal or political status in its central part ('in Serbia without provinces')." Moreover, he observed, "Serbs, who were the first South Slavs who succeeded in liberating themselves and forming their independent state, are the only nation in Yugoslavia which is deprived of its autonomy, unity, large parts of its territory and the right to be organized as a state."[21]

Adding insult to injury, in the view of these intellectuals, is the fact that once scattered among the other republics and provinces, the Serbian minorities there are not entitled to the minority rights guarantees of the Yugoslav Constitution. The explanation is simple. The constitution recognizes nations and nationalities. The former are the major groups that have their own republics (e.g., Serbia, Croatia, etc.), hence they are not minorities. The nationalities are the groups (e.g., Albanians, Hungarians, Italians, etc.) that do not have their own republics, and hence are minorities. By constitutional definition, therefore, the Serbs who live outside of Serbia are not minorities even when in fact they are. For example, in Kosovo, where they have been subjected to all sorts of brutalities at the hands of the Albanian majority of some 80 percent, the Serbian minority of less than 20 percent is not entitled to the minority guarantees of the Yugoslav Constitution. Mihailo Markovich points out that the "Serbs who live in other republics do not enjoy all those minority rights which they used to have under Austria-Hungary...."[22]

Cavoski has urged the amendment of the Yugoslav Constitution so that the Serbian people would "enjoy the same rights and freedoms, and the constitutional guarantees of those freedoms and rights that are enjoyed by the other peoples who make up the Yugoslav federation."[23]

Why did Serbian communists permit these things to happen? Markovich says that while other Yugoslav peoples could represent their respective interests, Serbian communists could not, because their "basic duty was to attack Serbian nationalism at every opportunity." It is characteristic, he continues, that in "1940 the Communist party of Croatia and the Communist party of Slovenia were created, but ... Serbian cadres were not allowed until the very end of the war to create a Serbian Communist party and the Anti-Fascist Council of Serbia."[24] In the course of the war, he concludes, Serbian Partisans and Communists were "naive, credulous, and a bit obsessed by their ancestors' guilt of 'great Serbian hegemonism'."[25]

As Markovich suggests, in the early years of the Tito regime even Serbian Communists went along with anti-Serbian decisions. Later they complained about the weaknesses of the Serbian element of the party. In the 1970s, for example, Milovan Djilas, a onetime close collaborator of Tito's, reminded me several times that the "Serbian cadre in the party is weak." And Dobrica Chosich, wartime political commissar and subsequently Serbia's leading novelist, said to me, "Only about 1965 did we discover that Tito hated Serbs. Prior to that time he managed to hide that hatred." More recently, he publicly raised the question of the Serbs' own culpability: "Why did we Partisans and revolutionaries for so long follow, praise, and worship those who deceived, subjugated, bribed, humiliated, and disgraced us in front of our children and the whole world?"[26]

Several Serbian intellectuals have emphasized Serbia's inequality in the economic sphere.[27] Mihailo Markovich points out that in several aspects of the economic picture - notably the degree of development in comparison to the other republics and the contributions to the fund for less developed areas - Serbia is left behind. Serbia, he notes, contributes 53.2 percent of its net accumulation to the fund for less developed areas, while Slovenia and Croatia contribute between 36 and 37 percent of theirs. Moreover, he observes, the value of basic industrial resources per worker in thousands of dinars is 2.7 in Serbia; 3.6 in Slovenia; 2.9 in Croatia; 3.3 in Bosnia-Hercegovina; 3.5 in Vojvodina; 5.0 in Montenegro; and 3.5 in Kosovo. In addition, consumption of kilowatts of electricity is less in Serbia than in the other republics and autonomous provinces (only Croatia falls below Serbia in this respect).

In an attempt to find the reason for Serbia's "relative poverty," Markovich examines several factors - poorer work productivity, poorer organization, lower efficiency, and a non-rational relationship between imports and exports - and provides statistics to show that none of these reasons hold.[28] Rather, he finds that the answer is basically political. Investment in Serbia has been less than in the other republics, while prices for certain goods and services have been kept artificially low in the other republics. For example, the price of electricity that Serbia exports to the other republics is kept artificially low, while Serbia has to pay world market prices for petroleum and petroleum derivatives that it gets from the other republics. All of this, he concludes, is the result of political decisions.

Closely related to much of the above was the 1986 abortive memorandum of the Serbian Academy of Sciences and Arts in Belgrade. The memorandum was prompted by what the vast majority of the Academy's membership perceived as the broad and serious crisis in Yugoslav society - political, economic, social, national, etc. A draft of the memorandum was stolen before it could be put in final form, and bitterly attacked in the Yugoslav press as being motivated by the spirit of "Serbian hegemonism." Hence it never officially saw the light of day.[29] The 74-page draft was not even referred to in the attacks by its right title ("The Crisis of the Yugoslav Economy and Society"). The most sensitive part of the memorandum is that dealing with Serbian grievances against the Yugoslav Communist Party, against Stalin and the Comintern, and against non-Serbian party leaders, such as Tito and Vladimir Bakarich (Croats) and Edward Kardelj (Slovene). Subsequently, the Serbian Academy defied the League of Communists by giving full support to the Academy's leaders and by denying that it incited Serbian nationalism.

VII

All of the foregoing must be viewed in the context of two major considerations: (1) The Serbs, the largest nationality group in Yugoslavia (close to 40%), contributed the most to the creation of Yugoslavia in the first place; (2) under the Tito regime, the Serbs were told in word and deed that they were the least deserving. Prior to World War I, the Serbs were the only ones that were independent (Serbia and Montenegro), and fought as allies of the Western Powers. Without the Serbian army and political organization, and without the determination of the Serbian political leadership, notably Prince Regent Alexander, there could not have been any Yugoslavia.

Serbian sacrifices toward the formation of a common South Slav state can hardly be over-estimated.

Under Tito, however, the Serbs were told that they were at fault for all the things that went wrong in the Yugoslavia of the interwar years. They were told that they had been guilty of hegemony, of being Great Serbs, of seeking to lord it over the other national groups. Communists (high and low), including the Serbian ones, never tired of their favorite cry - denouncing Serbian nationalism. At every turn, there was a conscious and persistent effort to make the Serbs feel inferior.

Why did Tito do it? Simply put, he feared the Serbs the most. They were the most numerous. They had a history of hostility to tyrants. During the Partisan struggle to seize power in the course of World War II, Tito had had no success in Serbia until near the end of the conflict, when Soviet forces drove the Nazis out of Belgrade and turned the capital over to him. Milovan Djilas, one of his closest wartime collaborators, reports that the Partisans could not have taken Belgrade without Soviet help, even with the 100 or so tanks that the Russians had given them.[30] Moreover, he says, that when they got into Belgrade, they did not find one single Communist there.[31] Throughout the war, on the other hand, Mihailovich was strong in Serbia. In the years after the war, Tito was sure that he had not made a mistake, because the Serbs, especially Belgrade, never warmed up to him or to Communist rule.

VIII

What does all this mean for the future of Yugoslavia? Without even touching upon the chaos in the Yugoslav economy, it is difficult to conclude other than that the outlook is grim. When the largest nationality group, and the one that has been most supportive of a common state, is as disaffected as it appears to be, the future for Yugoslavia cannot be bright.

No doubt speaking for a large majority of his compatriots, Mihailo Markovich, in setting forth some conditions for the continued existence of a common state, "to the extent that all of its people desire it," concluded:

> The present situation in Yugoslavia cannot be maintained....The only solution is a democratized and federalized Yugoslavia on the basis of full national equality. Those people who do not desire that type of equality show thereby that they are not prepared to live in union. Serbs should not be those who would prevent them from leaving the union.[32]

Prospects for peaceful change are not auspicious. As indicated above, a draft memorandum by a committee of the prestigious Serbian Academy of Sciences and Arts suggested ways out of the general Yugoslav crisis, which it said might have "such a catastrophic result as the dissolution of Yugoslavia as a state." When the draft was leaked to the authorities, the regime press attacked it as Great Serbian nationalism. About the same time, a group of prominent Serbian intellectuals, members of the Committee for the Defense of Freedom of Thought and Expression, addressed a plea to the Yugoslav parliament and to the Yugoslav public, urging eleven specific steps that would dismantle one-party communism in Yugoslavia and establish a democratic system. The party's reaction was predictable: it indicated, as it has done in recent years, that it wanted to find a solution to the crisis and to silence the critics. So far is has been unable to do either.

One of the stumbling blocks to a solution has been the political system that Tito bequeathed to the Yugoslavs, which has encouraged narrow nationality views. Under the collective presidency and the rotation system that is part and parcel of that system, all republics (and in effect, the autonomous provinces as well) share in the power structure. The system operates on the unanimity principle, which gives them a veto in virtually all important matters. The net result has been a good deal of political paralysis, modified from time to time by mutually acceptable compromises that may or may not be in accord with the constitution or the laws.

In the midst of the seeming paralysis, Slobodan Milosevich, who in 1987 emerged as the leader of the Serbian Communist Party, in the course of 1988 rapidly proceeded to mobilize the growing discontent. His basic demand is that Serbia be given equality in the federation, and specifically that it be given power over her autonomous provinces in Kosovo and Vojvodina.

Some of Milosevich's critics have suggested that he was a rabble rouser fanning the flames of discord. A more reasonable interpretation, however, is that he realized that unless something could be done about the Serbian grievances there was a threat not only to Communist rule, but to the survival of Yugoslavia as a state as well. Ironically, for the Serbian masses who have no use for a communist system, this was a dubious development. Without much doubt, they realize that for the time being no anti-communist (or even non-communist) leader would be permitted to arise. It is testimony to their desperation that they have responded to him as they have.

The increasingly oppressive economic situation, with inflation running over 200 percent, has provided a much safer basis for protests than nationality issues. This is not to say that economic complaints are not serious - among Serbs as among other Yugoslavs - but they should not be permitted to obscure the more basic and fundamental nationality grievances.

The other nationalities have also expressed their economic complaints, but they do not have nationality ones, except for the Albanians in Kosovo, who want the status of a republic or even the right to join Albania. At the same time, the non-Serbs are not too sympathetic to the Serbs. They fear that an amelioration of Serbian grievances would result in Serbian unity, with Serbia playing a predominant role in the federation. They like it the way it has been in the past - a divided and weak Serbia.

The Croats, the next largest nationality group, have exhibited no sympathy for Serbia's difficult position. The Slovenes, who historically have worked well with the Serbs, have become increasingly critical. And the leaders in Bosnia-Hercegovina have their hands full with their Islamic fundamentalists. Slovenia and Croatia, the two republics with the largest per capita income, believe (wrongly, in my opinion) that they could go it alone, that they do not need Yugoslavia. Most economists who know something of the country and with whose views I am familiar, are convinced that both Croatia and Slovenia need the Yugoslav market, that outside Yugoslavia they could not compete with Western European countries.

The Serbs have, however, found strong sympathy in Macedonia, which has its own Albanian minority. There is widespread sympathy also in Montenegro, but the Communist leaders there have been eager to protect their special privileges. The large number of Montenegrin intellectuals who live in Belgrade have been strongly supportive of the Serbian position and have been especially vocal.

The one thing that all Yugoslavs agree upon is that Communism has been a failure.

* * *

As the reader has been aware, the subject of this piece has been Serbian grievances and their impact on Yugoslavia's future. I was led to examine these because (1) until the recent past we heard very little about them, and (2) the Serbs, the largest nationality group and in the past the strongest supporter of the Yugoslav state, are having second thoughts about their past devotion to the idea of a common state, which suggests that this might be the most important development in present day Yugoslavia, with critical implications for United States foreign policy there and in the Balkans generally. Is Yugoslavia another Lebanon in the making?

NOTES

1. See Dimitrijie Djordjevic (ed.), *The Creation of Yugoslavia* (Santa Barbara, CA: Clio Books, 1980).

2. See my book, *The First Yugoslavia: Search for a Viable Political System* (Stanford, CA: Hoover Institution Press, 1983).

3. For a brief treatment, see Alex N. Dragnich and Slavko Todorovich, *The Saga of Kosovo: Focus on Serbian-Albanian Relations* (Boulder, CO: East European Monographs, 1984).

4. *Ibid.*, pp. 143-145.

5. April 9, 1986.

6. For example, see statement of Colonel Radislav V. Filipović to the Yugoslav and Serbian parliaments, printed in *Eparhiski observer* (Grayslake, IL), November 15, 1986. Also, see letter of Partisan commandant Ljubiša Veselinović to the Communist Central Committee, explaining his suicide in the middle of Belgrade, printed in *Naša reč* (London), June-July, 1986, pp. 16-17. The letter was published in a Yugoslav publication (*Svet*) April 18, 1986.

7. Veselin Djuretić, *Saveznici i Jugoslovenska ratna drama*, 2 volumes (Belgrade: Balkan Institute of the Serbian Academy of Sciences and Arts, 1985).

8. *Ibid.*, p. 6.

9. *Ibid.*, p. 13ff.

10. *Nož* (Belgrade: Zapis, 1983) and *Molitva* (Belgrade: Nova knjiga, 1985).

11. Serbian text printed in *Eparhiski observer*, October 1, 1986.

12. Serbian text printed in *Amerikanski Srbobran* (Pittsburgh, PA), February 26, 1986.

13. *Ibid.*

14. Batrić Jovanović, *Crnogorci o sebi: prilog istoriji crnogorske nacije* (Belgrade: Narodna knjiga, 1986).

15. For example, Mihailo Marković, "Jugoslovenska kriza i srpsko pitanje," (unpublished paper, Belgrade, August 1986), p. 17. Some of the same points were made by Dr. Radoslav Stojanović, "Inter-Ethnic Conflicts in Yugoslavia," (unpublished paper, College Park, MD, October 1987), pp. 29-35.

16. *Ibid.*

17. Zoran D. Nenezić, *Masoni u Jugoslaviji (1764-1980): Pregled istorije slobodnog zidarstva u Jugoslaviji, Prilozi i gradja* (Belgrade: Narodna knjiga, 1984), pp. 551-53.

18. See Kosta Čavoški, *Iz istorije stvaranja nove Jugoslavije* (London: *Naša reč*, 1987); Mihailo Marković, "Societal Development in Serbia after the Second World War," (unpublished paper, Belgrade, 1986), pp. 5ff; Radoslav Stojanović, *op. cit.*

19. Čavoški, *op. cit.*, pp. 14-15.

20. *Ibid.*, pp. 20-21.

21. Mihailo Marković, "Societal Development," pp. 3, 8, and 12.

22. *Ibid.*, p. 12. Also, see his "Jugoslovenska kriza," pp. 25-28.

23. *Naša reč* (February 1988), pp. 2-3.

24. Mihailo Marković, "Jugoslovenska kriza," p. 19.

25. *Ibid.*, p. 5.

26. *Književne novine*, June 1, 1987.

27. For example, Mihailo Marković, "Jugoslovenska kriza," pp. 20-25; Radoslav Stojanović, "Inter-Ethnic Conflicts," pp. 47-48.

28. Marković, *ibid.*, p. 23ff.

29. Texts of the draft were not published in Yugoslavia, but several were in the West, among them one by the American Serbian Heritage Foundation in Los Angeles and Serbian National Shield Society of Canada.

30. *Wartime* (New York: Harcourt Brace Jovanovich, 1977), p. 406.

31. *Ibid.*, p. 419.

32. Mihailo Marković, "Jugoslovenska kriza," p. 35.

SERBIA'S POLITICAL DEVELOPMENT AND WESTERN EUROPE'S POLITICAL TRADITION[*]

After being under Turkish colonial rule for nearly five centuries, Serbia regained her independence in the 19th century and in a few decades proceeded to establish a political system on par with the best in the Western political tradition.

At the outset, it is well to pause and to ask what is the Western political tradition. We all know it under the general name of democracy. It was essentially a march from monarchical absolutism to popular rule. This was a long process, in some countries taking centuries.

The classical example of the Western political tradition is England. As in other societies, England in its early history was ruled by an autocratic ruler - a monarch. Limitations on the monarch occurred in several stages. The beginning was Magna Carta in 1215, but it was several centuries later before Parliament was recognized as supreme (1688). Moreover, it was not until the 18th century that Parliament gained the power to hold the king's ministers politically responsible for their acts, i.e., the power to oust them if they failed to have the confidence of Parliament. This is what we call ministerial responsibility, i.e., the obligation of ministers to resign when their policies or proposals meet with defeat in parliament or in elections at the polls.

In some cases, even when parliaments won supremacy, they were not popularly elected bodies. In England, for example, it was not until the 19th century that the extension of the franchise made great strides. The best known steps in this direction were the reform acts of 1832 and 1867. It was not, however, until the early decades of the 20th century that England achieved universal suffrage. As the

---

[*] Author's copyright: *Serbia's Historical Heritage* (Boulder, CO: East European Monographs,1994), pp. 39-51.

suffrage was extended, i.e., as the House of Commons was democratized, the power of the upper house (House of Lords) gradually lost its power to veto acts of the House of Commons.

Hence the essence of the Western political tradition constituted the coming into being of constitutions that limited and channeled political power so that in the end the people were governed by ministers who were responsible to a popularly elected legislature.

We call such political systems parliamentary democracies. As we know, such systems are characterized by the existence of basic freedoms of speech, press, association, free elections, independent courts, and other guarantees.

Serbia's political history has been different than that of England, and yet there are some similarities. In the middle ages, Serbia was the strongest empire in the Balkans for over 100 years. Basically, Serbia was governed on the monarchical principle, with the monarch most often having the title of tsar. There were popular assemblies, but these were mainly of a consultative nature.

The political heritage of medieval Serbia was Tsar Dušan's Code of Laws,[1] named after Serbia's ruler. The first part of the Code of Laws was inaugurated in 1349 and part two in 1354. It was an independent Serbian creation, although Dušan may have borrowed or adapted certain principles from Byzantine law. The Code is a combination of public and private law, seeking to regularize and systematize social, economic, and political relations. It was probably made necessary as a way of recognizing the economic and social changes that had taken place. It was designed to protect the rights of peasants as well as the rights of the nobility. It included penalties, among other things, for homicide, arson, theft, drunkenness, swearing, bribery, and counterfeiting.

The Code also laid down rules for judges and for the clergy. Most important, the Code declared the supremacy of the law and that no one was above the law.

Unfortunately, Serbian political developments were stopped by the Ottoman victory over Serbia at Kosovo in 1389, and the annihilation of the Serbian state in the following century.

From the very moment of the beginning of their struggle to regain their independence, the Serbs were concerned with putting limits on their leaders' powers.[2] Although Karadjordje was the unquestioned leader of the Serbian uprising against the Turks in 1804, a council of the principal regional leaders was soon created, forcing Karadjordje to seek their counsel and approval.

Although the uprising collapsed by 1813, a new one erupted in 1815, under the leadership of one of Karadjordje's earlier regional leaders, Miloš Obrenović. Miloš proved to be an adept and shrewd manipulator of the Turkish Paša in Belgrade. Moreover, his own people were not initially inclined to question him or his tactics. By 1826, however, Miloš was forced to create a Council of State, even though he had the power to veto its acts.

A few years later, in 1835, some prominent Serbs demanded a new constitution, and one was written. But it never really went into effect, partly because of the intervention of Metternich (Austria) and Nicholas I (Russia), sworn enemies of constitutionalism. Of course, this suited Miloš.

Some who were not happy with Miloš's leadership conspired with Turkish authorities in Constantinople. This latter, while recognizing Miloš as Prince and the right of hereditary succession for the Obrenovićes, nevertheless granted to Serbia a type of constitution, known as the Hatisherif of 1838. It laid the foundations for the next twenty years of Serbia's political and governmental life. It divided power between Miloš and a Council in such a way that the latter had a veto over Miloš's actions. The Council leaders styled themselves as Defenders of the Constitution, i.e., defenders of the Hatisherif which gave them the upper hand over the Prince.

Miloš realized that he had been shorn of power and 1839 abdicated. His abdication was followed by the twenty-year rule of the Defenders of the Constitution, an oligarchical group that was initially popular. It should be noted that after Miloš's abdication, the Turks recognized Alexander Karadjordjević as hereditary prince of Serbia, but he had no more power than the Council was willing to tolerate.

Increasingly, over the years the Council and the Prince came into conflicts that were not easily resolved. Moreover, the Council oligarchy became alienated from the people, so that after 20 years of its rule, the members were scarcely known outside their offices.

In 1858, an assembly (Skupština) was called by mutual agreement of the Prince and the Council, each thinking it could outsmart the other. Instead, the Skupština ousted both and brought back Miloš Obrenović. Miloš lived less than two additional years, and was succeeded by his son Mihailo.

Prince Mihailo's reign (1860-1868) is generally described as benevolent or enlightened despotism. Nevertheless, popular stirrings were much in evidence, sparked in part by students recently returned from Western Europe. A Skupština had been established, but it met only every three years and lacked real legislative power. It managed, however, to address a number of subjects and to direct questions to Mihailo and his ministers. This was also the time that some rudimentary steps were taken that later led to the organization of political parties.

Following Mihailo's assassination in 1868, there being no direct heir to the throne, a grand nephew, Milan Obrenović, then a 14-year old student in Paris, was proclaimed Prince. During his minority, a three-man regency was chosen to exercise the royal powers. During that four year period, important and far-reaching steps were taken in the development of Serbia's political institutions. The principal leader in this effort was the First Regent, Jovan Ristić.[3] Ristić had studied in Germany and France, and had a doctorate from Heidelberg University. He had served under Mihailo in several capacities, including that of Serbia's representative in Constantinople.

Under Ristić's guiding hand, the Serbs for the first time established a constitution for themselves. While many felt that the constitution was something less than democratic, it was a great step forward in view of Serbia's past history. One of the most significant aspects of the Constitution of 1869 was the elevation of the National Skupština to the position of a real legislative body. No law could be passed, repealed, amended, or reinterpreted without its agreement. Moreover, the Skupština became a fixed institution with regular annual meetings. Three fourths of its members were elected under an essentially free universal manhood suffrage.

Even more important, in terms of parliamentary government as then practiced in England, was the recognition that ministers would be responsible to the Skupština. In other words, ministers would have to resign if the Skupština lost confidence in them.

Ristić had concluded that there never would be domestic peace unless political responsibility was transferred from the Prince to his ministers. By being guided by his ministers, the Prince would be above political struggles. If the people did not like what was going on, they could oust the ministers while the Prince would be untouched, because he was politically neutral.

As we all know, this is the essence of parliamentary government, which little Serbia was inaugurating in the 1870s, a time when such states as Germany, Austro-Hungary, Russia, and others could only dream of doing so.

Actually, the constitution provided the machinery, but it was Ristić, who as prime minister, began the process of establishing parliamentary government. After Milan came of age, Ristić became leader of the Liberal Party and as such he was one of Milan's first

prime ministers. In that position, he was successful in having cabinet
ministers appointed for the first time on the recommendation of the
prime minister.

Ristić's successor, Jovan Marinović, was the first Serbian prime
minister explicitly to recognize that a cabinet could not stay in power
if it did not have the confidence of the legislature. Subsequently,
when Ristić was again prime minister, he lectured the deputies on the
meaning of parliamentary government. In November 1879, he staked
the life of his cabinet on these words: "I am not afraid of a lack of
confidence. It could do nothing to my past, and it is not at all dis-
honorable to fall in parliament. In constitutional states, governments
do not fall except in parliament. It is not good where it happens
otherwise."

When Prince Milan reached the age of 18, the Regency came to
an end. Milan lost no time in making known his distaste for the
limitations on the Prince that the Constitution of 1869 had imposed.
Nevertheless, he by and large abided by them during the first decade
of his reign. After that he often ignored democratic principles and
managed to rule with the Progressive Party, the smallest of the three
major parties that evolved in the 1870s. Prince Milan found it
difficult to accept the principle that ministers should be the initiators
of policy, for which they alone would be held responsible. Moreover,
he did not believe that the people were really ready for democracy.

Milan's real political troubles began when it became evident in
the early 1880s that the Serbian people overwhelmingly supported the
Radical Party. The latter wanted more democracy rather than less. It
wanted an even more democratic constitution than that of 1869,
which Milan thought was too democratic. For his part, Milan was
convinced that the Radicals hated the dynasty, and conspired to deny
them the electoral victories that they had won.

It was soon evident, however, that the Serbian people were not
to be denied. In the late 1860s they had begun to organize and in the
1870s they formed political parties. At first it was the young
intellectuals who had studied abroad and had become imbued with
liberal-democratic ideas. They formed the Liberal Party. Soon the
more conservative elements combined to establish the Progressive
Party. The Radicals came into being in the late 1870s (formally in
1881). Their intellectual father was a young Serbian, Svetozar
Marković, who had studied in Switzerland. He styled himself a
socialist. The main founder of the party, however, was Nikola Pašić,
also a onetime student in Switzerland.[4]

The Radicals stressed democracy and self-government at all levels. They also called for freedom of speech, press, and association. They attacked bureaucracy and called for easing of the peasants' burdens. Moreover, they stressed the need to liberate Serbs who were still under foreign rule.

The Radical Party not only won the widespread support among the peasant masses but also among teachers and priests. Before long it also attracted literary figures and professors. In addition, merchants liked the idea that government should be less expensive.

The widespread and almost instantaneous success of the Radicals served to discourage the formation of minority parties and to cause the Liberals to fade. The young conservatives, the Progressive Party, inherited the support of many former Liberals. Unfortunately for them, they came into being as the Radicals were capturing almost universal support. Without popular support, the Progressives allied themselves with the palace, and in effect became King Milan's personal party.

In the 1883 elections, the Radicals won a great victory, but Milan disbanded the Skupština. Then, in fear of troubles, the regime sought to collect arms from the people. This provoked a rebellion in the Timok region, a Radical stronghold. The rebellion was brutally put down, while the Radical leader, Nikola Pašić, fled to Bulgaria, where he lived for the next six years.

Although Milan realized that his moves were not popular, it was not until he had launched an unsuccessful war with Bulgaria in 1885 that he concluded that he could not govern with the Progressives and that he should abdicate. He spent the next year or so in preparing the groundwork for the final act. He was primarily concerned with safeguarding the position of his son Alexander, a youngster of 13. He wanted to protect him from his mother, Natalie, whom Milan had divorced, and from the Radicals.

In the end, Milan promoted the adoption of a liberal democratic constitution, one of the most liberal constitutions in Europe of that day. In essence, it (1) clearly established a parliamentary system, (2) strongly protected civil rights, and (3) recognized certain political powers for organs of local government.

Milan guided the work of the constitutional commission that produced the new constitution. This was not the result of a sudden conversion to democratic parliamentary principles. As indicated above, he sought to protect his son by naming a royal regency that would rule until Alexander was of age, a right that the constitution gave him. The three-man regency was made up of two army generals personally loyal to Milan. The third regent was Jovan Ristić, even though Milan did not like him. But he was an experienced politician who had headed the regency twenty years earlier when Milan was not of age. Moreover, Ristić was no friend of the Radicals.

Milan was also motivated by his belief that the people were not ready for a liberal-democratic constitution, and that the result would be chaos. Within two years, he believed, the people as well as the Great Powers would beg him to return and to restore order. In the meantime, the regency would protect the dynasty from the Radicals, who in the process would be discredited, but would keep Natalie out of Serbia, while Milan would continue to mix in Serbian politics through men loyal to him.

At age 35, in early 1889, Milan left the Serbian throne, but Serbia was not to be free of his intrigues until his death in 1901.

Milan had miscalculated about future developments. First, the Serbs proved him wrong; they demonstrated the capacity to govern themselves. In the years of the regency (1889-1893), the Radicals had a clear majority in the Skupština, and the regents were constitutional rulers in the best sense of that term, leaving political decisions in the hands of ministers responsible to parliament. Much to Milan's chagrin, the chaos that he expected did not materialize.

In the first years of the new constitution, much needed legislation was passed: on freedom of the press; elections; ministerial responsibility; the Council of State; and the organization of the army. Moreover, the Radical cabinet made peace with the Orthodox Church and brought back Metropolitan Mihailo, whose ouster had been forced by Milan because he had refused to sign the decree of divorce from Natalie.

Secondly, Milan was not able to keep Natalie from seeing their son and thereby influencing him. Moreover, she sought to nullify the earlier divorce. At first Metropolitan Mihailo agreed, but Regent Ristić convinced him to change his mind. Natalie sent a memorandum to the Skupština, which prompted the Radical cabinet to forcibly expel her from Serbia, a very unpopular act, but the cabinet was more afraid of Milan than of Natalie or the public.

Even before Natalie was out of the way, Milan had other problems - mainly money - and he began to bargain with the Radicals. He did not like what the press was writing about him, but this was secondary to his need for money. He wanted six million dinars, but settled for something over one million, plus a loan of an additional two million. The latter was secured as a loan from the Russian Tsar, but in reality it was a gift. In return, Milan wrote a letter to the regency renouncing all rights under the constitution, including citizenship and membership in the royal household, as well as the right to educate his son Alexander. But Milan was not good about keeping promises.

The money Milan got was soon gone. He had also pawned his furniture and silver, as well as the jewels he had inherited from Mihailo. In desperation and completing sacrificing his self-respect, Milan turned to Natalie for help. He told her that he was going to commit suicide, and asked for 345,000 francs so as to pay off his debts and not leave a legacy of embarrassment to their son. She gave him 100,000, but on the condition that he not commit suicide and that he redeem the family jewels and give them to Alexander.

Faithful to his habits, Milan took the money and soon spent it. He even got a loan of 500,000 francs from the Turkish sultan, but this too was soon gone.

Milan finally realized that his financial woes could not be cured unless he could get regular payments from the Serbian treasury, which he knew the government would not authorize. Hence, the only road was a coup.

As indicated above, Milan was careful to engineer the appointment of a regency that would be loyal to him, through the selection of generals Kosta Protić and Jovan Belimarković, and Jovan Ristić, a known opponent of the Radicals and a supporter of the Obrenović dynasty.

The unexpected death of General Protić ushered in a crisis which was to prompt Milan to plan a coup. Under the constitution, a vacancy in the regency would by filled by the Skupština. Since the Radicals were in control, it was widely believed that Nikola Pašić, who had been amnestied in 1889 and returned to lead the Radicals, would be chosen regent. This was an outcome that Milan could not tolerate.

In 1890 Milan was in Serbia, and asked Regent Ristić to give him power "whether in one form or another," so that he could clean up certain Radical policies "if you will not." To this Ristić replied: "You know that I was the last to agree to your abdication.... If we have to give up power, you will not be the one to whom we will give it, but to the Large National Skupština." Milan went away angry, but continued to plot.

In April 1893, a well-prepared coup was executed by Alexander who although not yet 17, proclaimed himself of age. The Serbian people once more suffered a setback in their quest for democratic rule.

Following the Milan-engineered coup, Alexander ruled without much observance of democratic principles. First, he abolished the Constitution of 1888 and brought back the less democratic one of 1869. Secondly, he and his father put together various political combinations so as to keep the popular Radical Party out of power.

In practice, the young monarch found himself in the middle most of the time. He was getting contradictory advice from his father and his mother. Initially, he leaned toward his father's views: govern with anyone but the Radicals. Later, for about two years (1895-1897), he seemed under the influence of his mother: work with the Radicals and certainly not against them.

From 1897 to 1900, Serbia in effect had two kings, Alexander and Milan. The latter was made commandant of the army, with few limitations on his powers. The press was effectively muzzled; Alexander at one point said that if he could have his way he would introduce whippings for newsmen.

Late in Alexander's reign, two events shook Serbia. First, in 1899 there was an attempt on Milan's life, for which the Radicals were blamed. Had it not been for interventions by Russia and Austria-Hungary (each for different reasons), several Radical leaders, including Pašić, would have lost their lives.

The other event came in 1900: Alexander's decision to marry Draga Mašin, Natalie's lady-in-waiting, a widow ten or twelve years older than he. Both Milan and Natalie were opposed to the proposed marriage. When the news reached Milan, who was abroad, he resigned as commandant of the army, and in a letter to his son said that if this "impulsive act" was irrevocable, he would be the first to greet the government that would overthrow him. Ironically, Milan died six months later in Vienna, a grieving "old man" who had not reached his 47th birthday.

Milan's death lifted the burden of fear from the royal couple. Moreover, Alexander gained some popularity after it was announced a month after the marriage that Draga was pregnant. Soon, however, it became evident that this was a false and deliberate ruse, and the public was not amused.

Alexander tried to govern with several party combinations, but in the end resorted to personal rule. In the meantime, a conspiracy that had been in the making for some two years, chiefly among young army officers, resulted in the assassination of Alexander and Draga in 1903. This event marked the end of the Obrenović dynasty and the end of the 20-year struggle between the dynasty and the Radical Party.

The end of the Obrenović dynasty opened an extraordinary decade for Serbia. It was a decade of great achievements at home and abroad - a period of democratic rule, economic growth, and progress in education, literature, and the arts. It was a decade of balanced budgets and considerable territorial gains (result of the Balkan Wars) from the decaying Ottoman empire. But it was also a decade of domestic and foreign troubles.

The conspirators who ended the Obrenović dynasty turned power over to an all-party coalition, which in turn convened the existing parliament, which ratified the choice of Peter Karadjordjević as king, as well as the return of the Constitution of 1888, to be called the Constitution of 1903. Peter took an oath to defend the Constitution.

Peter I, grandson of Karadjordje, possessed a number of qualities that endeared him to his fellow Serbs. He had translated John Stuart Mill's essay *On Liberty*, prefaced by an introduction in the spirit of democracy. In 1870 he had fought in the French army in the war against Prussia. In 1876 he fought in the Serbian uprising (under an assumed name) in Bosnia-Hercegovina against the Turks.

Peter became a constitutional monarch in the best sense of that term, leaving the formulation of public policies to the freely elected political party leaders. Moreover, he earned the people's love and respect by his modest and frugal ways of life.

Serbia's new political system, characterized by a free and vigorous political life, won the admiration of many at home and abroad. The press was free. Elections were free. Civil rights were guaranteed. Political parties were free to organize and to campaign. And the people and the king accepted the results.

In domestic affairs, the new Serbian cabinets dealt with several thorny problems: (1) what to do about the conspirators whose brutal assassination of the Obrenovićes horrified many Europeans; (2) foreign loans, mainly for Serbia's rearmament; (3) the abdication of Prince George, heir to the throne; and (4) the problem of civil-military relations in a democracy. The Pašić cabinet found answers to the first three, but the fourth continued to plague the king and the cabinet into the World War I years.

In foreign affairs, the main problems were Austria-Hungary and Turkey. The former wanted Serbia to continue to be dependent upon Vienna. When Pašić did not turn to Austria-Hungary for a loan for arms, Vienna launched a trade war against Serbia. Pašić turned to France for a loan and received it. And although the trade war hurt, Serbia survived it, much to the distaste of the Vienna leaders.

After patient preparations, Serbia and her Balkan neighbors went to war in 1912 against the Ottoman empire and were successful beyond belief. The Turks were driven from the Balkan peninsula. Much of South Serbia was liberated. This was followed by Serbian-Bulgarian differences. By prior agreement, the two nations were to turn to the Russian Tsar for arbitration in case a dispute arose. Bulgaria refused to follow this course and in 1913 attacked Serbia, but the Serbs won a resounding victory.

Serbia and Montenegro were, however, denied some of the fruits of the Balkan Wars. Serbia was denied Bosnia-Hercegovina, occupied by Austria-Hungary under the terms of the Congress of Berlin (1878) but subsequently annexed. Montenegro was forced to give up Skadar, after having won it with considerable bloodshed. All in all, it was a remarkable decade - in many ways Serbia's golden decade even with the understandable disappointments.

It should be noted that with the end of the Obrenovićes, dynastic struggles in Serbia came to an end. Generally speaking, the Serbs respected their monarchs. At the same time, they expected them to respect the people and to rule in their interest. Perhaps this outlook was conditioned by the fact that Serbian monarchs, unlike the Bulgarians, Romanians, and Greeks (who brought foreigners from the great royal houses of Europe to be their monarchs), were native Serbs.

From this brief account of political developments in Serbia, it is clear that they were very much in harmony with Western Europe's political tradition. As the Serbs began asserting their independence from Turkey in the 19th century, the vast majority of them never lost sight of their ultimate goal - a political system that would make possible for them to decide questions of public policy in an established and orderly democratic manner.

NOTES

1. Probably the best work on the subject is Stojan Novaković, *Zakonik Stefana Dušana cara srpskog 1349 i 1354*(Belgrade, 1898).

2. For Serbia's political development, see my *The Development of Parliamentary Government in Serbia* (Boulder, CO: East European Monographs, 1978).

3. No one has done a political biography of Jovan Ristić, but see my brief article, "Jovan Ristić and Serbia's Struggle for Independence and Democracy," *Serbian Studies* (Spring 1990), pp. 57-66.

4. For the Radical Party and its leader, Nikola Pašić, as well as subsequent developments, see my *Serbia, Nikola Pašić, and Yugoslavia* (Rutgers University Press, 1974).

SERBIAN CULTURE IN KOSOVO IN PAST AND PRESENT TIMES*

The saga of Kosovo is a long, involved, and complicated one, and cannot be treated adequately in a brief essay presentation. Therefore, in what follows, I will attempt to summarize concisely and update the points developed in a book on that subject which I co-authored a few years ago.[1]

As I seek to depict some of the highlights in the historic evolution of Kosovo, I realize that much of this may have little meaning to many of this journal's American readers. I would therefore ask each one of them to imagine similar events taking place within a historic framework with which they are familiar - whether it be the United States or Canada or some other country - and I will come back to this point at the end of my remarks.

Kosovo is identified with the early years of the Serbian nation. It is often referred to as the "cradle" of Serbia, i.e., the place where the young Serbian state was born and nurtured, where the culture of the Serbian people flowered, where many of the historic monuments of that period have been preserved and can be seen today. Kosovo was the center of the Serbian Empire of the Middle Ages, the strongest empire in the Balkans for over 100 years. To subsequent generations of Serbs, Kosovo was to become holy ground, not unlike Jerusalem to others.

We can only speculate on what there was in Kosovo prior to the coming of the Serbs about the 6th century A.D. Certainly there is no anthropological or other evidence of an organized society in the Kosovo region prior to the establishment of the Serbian state. On the other hand, the evidence of Serbia's historic legacy is there for all to see.

Serbian Cultural Legacy Prior to the Turkish Conquest

Irrespective of where we might go in the world to study cultural achievements, we pose the question: what made them possible? In other words, what are the necessary conditions for cultural development? They are basically three. The first of these is a settled and organized society. Generally speaking, cultural activities

* *Serbian Studies*, Fall, 1988, pp. 71-83.

take place within an established setting, usually within the confines of a political unit or other social entity. In the case of the Serbs it was the medieval Serbian state which came into its own in the eleventh century.

The second prerequisite for cultural development is a leadership, usually political but often in combination with the religious, that is at least receptive to cultural manifestations. A political entity can encourage and facilitate cultural developments. It can impede them or pursue a neutral position. Fortunately for the Serbs, especially after the acceptance of Christianity, their leaders were eager not only to encourage the promotion of cultural works, but indeed to take a leading part in their realization.

The third condition for cultural growth is talented artists and artisans and other cultural workers. The Serbs, as every other people, had to begin somewhere. Most often in such situations the first step is to recognize shortcomings. The next step is to have the imagination and the initiative to seek to overcome them. Here again, the Serbian leaders, first of all Nemanja (1168-1196) and his youngest son, Rastko (later Saint Sava), took the lead. Nemanja realized that Serbia needed cultural manifestations that could easily be identified with the Serbian people, and he knew of the cultural richness of Byzantium as well as of his own Zeta littoral in the west. In the end it was under Sava's brilliant guidance that these two different artistic traditions were united to produce new and creative combinations that can easily be identified as medieval Serbian cultural creations.

Sava, a Mount Athos monk, scholar, and theologian, was eminently prepared to build the foundations upon which a national culture would grow within the environment of Eastern Orthodoxy. As a way of securely establishing Orthodoxy as a national faith, Sava gained autocephaly for the Serbian Church. A diplomat above all, who traveled widely, he knew most of the leading figures of the era: from emperors sitting on the various thrones of segmented Byzantium to the heads of churches and spiritual leaders of monastic communities, from Nicea and Jerusalem to the shores of the Adriatic and beyond. In his travels he became acquainted with architecture and religious art in churches and monasteries throughout Byzantium and all the way to the Holy Land. He was able to commission from Constantinople some of the most outstanding painters of the period.

Nemanja, who did not want to be remembered by castles or fortresses but by churches and roads, and Sava proved to be a magnificent combination: a pragmatic father to construct a viable framework and a sophisticated and artistically sensitive son to fill it with relevant content. Above all, Nemanja and Sava set a precedent which succeeding members of the dynasty (as well as the nobility and higher clergy) were to follow, the net result being untold cultural riches that continue to be the pride of the Serbs to this day.

In the book that I co-authored, mentioned earlier, there is a brief chapter that in the main discusses the surviving monuments - many were destroyed under the Turks - as Serbia's cultural legacy in Kosovo and adjoining areas.[2] It is not my place to pass judgment on the architectural style of the monasteries or on the quality of the artistic compositions that adorn their interiors. Even if I desired to do so, I do not have the needed qualifications. I cannot resist, however, reporting one or two observations by experts.

Art historians in general, and Byzantologists in particular, have written volumes dealing with the style and iconography of Serbian frescoes. On the whole, they agree that the paintings preserved on the walls of these churches constitute a continuity in Byzantine artistic expression during the period when the artistic output of Constantinople was severely curtailed due in large part to the political turmoil in the empire in the late 12th and early 13th centuries. Most scholars agree that Serbian art served as a link between the East and the West, transmitting to Western artists, eager to learn and to experiment, the venerable tradition kept alive in the superior Byzantine technique of frescoes and mosaics, as well as style. This flowering of Serbian art in the 13th and 14th centuries occurred just as Byzantium was undergoing an artistic revival and the West was on the threshold of the classical revival and the beginning of the Renaissance.[3]

The monastery *Gračanica*, built on the field of Kosovo, is considered by experts to be second to none among Serbian monasteries.[4] Some scholars dealing with Serbia's medieval cultural legacy give high praise to the monastic complex known as the *Peć Patriarchate*, so often referred to as the center of Serbian Orthodox Christendom. Other scholars have chosen to emphasize the majesty and serenity of the largest of all Serbian medieval churches, the *Dečani* monastery. Dečani contains more than a thousand compositions, with an estimated 10,000 painted figures. There are more than twenty biblical cycles on the walls, from Genesis to the Last Judgment. This is certainly the largest surviving iconographic complex ever created within the Byzantine sphere of influence.

Taken together, these Serbian churches and monasteries not only are a witness to the fact that the Kosovo region was ethnically the most homogeneous of Serbian territories in medieval times, but in addition, they constitute a vivid and dramatic visual presentation of the history of the rule of the Nemanjić dynasty. Moreover, some of the Serbian monasteries are today looked upon as world art treasures; at least Sopoćani and Studenica have been so designated by international art scholars.

The Saga of Kosovo under the Turks

After her defeat at Kosovo in 1389, Serbia rapidly fell under complete Turkish domination. As might be expected, one consequence was cultural stagnation and ultimately cultural decay. Although the Turks were in large measure willing to leave the Serbian peasants alone so long as tribute was paid and communications were not endangered, the Serbs were nevertheless left without leaders and without resources to carry out their cultural expressions. For the most part, the best that they could hope for was to preserve what they had. Soon, however, even this became impossible as vandalism and the elements took their toll.

A number of the most important monasteries (e.g., Mileševa and Sopoćani) bear scars of Turkish fires, to say nothing of natural disasters, yet surprisingly enough the beauty of many fresco decorations is scarcely diminished. Even under Turkish occupation one of the monasteries (Mileševa) for a brief time produced numerous liturgical books on its own presses. And for a time had its own school where a few Serbian children learned to read. Interestingly, one of the students who was taken from this school and placed in the Janissary corps subsequently rose to the rank of Grand Vizier in Constantinople - Mehmed Paša Sokolović, the builder of the famous bridge on the river Drina.

It should also be noted that after the Serbs were left without a state, the churches and monasteries over time became national centers, carriers of national identity. In large measure, Serbian Orthodoxy lost its churchly dogmatic character and increasingly accepted an ethnic attribute. As ill-equipped and inexperienced as the patriarchs were for this secular leadership role, they fought valiantly, especially in the period of 1557-1766, at the end of which the Patriarchate was abolished.[5] A noted church historian, in describing the devastating consequences for the Serbs of the actions of Islamized Albanians after the abolition of the Patriarchate in 1766, calls this period "the Second Kosovo."[6]

It is evident, therefore, that the saga of Kosovo after the Ottoman conquest was in essence one of continual setbacks for the

Serbs, not only in the cultural realm but ultimately also in terms of their physical existence. I say continual, because while the flow of the stream was in one general direction, there were times of relative calm. It should be noted that prior to 1389, where Serbs and Albanians existed side by side, they lived in considerable harmony. As late as the 15th century, the large majority of Albanians were Christians. So it is no surprise that at one time Serbs and Albanians paid homage to the same saints, worshipped in the same churches, and respected a past of shared values. Even today there are Albanians who can recall that their fathers would never begin any project on Tuesday, the day of the Serbian defeat at Kosovo.

The good neighborly and even brotherly association that had characterized the largest part of the history of Serbian-Albanian relations began to shift slowly after the two great migrations in 1683-1690 and 1717-1737 of Serbs to Austria and Hungary. While these migrations weakened the Serbs in Kosovo, many of those who had departed were reinforced by the movement to Kosovo of Serbs from other parts of the Ottoman empire, although a significant number of these had been converted to Islam. Nevertheless, until about the middle of the 18th century the Kosovo area was ethnically homogeneous. The Islamization of the Albanians (about half of all of them had been converted by the end of the 16th century), was followed in the 18th century with an influx of Albanians into Kosovo in large numbers.

Instigated in part by the Ottoman authorities, this movement of Albanians sharply reversed the nature of their relations with the Serbs, and was the beginning of oppression of the latter by the former. This oppression reached such proportions in the last decades of the 19th century and the early years of the 20th that it could properly be referred to as genocide. The Albanian atrocities are recorded in massive source materials, mainly in reports by consuls of European powers in Bitolj, Skoplje, Prizren, and Priština, and in the protests to the Porte by these European states. The reports by European consuls are supplemented by extensive reports by Serbia's consuls in these same cities.[7]

I have examined ten or more of the latter reports, dealing mainly with the first decade of this century. They are specific as to persons, time, and place. They report on murders of Serbs, rape, pillaging, arson, and attempts to force Serbs to leave their lands. Some of the reports indicate that incidents were called to the attention of Turkish officials, who promised to help, but usually that is where the matter ended. Similarly, the diplomatic protests of the European powers to the Porte also bore no fruit, but at least authentic documents remain testifying to the crimes committed against the Serbs in the Kosovo region.

This sad saga of Kosovo was bitterly aggravating and deeply disappointing to Serbia's leaders in Belgrade. Aggravating because while in the course of the 19th century the Serbs were successful in regaining their independence and in building a democratic political system, they were not in a position to be of much help to their brethren outside Serbia, especially in Kosovo, or Old Serbia, as it was called. Disappointing because the Serbian leaders had believed that the Albanians, as other Balkan people, would make common cause in driving the Turks from Europe. Serbian naivete was made evident in the wars that Serbia and Montenegro waged in 1876-77 and 1877-78 against the Turks, when the Albanians fought to defend the Ottoman empire.

Albanian actions can best be understood if we recall that in the latter half of the 19th century they had managed a formal unity among the major factions among them and in 1878 formed the Prizren League. Although great differences continued among them, by and large the Albanians remained loyal defenders of the Ottoman empire, and hence they had few fears of the Turks. If the latter should be forced to leave Europe, the Prizren League leaders believed that Serbia, Montenegro, and Greece would be the main barriers to the formation of a large Albanian state. Admittedly, this is far from being an adequate exposition of Albanian actions and aspirations in the 19th century.[8]

As is generally known, one result of the Balkan wars of 1912 and 1913 was that Kosovo was liberated and that Serbia and Montenegro also liberated other areas, but the Great Powers denied them some of their important gains. Another result was that the Great Powers were instrumental in the creation of an Albanian state in 1912. In the process of creating an Albanian state, however, the Great Powers denied to the Serbs some historic lands, notably the city of Skadar, which Montenegrin forces had succeeded in taking. Just as the Serbs began establishing their rule in the Kosovo area came World War I, and in 1915 the Serbs were forced to flee their homeland in the face of the oncoming German armies. Once again, Kosovo Serbs were left to face new persecutions from several sources, including Albanian and Bulgarian.[9]

Kosovo in the First Yugoslavia

After the formation of the new state, The Kingdom of the Serbs, Croats, and Slovenes, the leaders in Belgrade were forced to give Kosovo a rather low priority. The enormous problems of beginning to govern a newly constituted state, with serious nationality problems which soon surfaced, to say nothing of seeking to recover from the ravages of war, left little time for anything else.

Even when the Yugoslav government leaders turned their attention to Kosovo, they again seemed to suffer from a form of naivete in dealing with the Albanians in the Kosovo region. The Yugoslav government thought that it could establish stability and harmony with agrarian reforms, i.e., breaking up the landed estates of Albanian or Turkish begs, who had prospered under Ottoman rule, and giving land to Albanian peasants and to Serbs and other Yugoslavs who were willing to come to Kosovo. Instead of a solution, this approach led to more bad blood between Serbs and Albanians.

In terms of Serbian culture in Kosovo, some modest successes were realized, largely through efforts of the Serbian Orthodox Church. Important restoration work was done at the Sopoćani Monastery, the Peć Patriarchate, as well as the monasteries of Banjska and Kalenić. In addition, surveys and some archeological excavations were carried out at other places, among them Tsar Dušan's church, Holy Archangels near Prizren, and at Stobi near Skoplje.

Present Times

What can we say about Serbian culture in Kosovo in present times? I interpret present times to mean the period since World War II. On the one hand, the Yugoslav Communist regime did a great deal by way of restoring Serbian cultural monuments as well as cultural objects in other parts of the country. In this the government was stimulated by a general world-wide interest in and increase in this type of activity, as well as by the more advanced knowledge concerning techniques of such restorations. On the other hand, the regime in Belgrade left political control in Kosovo to Albanian Communists, many of whom joined the Party near the end of the war when they saw that their dream of an Axis-sponsored large Albania would not be realized.

Having said the above, it is still valid to conclude, it seems to me, that as far as Serbian culture in Kosovo in this period is concerned, it is a long and painful story. In brief, there has been a reversion to a situation similar to Turkish times, only worse. Without stopping to detail the actions of the Tito regime in promoting conditions that led to the persecution of Serbs in Kosovo[10] and to attempts to annihilate their cultural past, we can say that although Kosovo was made an autonomous province of Serbia, the government of Serbia, by design or otherwise, has had virtually no control over what was happening in the Kosovo region.

Although the Yugoslav government was aware of what was going on in Kosovo, there was no outcry or protest. For example, at least by the early 1970s, long-established Serbian professors at the University of Priština were told that they could stay in their positions only if they learned Albanian. There were few voices crying in the wilderness even in the 1960s, notably that of novelist Dobrica Ćosić, attempting to call attention to what was going on in Kosovo. Ćosić was rewarded by expulsion from the Central Committee of the Serbian Communist Party. In the meantime, over 200 professors were brought to Priština University from Albania. And all sorts of textbooks were brought from Albania. The Yugoslav public still has not been told who invited the professors from Albania and who made possible the importation of those textbooks.

Not until the demonstrations by the Kosovo Albanians in 1981, and their public demand for the status of a republic and even the right to join their motherland Albania, did anyone in Belgrade dare even mention the suffering of the Serbs of Kosovo. Since that time much has been publicly noted about various actions of Albanians of Kosovo to force Serbs to leave the area and to obliterate their cultural heritage there. Actions against the Serbs included unlawful seizure of properties, vandalizing of churches and cemeteries, physical violence against Serbian priests and their domiciles, arson, rape, etc.[11]

Instead of the situation getting better since 1981, it has become worse. In the summer of 1987, a scandal - some refer to it as "administrative genocide" - came to light when Serbian Orthodox Church authorities in Peć discovered at the local cadastral office that many Serbian Orthodox churches had disappeared from the face of the earth. Someone had simply eliminated them and listed them as mosques. The Peć Patriarchate was listed simply as an ordinary "religious object." Both Serbian Orthodox churches in Lipljan, which are under state protection as cultural-historical monuments, had in the books become mosques. In the village of Livadj, populated exclusively by Serbs, the Orthodox church is administratively a mosque. And in the villages of Dobrotin and Donji Gušteric, also exclusively populated by Serbs, their churches have become "ordinary buildings."

In the cadastral books of the Uroševac region there are no longer any Orthodox churches in the villages of Nekodin, Gornji Nerodim, and Bavljak. They have become mosques. And in Uroševac itself the large Orthodox church "went over to Islam." A similar story is to be found in the Gnjilska opština. One church there was simply eliminated and transformed into a "cemetery."

The pearl of Serbian medieval culture, the monastery Gračanica is listed as general public property. Another pearl of Serbian culture, the 650-year old Monastery of Dečani, has been transformed into an "ordinary building."

In some areas Serbian Orthodox churches have become "pasture lands." One cemetery has become the property of the state forestry enterprise, while another one is listed as the property of a state school. In still another case, the cemetery is listed as "private property."

As might be expected, these actions against Serbian history and culture evoked bitterness among Serbs. They only official explanation is that these were unintentional mistakes or foreign mistakes or of a technical nature. In one place they blamed it on the computer, and in another on a secretary. Not one culprit was named, as if the mistakes were made by themselves.[12]

In April 1987, Slobodan Milošević, the head of the Presidency of the Serbian Communist party, went to Kosovo to hear complaints from Serbs. Over 15,000 came, but only some 300 pre-selected Serbs could be accommodated because of the size of the building. The meeting lasted 13 hours and 78 persons spoke. The majority of them openly attacked the Communist regime. From the excerpts printed in the Party organ Borba, a few sentences are sufficient to get a flavor of the proceedings:[13]

> Serbian man: "I know why Germany was divided after the war, but why was Serbia divided?"

> Serbian man: "We do not need guarantees... heads will fall, because it is impossible to endure and to permit the beating or our children and women."

> Serbian woman: "Either there will be some order in Kosovo, or by God we will take up arms again if need be."

Serbian man: "Serbs want to live together with Albanians... but here counterrevolution is being financed from the federation."

Serbian woman: "From the establishment of Priština University there has been a process of ethnic epuration of Kosovo and the process of cultural purity."

Serbian man: "How is it that Yugoslavia protests one-language signs in Austria but agrees to it in Kosovo?"

Serbian man: "How is it that according to the 1974 Constitution Serbo-Croatian is also an official language in Kosovo while in the constitution of the Province it is not obligatory?"

Another man asked about the erection of a monument to the Prizren League, which he characterized as a fascist organization that sought to tear Yugoslavia apart. He also asked why the program of the Albanian nationalist group, Balli Combetar, was being carried out in Kosovo. There was also condemnation of Serbian Communists in Kosovo who "served with the Albanians" in putting their personal interests ahead of the national interest.

The open use of the term genocide is to be found even in some Yugoslav newspapers, as well as expressions of amazement that after six years there has not been a single resignation either in Kosovo or at the top in Yugoslavia that would bear witness to a feeling of responsibility. Instead, the authorities "continue with the same announcements in which they avoid naming criminals."[14] One member of the Writers of Serbia opined: "There is no Serbia. If there were, what is happening in Kosovo would not be taking place."

Ironically, in the same month (June, 1987) a similar stance was taken by the Presidency of the League of Yugoslav Communists (LCY) after the LCY's 13th Congress, when it concluded that the "most difficult part of the problem of Kosovo and the whole of Yugoslav society is to be found in that the policy of the LCY is not being implemented."[15] It seems fair to ask, who is failing to implement it? Can anyone doubt that it is the Kosovo Albanians with the help of their agents among the Serbian Communists?

A month or so earlier, at an "ideological" plenum of the Central Committee of the LCY, a member by the name of Dušan

Dragosavac said: "If we cannot quickly overcome genocide... then I see as the only way out an urgent convoking of an extraordinary Congress of the League of Yugoslav Communists and the calling of free elections with multiple candidates, so that men can come to the top who can bring an end to the genocide."[16]

What of the Future?

At this stage it is quite appropriate to ask: what of the future? Rather than speculate about the future, I should like to emphasize the seriousness of the Kosovo situation. My readers will recall that at the outset I asked them to think within a framework of situations close to home, Canada or the United States, that would make more meaningful for them the things that I was going to say. As I have thought about it, however, I had to conclude that in Canada and in the United States we do not have any really comparable situations. The United States and Canada are relatively young states, and do not have anything in their history that could help in giving us a better insight into the saga of Kosovo.

Nevertheless, one could try to imagine that a few hundred years into the future Mexicans became the overwhelming majority in Texas, and embarked on a campaign to push all non-Mexicans out, engaging in pillage, arson, rape, and similar acts. One could imagine further that the Mexicans desecrated the Alamo or destroyed it, or imagine also that although they were United States citizens they did not think of themselves as Americans, and insisted on Spanish as the only valid language there.

I have used Texas, but some would say that California would be an even more appropriate example. Still, in either case, the imagined Mexican actions would be more understandable, because of their one-time sovereignty in Texas and California.

Instead of Texas or California, let us come east, and imagine that at some future time a certain group of citizens of the United States desecrated the historical monuments in Boston, Concord, or Lexington. Or imagine a similar desecration of the many monuments at Gettysburg.

Those of us more familiar with Canadian history can also do some imagining. Imagine that one day a separatist Quebec movement were doing what the Kosovo Albanians have been doing, engaging in all sorts of acts to force English inhabitants out, to eradicate traces of English cultural manifestations, doing away with the English language, and refusing to play a constructive role in Canadian society.

If one can imagine any of the situations that I have asked my American readers to imagine, then one can have some appreciation of how the Serbs feel about what has been happening in Kosovo.

There is no denying the fact that today Albanians make up close to 80 percent of the population of Kosovo. It is ironic that they, who for many years talked about minority rights, have in recent decades been the prime violators of minority rights in Yugoslavia. The first prerequisite for any peaceful outcome, it seems to me, is for the Kosovo Albanians to act as Yugoslavs - as constructive citizens of their adopted land, which they seem disinclined to do, despite all the revelations of the past six or seven years. If indeed they continue on the course they have been following, then not only will Serbian prospects (cultural and otherwise) be bleak in Kosovo, but also the logical result is apt to be a two Albanias situation, with all the ominous consequences of the two Koreas and the two Germanies. Even more likely is a "northern Ireland" plight in the making.

NOTES

1. Alex N. Dragnich and Slavko Todorovich, *The Saga of Kosovo: Focus on Serbian-Albanian Relations* (Boulder, CO: East European Monographs, 1984). Two recent and excellent detailed works are: Dimitrije Bogdanović, *Knjiga o Kosovu* (Belgrade: Serbian Academy of Sciences and Arts, 1986), and Hieromonk Antanasije Jevtić (ed.), *Zadužbine Kosovo: spomenici i znamenija srpskog naroda* (Belgrade: Serbian Orthodox Church, 1987).

2. See chapter 3 of *The Saga of Kosovo*.

3. See Gabriel Millet, *Le peinture du Moyen Age en Yougoslavie* (Paris: Boccard, 1954); Svetozar Radojčić, *Staro srpsko slikarstvo* (Belgrade, 1966); David Talbot Rice, *Byzantine Painting: The Last Phase* (London, 1968); Vojislav J. Djurić, "Istorijeskc kompozicie u sprskom slikarstvu srednjeg veka i njihove književne paralele," *Zbornik radova Vizantološkog instituta*, 10 (1967), pp. 121-148; Milan Kašanin, *Srpska književnost u srednjem veku* (Belgrade, 1975). Also see Vasa D. Mihailovich (ed.), *Landmarks in Serbian Culture and History* (Pittsburgh, PA: Serb National Federation, 1983), and Jovan Deretić, *Istorija srpske književnosti* (Belgrade: Nolit, 1983).

4. Slobodan Čurčić, *Gračanica: King Milutin's Church and Its Place in Late Byzantine Architecture* (University Park, PA: Pennsylvania State University Press, 1979).

5. *Saga of Kosovo*, p. 63.

6. *Ibid.*

7. In 1986 and 1987, the Serbian Orthodox Church organ in Belgrade, *Pravoslavlje*, reprinted many of these reports, which are in the Archives of Serbia. For a sample, see the issues for November 15, December 1 and 15, 1986; and February 1 and 15, March 1 and 15, April 1 and 15, May 1, and 15, June 1 and 15, 1987. A noted historian, Jovan Cvijić, estimated that 150,000 Serbs were driven from Kosovo between 1876 and 1912, *Balkanski rat i Srbija* (Belgrade, 1912), p. 8.

8. For more detail, see Bogdanović, *Knjiga o Kosovu.*

9. See Bogdanović, *Knjiga o Kosovu* and Jevtić, *Zadužbine Kosovo*, as well as *Saga of Kosovo.*

10. For an account of the expulsion of Serbs from Kosovo during the Second World War and preventing their return, as well as encouraging Albanians to move into Kosovo, see Bogdanović, Jevtić, as well as chapter 14 of the *Saga of Kosovo.*

11. For details, see *Saga of Kosovo*, chapter 14.

12. See article in *Pravoslavlje*, July 1, 1987, p. 10.

13. *Borba*, May 8, 1987, and *Ilustrovana politika*, May 5, 1987.

14. Appeal of the Union of Writers of Serbia in *Književne novine*, June 15, 1987.

15. *Politika*, June 11, 1987.

16. *Borba*, May 23, 1987.

YUGOSLAVIA IN HISTORICAL PERSPECTIVE[*]

Yugoslavia was born on 1 December 1918, the result of the fortuitous confluence of three indispensable circumstances: the desire of the South Slavs to unite, the decay of the Ottoman Empire, and the dissolution of the Habsburg empire. The first of these - the dream or idea of unification of the South (*Yug*) Slavs (mainly Serbs, Croats, and Slovenes) - was spawned almost exclusively by the intellectuals among them, mainly in the latter half of the nineteenth century. The idea evoked an enthusiastic response among the politically aware youth but was scarcely noted by the vast peasant masses.

The supporters of South Slav unity stressed the fact that the people had much in common - language, first of all. Moreover, they noted that the people were mainly Christian. The Serbs were largely Orthodox, having received their Christianity from Byzantium, while the Croats and Slovenes acquired theirs from Catholic Rome. A large number of South Slavs, mainly in the province of Bosnia, were of a Muslim faith that came from conversions during the centuries of Ottoman occupation.

Those who espoused the South Slav idea increasingly pointed with pride to Serbia, which in the nineteenth century had regained its independence and rapidly developed a parliamentary democratic system that, in 1903, was unmatched on the European continent, except perhaps in France and one or two small countries. Consequently, Serbia was a political magnet for the Slovenes, Serbs, and Croats still living under foreign rule.

Contrary to some assertions, the Serbs were not politically shaped by the "backward East." All of Serbia's leaders, who in the latter half of the nineteenth century and the beginning of the twentieth directed the country's development toward freedom and democracy, spent a great deal of time in western Europe, where they received a mature appreciation of democratic ideas and the functioning of parliamentary systems.

The second prerequisite for the formation of a South Slav state, the decay and disintegration of the Ottoman Empire, was well on its way before the turn of the century. In the Balkan wars of 1912, Serbia and its allies drove the Ottoman Turks out of Europe.

---

[*] *Mediterranean Quarterly*, 3 (Summer, 1992), pp. 5-19. Reprinted with permission.

The third circumstance that would make possible the creation of a Yugoslav state, the dismemberment of the Habsburg empire, seemed merely a dream before the First World War, and even when war broke out the dissolution of that empire was far from certain. Despite the odds, soon after Austria-Hungary's attack on Serbia in 1914, the Serbian cabinet, under the leadership of Prime Minister Pashich, declared in December that its major war aim, after victory, was the liberation and unification of all Serbs, Croats, and Slovenes. Regarded by some as an act of bravado, the declaration was confirmed by the Serbian parliament, and the message was conveyed to Serbia's allies.

The First World War

In subsequent wartime negotiations between the Serbian government and the Yugoslav Committee (made up mainly of Slovenes, Croats, and Serbs from the South Slav areas of Austria-Hungary), an agreement was reached in July 1917 on the creation of a common state, to be known as the Kingdom of the Serbs, Croats, and Slovenes. Because the meetings took place on the Greek island of Corfu, the agreement came to be called the Corfu Declaration.

Full of sentiments of unity, brotherhood, and common interests, the agreement contained fourteen specific points dealing with the organization of the future state. It was to be a "constitutional, democratic, and parliamentary monarchy with the Karadjordjevich [Serbian] dynasty at the head." The final point of the declaration stated that a constituent assembly would adopt a constitution "by a numerically qualified majority," a somewhat vague and imprecise provision that was nowhere defined.

Aside from the dynasty, Serbia did not ask for any privileged status or veto power, a stance quite different from, for example, the actions of Prussia when it was uniting Germany. Serbia gave up its democratic constitution, convinced that a constituent assembly would produce a democratic one for the new state. In addition, Serbia yielded its flag, coat of arms, and other national symbols.

In 1915, between Serbia's declaration of war aims and the Corfu Declaration, Britain, France, and Russia concluded the secret Treaty of London, which promised to Italy certain Austro-Hungarian areas along the Dalmatian coast and the northern Adriatic (areas mainly populated by South Slavs) as a reward for Italy's joining the Triple Entente in the war against Germany and Austria-Hungary.

While the Allies had a high regard for Serbia's brave stand against Austria-Hungary, they realized that the creation of a South Slav state would make it impossible for them to keep their promises to Italy. Consequently, they treated the Corfu Declaration with studied coolness. As compensation, however, they indicated to Pashich that they were willing to see the establishment of a Great Serbia, which would include Bosnia-Hercegovina and large parts of the southern Dalmatian coast, but Pashich chose to stand by the Corfu Declaration.

Serbia's hopes for the realization of its goals were severely weakened in 1917 when Russia, its special patron, was knocked out of the war by the Bolshevik revolution. In addition, several Allied proclamations in early 1918 gave little comfort to Serbia. In these pronouncements, Britain, France, and their new ally, the United States, mentioned the rights and aspirations of the Poles, Czechs, and others, but made no reference to the declared aspirations of the South Slavs.

When Pashich's query as to whether the omission was accidental or intentional was "leaked," he came under attack from British pro-Yugoslav publicists and members of the Yugoslav Committee who feared he was ready to accept the Allies' offer of creating a Great Serbia. They charged him with abandoning the Yugoslav idea. Denying the charges, he issued statements in October 1918 to the British press in which he declared that "the Serbian people cannot wish a dominant position in the future kingdom," but that it was Serbia's duty to liberate all Serbs, Croats, and Slovenes. After that they would be free to join Serbia or "create small states as in the distant past." This was not good news for the members of the Yugoslav Committee, because the South Slavs they purported to represent might continue to live under foreign rule.

By this time, South Slav politicians were being overtaken by events. In November 1918, an overwhelming number of districts in Vojvodina and Bosnia-Hercegovina decided in favor of uniting with Serbia, as did the national assembly in Montenegro. Most critical for the Croats and Slovenes was the occupation of key areas of the northern Adriatic by Italian troops seeking to assure to Italy the promises of the Treaty of London.

In light of these developments, delegates of the National Council, acting for the recently proclaimed state of Slovenes, Croats, and Serbs in Zagreb, rushed to liberated Belgrade and proposed that provisional authorities be established under Prince Alexander, pending the writing of a constitution for the new state. This was accepted by Alexander and his ministers, and on 1 December 1918 the Kingdom of the Serbs, Croats, and Slovenes was proclaimed.

It is of more than passing interest that the Croats and Slovenes were able to leave as citizens of the Austro-Hungarian Empire and be accepted with equal rights as citizens of a victorious Kingdom of the Serbs, Croats, and Slovenes. Croatian and Slovenian soldiers and officers who had fought for Austria-Hungary were even accepted into the army of the new Yugoslav state.

The First Yugoslavia, 1918-1941

The newly created state faced unbelievable hurdles.[1] The Serbs, Croats, and Slovenes, as well as Italian, Hungarian, Albanian, and other minorities, were together in a new political entity. Serbia had a great deal of experience in democratic government, but other parts of the state had precious little or none. Moreover, the citizens had lived under several different legal systems. Economically, the new kingdom was predominantly peasant. Serbia was a land of small landholdings, while in parts of Croatia and Slovenia, there were some large estates. Serbia and Montenegro were badly devastated by the war and had almost no industry. Croatia and Slovenia, as parts of the Habsburg domain, had a modest industrial base.

While the new state was founded on a private enterprise economy, the bulk of working capital was centered in Zagreb, with the result that investments in industry flowed toward Croatia and Slovenia. The Yugoslav political authorities encouraged this, because it made sense to rely on industrial growth where modern industry already existed. Interestingly, Communist planners in the second Yugoslavia, after the Second World War, also accelerated industrial investments in Slovenia and Croatia, although not entirely for the same reasons. This direction of economic development in the first and second Yugoslavias goes a long way toward explaining why these two areas became more prosperous than other regions.

Organizing governmental authority was a difficult task. The provisional parliament and cabinet, laboring fruitlessly for two years, gave way in 1921 to a constitutional assembly. Unfortunately, the political leaders who had represented Croatia in the provisional parliament were soundly defeated by the Croatian Peasant Party, led by Stepan Radich, who decided to boycott the constituent assembly. While the assembly was in session, Radich changed the name of his party to the Croatian Republican Peasant Party and openly campaigned for an independent Croatia.

Nevertheless, in June 1921 the kingdom had a democratic constitution with a parliamentary system. It provided for a unitary state with a strong central government and limited powers to local governments. Radich, however, refused to have his party's deputies take their seats in the national parliament. He was subsequently imprisoned briefly for anti-state activities, but in 1925 he accepted the constitution, the monarchy, and the political order, and even dropped the word *republican* from his party's name. At the same time, his party joined a political coalition headed by Nikola Pashich of the Radical Party, who had been prime minister since early 1921 and had presided over the drafting of the constitution. Within a brief period, Radich went from being a prisoner in the dock to a minister in the cabinet.

The bright hopes stemming from this arrangement were soon dashed. Pashich left his post as prime minister in April 1926 and died in December. The new cabinet of the Radicals plus Radich entered stormy waters, with Radich and his party colleagues increasingly engaged in obstructionist tactics in parliament. In the difficult days of early 1928, a Radical deputy from Montenegro shot Radich and several of his colleagues during a parliamentary session. Two died almost immediately, but Radich recovered, only to die in August of secondary infections from his diabetes. The Croatian deputies and their political associates left parliament.

For a time, Alexander, who had become king in 1921, made several efforts to find a political solution, including making the leader of the Slovene People's Party, Anton Koroshets, prime minister. In January 1929, however, the king took personal power, convinced that the system of parliamentary democracy had failed to create a consensus. Declaring that his move would be temporary, he ruled mainly through non-political ministers, seeking to impose consensus from above. He changed the name of the country to Yugoslavia and divided it into nine administrative regions, called *banovinas*, after a Croatian term meaning governor, in an effort to eliminate narrow historical entities. This was in accord with his earlier pro-Yugoslav orientation of giving his three sons Serbian, Croatian, and Slovene first names.

Alexander presented the nation in 1931 with a new constitution, seeking to reestablish democracy in the somewhat limited form that came to be called "guided democracy" in the period after the Second World War. In foreign affairs he was instrumental in the creation of the Little Entente in close collaboration with France. It was while on an official visit to France in October 1934 that he was assassinated by members of the Internal Macedonian Revolutionary Organization (IMRO) in a well-organized plot coordinated between IMRO and the Croatian extremist movement known as the Ustashe, which was led by Ante Pavelich, who had fled to Italy in the early years of the king's personal rule.

Because Alexander's eldest son, Peter II, was only eleven, the king's first cousin, Paul Karadjordjevich, became prince regent. Under pressure of domestic and foreign events, Paul was determined to solve the Croatian problem and to keep Yugoslavia out of an impending world war. He negotiated with Radich's successor, Vladko Machek, who had no Croatian blood (his father a Slovene and mother Austrian-Polish). Negotiating with Machek was not easy, because Machek was at the same time carrying on talks with Mussolini's foreign secretary, Galeazzo Ciano. In August 1939, an agreement known as Sporazum was signed, giving Croatia a large autonomous unit called Croatian Banovina. While Machek was at least temporarily satisfied, the Slovenes and the Serbs, especially the latter, were unhappy. Nevertheless, plans were under way to create Slovenian and Serbian units when the war intervened.

Because of a seeming lack of policy on the part of Britain and France and the increase in Italian and German power on the Continent, Paul and his political associates believed that Yugoslavia could stay out of war only if some accommodation was made with the changed international situation. After resisting Hitler's pressure for nearly two years, Paul agreed to adhere to the tripartite pact between Germany, Italy, and Japan (the Axis powers), but under conditions that did not infringe on Yugoslavia's sovereignty.

Paul was overthrown in March 1941 by army officers holding the mistaken belief that he had betrayed his country. Although the new government announced it would adhere to all of Yugoslavia's international obligations, Hitler was not appeased and soon launched a military strike, overcoming Yugoslav resistance in two weeks. Yugoslavia was then partitioned among the Axis and its allies.

Mussolini's troops brought with them Ante Pavelich and his Ustashe, which established an Axis satellite, the so-called Independent State of Croatia. The more than two million Serbs in that state, according to some Ustashe documents, were to be dealt with as follows: one-third to be killed, one-third converted to Catholicism, and one-third driven to Serbia. Many historians think that the actual results of Croatia's policy approximated this formula. In any case, most experts on this period of Yugoslavia's history believe that the number of Serbs killed in a most brutal fashion was about seven hundred thousand. In addition, some sixty thousand Jews also were killed, along with a smaller number of Gypsies. Many Serbs fled to the hills, where they were a source of recruits for guerrilla resistance movements.

The Second Yugoslavia

The second, or Tito's, Yugoslavia emerged as the result of victory in the wartime civil war.[2] Although Tito (Josip Broz) and his Communist comrades disguised their Partisan Liberation Movement as broadly democratic, they were always in control, and once in Belgrade, they set up a Communist dictatorship in spring 1945. On their way there, they had cleverly manipulated Western sources for considerable aid, helped by open or hidden Communists in Western intelligence services. In the process, they discredited the non-Communist guerrilla movement led by General Drazha Mihailovich, the first to raise the flag of underground resistance to the Axis. Even this would not have been enough to secure a victory for the Communists, by their own admission, if it had not been for the Soviet Red Army, which liberated Belgrade and turned the capital over to Tito. Some of his units had joined the Soviets along the way.

Once in power, Tito and his comrades proceeded to organize Yugoslavia on the Soviet model.[3] They installed a dictatorship with all power in the Communist party. As in the case of the Soviet

Union, they were merciless toward their real or imagined opposition. Moreover, they set up a Soviet-type federation. The country was divided into six republics - Serbia, Croatia, Slovenia, Macedonia, Montenegro, and Bosnia-Hercegovina. The last represented a special case because of the large population of Serbs and Croats who had converted to Islam during the centuries of Turkish rule. Montenegro, populated almost exclusively by Serbs, was made a separate republic mainly because so many of Tito's supporters came from there and wanted it that way.

Serbia was a special case, in large part because it had been the stronghold of Mihailovich's supporters, while the Tito partisans had little support. Moreover, Serbia had a history of hostility to tyrants. Hence, it had to be weakened. To this end, not only were many Serbian areas left out of the Republic of Serbia, but also within its borders were created two autonomous provinces, Vojvodina (with a large Hungarian minority) and Kosovo (with an Albanian majority).

On the economic front, the Yugoslav Communists emphasized collectivization of agriculture and nationalization of the industrial and commercial sectors. As in other Communist-ruled countries, collectivization of agriculture was unpopular and unproductive. Fortunately, the leaders early recognized the folly of collectivization, and by the mid-1950s they permitted peasants to leave collectives.

For more than a decade, the economic tsar of Tito's Yugoslavia was a Slovene, Boris Kidrich. When he died, another Slovene, Franz Leskoshek, took over. In addition, Tito's closest political collaborator was yet another Slovene, Edward Kardelj. Slovenian party stalwarts such as Stane Dolancts and Matija Ribichic also occupied positions at the highest levels. Tito's closest Croatian political comrade was Vladimir Bakarich. It seems significant that no Serb in the party structure held any position of appreciable importance in the economic sphere.

Following their expulsion in 1948 from the international Communist camp (Cominform), Tito and his comrades at first tried to demonstrate that they were not deviationists, as Moscow had charged, but loyal Marxist-Leninists. Although Tito's real crime was not an ideological one but that of resisting Soviet domination, he sought to show that it was the Soviet Union that had deviated. Admitting that it was wrong in copying the Soviet model, Yugoslavia's leadership began altering the system. The party's name was changed to the League of Yugoslav Communists (LCY), suggesting that it was going to follow the path of persuasion instead of dictatorship.

Moreover, Tito and his comrades inaugurated some controlled decentralization, mainly in the economic area, and adopted some aspects of the market mechanism. In addition, they introduced workers councils, subsequently expanded under the term *self-management*, but neither economic decentralization nor self-management produced the desired results.

In foreign relations, Tito conceived of the concept of nonalignment, for which he received a good deal of support from a number of Third World countries. At various congresses of the nonaligned states, however, they were often "nonaligned" on the side of the Soviet Union, and unity was not always present.

Post-Tito Yugoslavia

Before Tito died in 1980, many of his chickens were coming home to roost. He had built up a foreign debt of more than twenty billion dollars. The standard of living, which had improved in the early 1970s, began to go downward. Economic and political differences among the leaders of the various republics had in the past been resolved by Tito, who was acceptable as the supreme arbiter, but after his passing, impatience and restlessness grew. Tito had planned, through the constitution of 1974, to avoid struggles among his heirs. Basically, what the constitution did was make impossible any important decisions unless there was virtual unanimity among the representatives of the republics and autonomous provinces.

In case of emergencies, when the legislature and prime minister were unable to act, the collective presidency of eight persons could make decisions. Very often, political paralysis was resolved by adopting measures in the most general or abstract terms, so that the representative of each unit could go back home and interpret them liberally. Despite these precautions, many unresolved problems made for a disintegrative process.

As economic stagnation became more and more pronounced in the middle and late 1980s, two of the more affluent republics, Slovenia and Croatia, increasingly blamed the other republics, especially Serbia. They argued that they were contributing far more to the federal budget than they received in return, seemingly unaware that their relative prosperity was due in large part to the disproportionate industrial investments in their regions during the first and second Yugoslavias. Moreover, they refused to recognize that the hard currency tourism was bringing in was made possible by the meats and other foodstuffs to be found on tourist tables and which had come from the other republics, mainly Serbia. It is instructive to note that in 1991 the average per capita income in Slovenia was $12,618, in Croatia, $7,179, and in Serbia only $4,870.

At the same time, the LCY, which in earlier years had been able to dictate decisions, became hopelessly split along nationalist lines. This was to be evident as Communist regimes were collapsing in other parts of Eastern Europe. An extraordinary congress of the LCY, held in January 1990, failed to resolve differences. There was agreement that the party should give up its monopoly of power and that a multiparty system should be adopted. Before this and other resolutions could be formalized, however, the Slovenian delegates walked out, a move supported by the Croatian representatives. The congress was adjourned indefinitely, and for all practical purposes the national party came to an end.

Elections at the republic level were held later in 1990 in Slovenia and Croatia, the outcome being that hastily formed coalitions, led by well-known former Communists - in Croatia, Tito's one-time general, Franjo Tudjman, and in Slovenia, Milan Kuchan, a member of the LCY and a Marxist theoretician - were victorious. Almost immediately they began categorizing the results as a victory for democracy, whereas in fact the new governments were most authoritarian and brooked no opposition. Subsequent elections in Bosnia-Hercegovina resulted in a three-way split in power, closely proportionate to the population's division between Muslims, Serbs, and Croats. In Serbia and Montenegro, the Communists were victorious but replaced the name Communist with Socialist. In Macedonia, former Communists were elected. The Albanians in Kosovo boycotted the elections.

As dissatisfactions were being voiced in recent years, particularly by the Slovenes and Croats, the Serbs were also making known their discontent. They could do so only after Slobodan Miloshevich became head of the Serbian Communist party in 1986 and opened the Pandora's box of a decades-long persecution of Serbs in Kosovo by the Albanian majority there. The Slovenes and Croats were critical of Miloshevich, asserting that he was making too much of the issue, but in fact the persecutions were brutal and extensive both as to persons and properties, including churches, forcing thousands of Serbs to flee from their homes and their historical homeland.

Moreover, the Serbs did not forget that the Kosovo Albanians had joined with Mussolini's puppet Albania to form a Great Albania. And when Italy had met military defeat in 1943, these same Kosovo Albanians had formed a special regiment, the SS Skenderbeg, to fight alongside the Nazis. Moreover, the Serbs were made aware that those of their compatriots who had been forced to leave Kosovo in the course of the Second World War, by official decrees of the Tito regime, were not allowed to return after the war. At the same time, at least one hundred thousand Albanians had been encouraged to move from Albania to Kosovo. In this way, Tito had fulfilled his wartime promise to compensate them for their help in his grab for power, even though their assistance was actually next to nothing.

In any case, Miloshevich's action opened the way for Serbs to ventilate many other grievances from the Tito period. They pointed out that they had sacrificed the most for the common state, without any recognition from others. On the contrary, they were being blamed for all failures in the first as well as the second Yugoslavia. Consequently, Serbian intellectuals began questioning the wisdom of Serbia's continuing commitment to an integral Yugoslavia as long as others did not want to live in freedom and equality.

In 1990, Croatia and Slovenia demanded that Yugoslavia be organized as a loose association of sovereign states; otherwise, they would secede. In the political stalemate of mid-summer 1991, Slovenia declared that it was seceding, and Croatia followed suit. The central Yugoslav government declared these actions illegal (the Yugoslav Constitutional Court subsequently agreed) and sent troops to control border crossings in Slovenia, with no small amount of bloodshed. Subsequently, a cease-fire agreement was signed with Western European assistance, and Yugoslav troops were withdrawn.

More bloodshed occurred in Croatia, between Croatian militia and armed groups of Serbs insistent on protecting the Serbian minority of from six hundred thousand to eight hundred thousand living in that republic. These Serbs had indicated that if Croatia were to remain a part of Yugoslavia, they would be satisfied with cultural autonomy. If Croatia were to leave Yugoslavia, however, they were determined to be annexed to Serbia.

The Slovenian-Croatian draft of a new constitution did not offer much hope. Under it, the national government would have consultative powers, making it even weaker than the national government under the early American Articles of Confederation. Under such a system, Serbian interests anywhere outside Serbia could not be protected by the national government or by the government of Serbia. With about 30 percent of the Serbs living outside Serbia, it was highly unlikely that Serbia could ever accept such a constitution.

Ironically, Tito, who had a Croatian father and Slovenian mother, and his Serbian, Croatian, Slovenian, and other South Slav Communist comrades, who prided themselves on being proponents of "Brotherhood and Unity," achieved exactly the opposite result.

The Aftermath

The precipitous declaration of independence, first by Slovenia and Croatia and subsequently by Bosnia-Hercegovina, led to civil war. The preamble of the Yugoslav constitution mentions the right to self-determination, including the right of secession, but the body of the document does not provide any procedure by which secession can actually take place, although it does make it amply clear that it could not be done unilaterally.

Adding to the tragedy was the haste with which the European Community (EC), under strong pressure from Germany and Austria, extended diplomatic recognition to Slovenia and Croatia. To the Serbs, who had fought against the Germans and Austrians in two world wars, the German policy had all the earmarks of a plan to achieve politically and economically what it had failed to attain militarily.

Ironically, the action of the EC states took place while they still had accredited diplomats to the existing Yugoslav national government. Moreover, several key positions in the Belgrade central government were held by non-Serbs: Prime Minister Ante Markovich, a Croat; Foreign Minister Budimir Lonchar, another Croat; General Veljko Kadijevich, minister of defense and supreme commander, son of a Croat-Serb marriage; Deputy Commander

Stane Brovet, a Slovene; and Chief of the Air Force Zvonko Jurjevich, yet another Croat. While the army's officer corps was predominantly Serbian, the high command was 38 percent Croatian, 33 percent Serbia, 8.3 percent Slovenian, 8.3 percent Macedonian, and 4.1 percent Muslim. In addition, in 1991, a Croat, Stipe Mesich, became president of the collective presidency, following several months during which he had failed to get confirmation because of his now prophetic statement that he would be the last Yugoslav president.

In all central government positions, the Yugoslav Communists used the "key," or quota: positions would be apportioned roughly in accord with the size of each ethnic group. This was true, for example, of diplomatic appointments. The Serbs pointed out, however, that while they got their share of these, a Serb was rarely appointed to an ambassadorship in one of the large countries in the West. In addition, no Serb had been appointed to the prime minister-ship in the past decade, except for a Serb from Bosnia-Hercegovina. The foregoing examples of affirmative action would seem to contradict charges of Serbian domination of the Yugoslav national government.

The actions of the EC countries, joined by the United States after a period of insisting that recognition could come only after the Yugoslav republics had reached political settlements, raised interesting questions of international law. The most important of these was whether several sovereign states had a right to aid in the destruction of another member state of the international community, particularly when no member of this community was threatened by developments in Yugoslavia. In addition, the EC had acted after offering its "good offices," purportedly with the aim of seeking a peaceful resolution of differences, but then took sides before any meaningful negotiations could take place, declaring publicly that recognition of Slovenia and Croatia was forthcoming, thus aiding and abetting them in violation of the Helsinki Accords' provision against changing boundaries by force.

Aside from legal questions, it seemed obvious that the EC was acting without much knowledge of Yugoslav history. The EC leaders proceeded on two faulty assumptions. The first was that the boundaries of the republics could not be altered. These boundaries did not exist before the Tito regime, and it should have been clear that, when the Tito structure came tumbling down, the Serbs, who were scattered so that a third of them did not live in the Republic of Serbia, would no longer accept Tito's punitive territorial divisions. Second, while respecting the wishes and interests of the secessionist republics, the EC and the United States assumed that the interests and wishes of Serbia could be ignored. Proceeding on the basis of these unsound assumptions was an unfailing formula for disaster.

The evolution of events in Yugoslavia, as well as in the former Soviet empire, leads to the larger question of the impact of the creation of many mini-states. In the earlier decades of the twentieth century, the trend seemed to be toward larger national units. Self-determination may constitute a victory for small powers, but can this victory be permanent? Could such states produce viable political systems? Additionally, is it responsible to extend diplomatic recognition to certain geographic units that have never had their own states, especially in such complex and volatile areas as Bosnia-Hercegovina and Macedonia - particularly when such actions adversely affect relations with other peoples, such as the Serbs, who are the only proven Western allies among the Yugoslavs? Some Western European and American pundits have asserted that states should be able to recognize self-defined communities. Logically, under this formulation, the self-defined Serbian communities in Croatia and Bosnia-Hercegovina could expect recognition, as could the Albanians in Serbia's Kosovo province. Where does this type of action lead?

And how are outside nations to judge the actions of those who seek to prevent secession? Should they condemn only those who fail to overcome insurgency and secession, as in the case of Yugoslavia, and not those who succeed in suppressing such rebellion, as the Union did in the American Civil War, despite incomparably larger casualties over a four-year period in the latter case?

And what are the circumstances that would lead the U.S. Secretary of State in 1992 to consider recognizing Yugoslav Macedonia when another American Secretary of State declared in 1944 that the United States government "considers any talk of a Macedonian nation, Macedonian fatherland, or Macedonian national consciousness to be unjustified demagoguery representing no ethnic or political reality?"[4]

The tragedy of Yugoslavia has been matched by the equally sad and pathetic attempts at crisis management by leaders of the Western international community.

NOTES

1. For a full treatment of this period of Yugoslavia's history, see Dragnich, *The First Yugoslavia: Search for a Viable Political System* (Stanford, CA: Hoover Institution Press, 1983).

2. For the latest works on Tito's struggle for power, see Michael Lees, *The Rape of Serbia: The British Role in Tito's Grab for Power, 1943-1944* (New York: Harcourt Brace Jovanovich, 1990); and David Martin, *The Web of Disinformation: Churchill's Yugoslav Blunder* (New York: Harcourt Brace Jovanovich, 1990). Both books were reviewed by this author in *Mediterranean Quarterly* 2 (Spring 1991): 105-109.

3. For an account of the early years of the Tito regime, see Dragnich, *Tito's Promised Land: Yugoslavia* (New Brunswick, NJ: Rutgers University Press, 1954). For a longer overview, see Dennison Rusinow, *The Yugoslav Experiment, 1948-1974* (Berkeley: University of California Press, 1977).

4. Circular airgram from Secretary of State Edward Stettinus to certain diplomatic and consular officers, 26 December 1944.

THE TRAGEDY OF YUGOSLAVIA*

Yugoslavia, if we have been inclined to believe what news stories and commentaries have offered us, was a conglomerate of feuding ethnic groups put together in 1945 by Communist leader Josip Broz Tito. Others have referred to it as an artificial creation of the Versailles peace conference in 1919. If we are to understand the tragedy that has been unfolding there in the past year or two, it is necessary to know something of Yugoslavia's history.

The Yugoslav state was created on December 1, 1918, prior to the convening of Versailles, by men who were seeking the realization of an idea long nurtured by South Slav intellectuals, mainly Croats and Serbs. Although the idea did not have deep roots among the masses, the South (*yug* means south) Slavs had several things in common - language, Christian religion (even though the Slovenes and Croats were Roman Catholic and the Serbs Orthodox), and a closely related ethnicity.

On the other hand, their political experiences had been different. The Slovenes and Croats were still under foreign and non-democratic rule which had lasted for centuries, while the Serbs had regained their independence from long Ottoman reign by mid-nineteenth century, and rather rapidly developed a model democratic parliamentary political system. By the beginning of the twentieth century, Serbia's political system was at least on par with that of France and one or two small democratic states in Europe. The remaining European countries, including Russia, Germany, and Austria-Hungary, were still in various stages of authoritarian rule.

While Serbia had been a sort of magnet for the South Slavs in the Habsburg empire, no advance preparation for a common state had been made, and it was only Austria-Hungary's attack on Serbia in 1914, and the prospect of the former's collapse, that provided the opportunity for a hasty union.

Serbia's guiding hand in the creation of the First Yugoslavia cannot be disputed. Shortly after the onset of World War I, Serbia declared as its major war aim (next to victory) the liberation and

* *Vanderbilt Magazine* (Winter, 1992), pp. 27-29. Reprinted with permission.

unification of all Serbs, Croats, and Slovenes. Moreover, Serbia inspired the creation of the Yugoslav Committee, made up of South Slavs from Austria-Hungary and chaired by Croat Ante Trumbich, to aid in the propagation of the idea in Allied capitals.

In July 1917, Trumbich and Serbian Prime Minister Nikola Pashich met on the Greek island of Corfu and concluded an agreement on the nature of the forth-coming Yugoslav state, to be known as the Kingdom of the Serbs, Croats, and Slovenes. It was to be a parliamentary constitutional monarchy, with the Serbian king as monarch. The agreement came to be called the Corfu Declaration.

Pursuant to that agreement, Croat, Serb, and Slovene representatives from the Croatian city of Zagreb came to Belgrade, and in a meeting on December 1, 1918, with the Serbian ministers and Prince Alexander Karadjordjevich, declared the coming into existence of the Kingdom of the Serbs, Croats, and Slovenes. It was made up of the two Serbian states (Serbia and Montenegro), and the South Slav provinces of Austria-Hungary - Slovenia, Croatia, Bosnia-Hercegovina, and Vojvodina.

The delegates from Zagreb were in somewhat of a hurry because the impending collapse of Austria-Hungary and Germany threatened to leave many of their compatriots under foreign rule. The Allied Powers, in the secret Treaty of London in 1915, had promised to Italy large areas of the northern Adriatic and Dalmatia as a reward for joining the Allied camp.

Parenthetically, it needs to be added that pursuant to that treaty, Serbia was offered a Great Serbia on the proverbial silver platter, if she should give up the dream of a Yugoslav state, thus enabling the Allies to fulfill their promises to Italy. Such a Serbia would have included Bosnia-Hercegovina, parts of Dalmatia, as well as the Serbian-populated areas of Croatia that have recently been the scene of bitter fighting. With the benefit of hindsight, Serbia's refusal of the offer constitutes a bitter tragedy.

In 1919, following the declaration of a common state, a Provisional Parliament was established, with the primary task of drafting a constitution for the new state. After nearly two years of mainly fruitless work, the Provisional Parliament called for elections in November 1920 for delegates to a Constituent Assembly to do the constitution-making.

The latter effort got off to a bad start, mainly because the men who had represented Croatia in the Provisional Parliament were defeated by Croatian nationalist forces, represented by the Croatian Republican Peasant Party, led by Stjepan Radich, who wanted an independent Croatia and therefore decided that his Party's delegates should boycott the Constituent Assembly.

Nevertheless, a democratic constitution was adopted in 1921 by an absolute majority of the elected delegates (including the Croatian ones), which constitutional experts believed met the Corfu provision requiring a "numerically qualified majority," otherwise undefined.

Again, the newly elected Croatian members of Parliament refused to take their seats, and it was not until 1925 that Radich and his Croatian Peasant Party (they dropped the word "Republican" from the name), recognized the monarchy, and accepted the Constitution, and took their seats. Subsequently, Radich even became a cabinet minister.

When Nikola Pashich, longtime prime minister of Serbia and prime minister of the new state from 1921 to 1926, left the political scene shortly before his death, obstructionism and general turmoil became the rule in parliament. It was during one of these tumultuous sessions in 1928 that Radich and several of his party deputies were shot by a Serbian deputy from Montenegro. Some died on the spot, while Radich recovered, only to die several months later of a secondary infection of his diabetes.

The Croat deputies withdrew from parliament and efforts at several cabinet combinations seemed to get nowhere, thus ending what had been a promising beginning in Yugoslav democracy.

King Alexander sought to end the chaos by taking power into his hands on January 1, 1929. He declared all political parties dissolved, and undertook to rule through cabinets headed by persons loyal to him. He also changed the name of the state to Yugoslavia, and divided the country into nine administrative areas named after waterways (all but one rivers) as a possible way of minimizing ethnic identities. In 1931, he engineered what after World War II came to be called "guided democracy." The experiment was short-lived because Alexander was assassinated in 1934 while on a state visit to France in what was a well-planned plot, organized by extremist Croats.

Since Alexander's son was a minor, royal authority was vested mainly in Alexander's first cousin, Prince Paul. He faced two critical problems: how to create a viable political order, and how to keep Yugoslavia from becoming involved in the impending Second World War.

Paul lost no time in initiating a series of talks (through his ministers) with the leader of the Croatian Peasant Party, Vladko Machek, which led to an agreement in August 1939 that established a Croatian territorial unit (known as *Banovina*), giving the Croats considerable autonomy - in fact the first move toward federation. The next item on the agenda was the creation of similar Serbian and Slovene units, but with the outbreak of war in the following month, the projected reforms were shelved. While we shall never know, it seems reasonable to conclude that the Yugoslavs were on the way toward the resolution of their basic political problems had it not been for the world conflict.

Prince Paul sought to keep Yugoslavia out of the war, but in the final analysis found that he could do so only by accepting a somewhat watered-down version of Hitler's Tri-Partite Pact, which promised to respect Yugoslavia's neutrality. Unfortunately, Yugoslav army officers, aided and abetted by British agents, overthrew the regency of Prince Paul, a popular act, mainly in Serbia, where the populace was whipped up by allegations that Paul had put Yugoslavia in the same boat as Hungary, Romania, and Bulgaria as Axis partners. When the revolutionaries read the agreement, they concluded that there was nothing there that they could not accept, but it was too late. Hitler could not permit the upstarts to get away with insulting Germany, and in a matter of days launched an attack that in two weeks put an end to the first Yugoslavia.

Aside from the ravages of armed conflict, Yugoslavia suffered three terrible consequences - really catastrophes - as a result of the Second World War. The first one was the establishment in April 1941 of the so-called Independent State of Croatia, an Axis satellite whose terror against non-Croats knew no bounds, so that even the Germans and Italians were appalled. The movement governing Croatia, known as the *Ustashe*, was similar to the Nazi and Fascist ones. In the early years of that regime, the *Ustashe* and their henchmen were responsible for massacring some 700,000 Serbs (men, women, and children) in particularly bestial ways, as well as some 60,000 Jews and a smaller number of Gypsies.

It was these massacres that struck fear in the hearts of some 600,000 to 800,000 Serbs living in Croatia when the movement was launched to create another independent Croatian state. The regime that came into power in 1990, under former Communist general Franjo Tudjman, did little to allay those fears. On the contrary, Tudjman portrayed Axis satellite Croatia as the understandable urge of the Croats to have their own state. In addition, some of the trappings of that state were imitated by him, including measures that discriminated against Serbs, while at the same time asserting that Croatia had set up a democratic system.

When in 1991 the Croatian authorities declared that Croatia was seceding from Yugoslavia, the Serbian inhabitants made it known that they wanted no part of such a state, and began an armed rebellion. This was a bit reminiscent of those Virginians who wanted to remain a part of the Union, and in 1863 constituted the state of West Virginia. But this is getting ahead of the story.

The second and related catastrophe was the civil war that evolved from two competing guerrilla movements - the Chetniks, led by Colonel (later General) Drazha Mihailovich, and the Partisans, led by Communist Josip Broz Tito. Mihailovich was at a serious disadvantage from the beginning, because his only aim was to aid the Allies and to leave questions about the future organization of the state to the electorate after the war. The Communist-led Partisans, on the other hand, were primarily dedicated to the seizure of power, and committed all of their energies to that goal. Ultimately, they convinced the Western Allies, primarily Britain, whose voice was dominant in the matter, that they and not Mihailovich deserved their sole support. The Partisans even charged Mihailovich of collaborating with the enemy, a charge that scholars, including Yugoslav Communist ones, have in subsequent years disproved.

When Soviet troops captured Belgrade and turned over the capital to Tito in 1944, he began establishing a Communist regime. In 1946, Mihailovich was captured and, after a "show trial," executed. This ended the civil war, which was not only costly in lives and property, but perhaps more importantly, it left bitter scars that did not heal.

Parenthetically, it should be noted that in the 1920s, the Yugoslav Communists followed the line of the Moscow-directed Communist International (Comintern) in regarding Yugoslavia as an artificial creation - "a prison of nationalities" - and called for its dismemberment. In the 1930s, the Comintern line changed and the Yugoslav Communist Party fell in line. It was in the late 1930s that Josip Broz Tito, whose underground name for a time was Walter, became General Secretary of the Party.

The third major catastrophe for Yugoslavia was the Communist system, three aspects of which need brief comment - political, economic, and ethnic.

The political dictatorship, patterned after the Soviet one, provided for a pseudo federation of six republics and two autonomous provinces, as well as for "democratic" institutions which were completely under the control of the Communist Party. After the break with Stalin in 1948, there was hope for change, and some "mellowing" of dictatorial rule did take place, but the primacy of the Communist Party was never altered. Seeking to avoid a struggle for power after his death, Tito in the late 1970s established a collective presidency of eight persons, and modified the other governmental bodies so that virtual unanimity was required for all decisions of consequence.

In the decade after Tito's death in 1980, his heirs sought to hold the system together, but in the end failed, because the system bequeathed to them led to political paralysis. Increasingly, the Communist Party (since 1952 called The League of Yugoslav Communists) tended to split along republic (ethnic) lines, and at an Extraordinary Congress in 1990, hopelessly divided, it breathed its last. From then on, the country itself began coming apart.

The economy, as in other Communist-ruled countries, turned out to be a failure. Some major economic objectives were reached, but with much waste and at heavy costs. Soon after the break with Moscow, Tito did de-collectivize agriculture, but the much touted workers' councils and the self-management system failed to achieve expectations. Moreover, Tito's decentralizing of the economic system led to the republics engaging in ruinous competition and autarchy. In the decade of the 1980s, the economy went downhill, with a huge foreign debt, high inflation, and a decline in the standard of living.

Bickering between and among the republics as to who was responsible for the sad state of economic affairs contributed to much controversy. Slovenia and Croatia claimed that they were being exploited for the benefit of the less well-to-do republics, and blamed Serbia most of all. Serbia, for her part, reminded Slovenia and Croatia, quite correctly in view of my own studies, that they had received favorable economic treatment in the First as well as Tito's Yugoslavia, pointing out that in 1991 the average per capita income in Slovenia was $12,618, in Croatia it was $7,179, and in Serbia only $4,870. By 1991, however, rational dialogue seemed no longer possible.

Contributing to much of the political and economic bickering was the legacy of Tito's ethnic or nationality policy. He and his Communist comrades believed that they could solve the problem of past ethnic discords by dividing the country into nationality groups or republics, the first time this had been done in Yugoslavia. Some of the resulting boundaries were not rational. While Tito's handiwork may have been popular with those who wanted a separate Macedonia or Bosnia-Hercegovina, it created serious dissatisfactions, especially among the Serbs, who had been the strongest supporters of a common state and had sacrificed the most for it. Some 35 percent of them were left in other republics. Moreover, inside the republic of Serbia itself two autonomous provinces were created. One was Vojvodina, where a Hungarian minority was present, the other was Kosovo, where the Albanian minority had become a majority.

Tito made no secret of his determination to weaken Serbia, asserting that it was responsible for all the woes that had befallen pre-war Yugoslavia. More importantly, Tito's Partisans had little support in Serbia, which was the center of the Mihailovich movement, and which had a history of hostility to tyrants.

While a part of the republic of Serbia, these provinces were subject to little or no control by Serbian authorities. This was a bitter pill, particularly the status of Kosovo, the cradle of the medieval Serbian state, where Serbia's noted religious and cultural monuments were located. Not only had Tito encouraged more and more Albanians to move into Kosovo, leading to an Albanian majority of nearly 90 percent, but in addition tolerated the desecration and destruction of many of the Serbian Christian monuments by the

Kosovo Albanians who also forced thousands of Serbs to flee for their lives.

Not until Slobodan Milosevich became head of the Serbian Communist Party in 1986 were the Serbs able to ventilate their grievances and to call for justice. The Serbian masses, although anti-communist, were grateful to Milosevich for asserting control over Kosovo, and for making it possible for them to voice their complaints and to articulate their aspirations.

Although the Serbs had been the strongest supporters of a Yugoslav state, they began to realize just how costly the Yugoslav experiment had been to them and to have serious doubts about the wisdom of that commitment. Nevertheless, they were willing to listen to Slovene and Croat proposals for change. When these turned out to be a constitutional structure that was even weaker than the American Articles of Confederation, the Serbs indicated that they were prepared to let Slovenia and Croatia go their separate ways. In the case of the latter, however, the Serbs insisted that the 600,000 to 800,000 Serbs in Croatia should not be forced to leave Yugoslavia against their will, and called for some changes in the boundaries that had been Tito's work.

The failure of the secessionist Croatian government to consider the clearly expressed will of the Serbian minority, insisting that it remain a part of an independent Croatia, and Serbia's determination to help their compatriots, led to civil war.

Whatever the outcome of this tragedy, one thing seems fairly evident: ironically, Tito and his Communist comrades, who prided themselves on the slogan of "Brotherhood and Unity," achieved the exact opposite. More than that, their whole path seems to have been one of political folly.

Finally, lest we become overly euphoric about the victory of democracy, which I believe all peoples of Yugoslavia want, we must keep in mind that for the time being most key positions in the bureaucracy of all republics - despite claims of democracy - are controlled by Communists or former Communists under other political designations. All opposition groups operated under the most severe handicaps. The ultimate battle for democracy is yet to be won, and very likely will take some time.

THE WEST'S MISMANAGEMENT OF THE YUGOSLAV CRISIS*

The efforts of the European Community (EC) and the United States to manage the crisis in Yugoslavia as that country began to drift toward civil war presents us with an interesting case of collective action that has been anything but successful.

Following the declarations of sovereignty in mid-1990 by the republics of Slovenia and Croatia, with strong suggestions that they intended to secede from Yugoslavia, the EC offered its good offices in the ostensible hope of an orderly and peaceful resolution of the crisis. The crisis had been building for several months, as the handiwork of Communist dictator Tito had begun to unravel. Thus, the EC and the United States were not caught unaware of Yugoslav developments.

From the beginning, however, EC policy-makers' decisions demonstrated that they knew little or no Yugoslav history. Many of the EC leaders seemed to assume that Yugoslavia began with Tito's Communist party regime. They knew of the Yugoslav republics but apparently did not know how they came about or if the boundaries between them had been satisfactory to all ethnic groups.

Strange as it may seem, they were also ignorant of the fact that the first Yugoslavia (pre-Tito) had not been divided into republics or other ethnic units. The Yugoslavia of the interwar years was a unitary state. Initially, there were thirty-three administrative districts, but in 1929 these were reduced to nine (a tenth embraced the capital, Belgrade). The nine were known as *banovine* (after a Croatian term meaning governor); they were named after waterways and were designed to cut across ethnic and regional differences. A provisional modification was made in 1939, dictated mainly by international developments.

After the assassination of King Alexander in 1934 as a result of a carefully laid plot by Croatian extremists, the country was ruled under a Royal Regency because the heir to the throne was not of age. In 1939, with war clouds on the horizon and with the Croat leader threatening to use Fascist Italian and Nazi German help to break

---

* *World Affairs*, Fall, 1993, pp. 63-71. Reprinted with permission.

away from Yugoslavia, Prince Regent Paul made a hasty agreement with the Croats that combined two of the banovinas where most of the Croats lived, but also contained over one million Serbs. This provisional agreement gave considerable powers to the Banovina of Croatia, but it never received the legal sanction of ratification by the national legislature, as required by the agreement. The coming of the Second World War put an end to further domestic political changes, and in April 1941 the Axis Powers destroyed the first Yugoslavia.

The only so-called independent entity on Yugoslav soil during World War II was the Axis puppet Croatian state, whose minions massacred some 700,000 Serbs, 60,000 Jews, and 20,000 Gypsies. After the war, no Yugoslav Communist leader apologized for the acts of the Axis puppet regime, no retribution was visited on Croatia, and no payments were made to aggrieved parties or their relatives. This was in sharp contrast with the postwar German government, which condemned the Nazi regime and apologized for its acts.

With the creation of the second Yugoslavia (Tito's), the country was divided into six republics (plus two autonomous provinces in the republic of Serbia). This arrangement was supposed to solve the nationality problems that had been a divisive force in Yugoslavia's brief history.

In the pre-Communist years, Yugoslavia was said to consist primarily of three ethnic groups - Serbs, Croats, and Slovenes. Because Tito and his Communist comrades blamed the Serbs for all the failures of the first Yugoslavia, and because Communist guerrillas had little success in Serbia (Colonel Draza Mihailovic was the leader of the non-Communist guerrilla movement in Serbia), they were determined to punish this largest ethnic group and the strongest supporter of the common state. They weakened Serbia by creating a second Serbian republic - Montenegro - an independent state prior to the First World War. The fact that many of Tito's generals and political supporters came from Montenegro played a significant role in its establishment as a separate republic.

Second, as a way of further weakening Serbia, Tito created the republic of Bosnia-Herzegovina, where the Serbs were the largest ethnic group (the Croats were half as numerous as the Serbs). In 1971, he used the presence of a large Muslim population, descendants of Serbs and Croats (mainly the former) who had been converted to Islam during the centuries of Ottoman rule, to create a new ethnic identity (Muslim), ironically based on religion. That move made the Muslims the largest group in the republic.

Tito also created a separate republic of Macedonia (once known as South Serbia), partly to punish the Serbs, partly to foreclose Bulgarian claims to parts of that area, and partly to lay claim to Greek Macedonia. As already mentioned, he created two autonomous provinces inside Serbia, Kosovo (cradle of the Serbian nation and at the time of the Ottoman conquest in the fourteenth century ethnically solid Serbian, but by 1946 equally divided), and Vojvodina (with a large Hungarian minority).

During his rule, Tito managed to sweep nationality questions under the rug, insisting that the problems were solved, and thereby foreclosing further dialogue on this issue. After Tito's death in 1980, however, differences among the republics grew, increasingly taking on nationalist overtones.

While threats to Yugoslavia's survival were in evidence in the bickering between the republics in the late 1980s, the first concrete sign came in January 1990, when the extraordinary congress of the national party broke up in disarray. This was followed by Serbia's assuming basic political powers in her autonomous provinces, Kosovo and Vojvodina, limiting or revoking their autonomy. Soon thereafter, in elections in Slovenia and Croatia, recycled Communists, posing as nationalists, were victorious. These were followed, as indicated above, by Slovene and Croat declarations of sovereignty and hints of intentions to secede.

At the same time, General Tudjman's regime in Croatia reduced the Serbs to a minority status, whereas in the Tito period they had been considered constituent peoples and hence on the same level as the Croats. Moreover, under Tudjman the Serbs were subjected to discriminatory acts in employment and in civil rights. Crude examples of the latter were nocturnal shootings, hate slogans painted on their houses, and threatening telephone calls in the middle of the night. Eventually, over one hundred thousand Serbs abandoned their homes and sought refuge in Serbia, Montenegro, and Bosnia-Herzegovina.

A short time earlier, Slovenia and Croatia had proposed a reorganization of Yugoslavia as a confederation. Under their proposal, the central government would have basically consultative powers, even weaker than the U.S. federal government under the

Articles of Confederation, which had proved utterly unworkable. Because the national government would have no power to protect the large number of Serbs who would be left outside Serbia - between 600,000 to 800,000 in Croatia and 1.5 million in Bosnia-Herzegovina - the Slovene-Croat proposal was not acceptable to Serbia.

In June 1991, Slovenia and Croatia issued independence pronouncements. Slovenia took control of border posts on the Austrian and Italian frontiers, taking the first steps in violation of the Helsinki Accords' proviso that international boundaries could not be changed except by peaceful means. The European Community sponsored a meeting of the presidents of the Yugoslav republics on the island of Brioni (Tito's favorite retreat) and called for a ninety-day suspension of the independence declarations and a withdrawal to barracks of all federal troops. At the same time, EC foreign ministers obtained Slovenia's promise to remove its border signs and flags during that period and share border authority with the federal government. While the Slovenes made a half-hearted attempt to share the border post authority, they did not remove Slovenian flags or signs.

At the end of the three-month delay period, Slovenia and Croatia declared formal secessions, and the EC did nothing. The Yugoslav government declared the Slovene and Croat acts unconstitutional (later confirmed by the decision of the Yugoslav Constitutional Court), and ordered Yugoslav army troops in Slovenia to reclaim the border posts. The Slovenian militia, joined by irregulars, resisted fiercely, firing the first shots in what was to evolve into a civil war. They even seized foreign freight trucks in international transit to block highways. The result was a setback to the Yugoslav army and its withdrawal from Slovenia.

Unlike Slovenia, Croatia had a large Serbian minority, which did not cherish being in an independent Croatian state, particularly in view of their memories of what happened to their compatriots the last time that Croatia was independent. These Serbs took up armed resistance, which was aided by the Yugoslav army units that were in the territory. At the same time, Croatian armed units struck at Yugoslav army garrisons in Croatia.

The reaction in the West favored the continued existence of the Yugoslav state, but as the situation deteriorated in 1991, the reaction changed to one of respecting the wishes of the peoples of Yugoslavia.

The European Community offered its good offices, which was accepted, and soon a mission was on its way to Yugoslavia, headed by Lord Carrington. Considerable differences in approach soon emerged, however, between the United States and European Community, and within the EC itself. The attitude of the United States, as expressed by Secretary of State James Baker, was that if Yugoslavia was to break up, the United States would wait until the different groups had resolved their differences through political settlements, and only then would the question of recognition be considered. At the same time, he personally warned the Slovene and Croat presidents that if they seceded unilaterally there would be civil war. Similarly, Lawrence Eagleburger revealed in August 1992 that he had also warned that in case of unilateral acts of independence, there would be "civil war of massive proportions."

The EC, prodded by Germany and Austria, showed no such restraint. For a time, the majority of EC countries had reservations about acting in haste and some suspicion of German motives was expressed unofficially. The Germans, even before the Carrington mission had sufficient time to test its efforts in negotiation, were pushing for recognition of Slovenia and Croatia. It is interesting to note, however, that the German and Austrian ambassadors in Belgrade recommended against the actions that their governments insisted on taking.

At the EC meeting in Maastricht in mid-December 1991, the initial vote on recognizing Slovenia and Croatia as independent countries was eight to four against. But German Foreign Minister Hans Dietrich Genscher declared that they would not leave the table before they got unanimous support for recognition. It was then 10 P.M. By 4 A.M. the next morning, he had his way. Having given in on some monetary issues, Genscher reportedly said, "now you owe me one," whereupon he had his way. In addition, it was reported that a German foreign office person had told newsmen: "We will move ahead whether any, all, or none of the European states join us." Cyrus Vance, Secretary of State under President Carter who had been sent by the United Nations to seek a cease-fire between the fighting parties in Croatia, as well as UN Secretary General Perez de Cuellar, told Genscher that premature recognition of Slovenia and Croatia could "intensify and widen the war."

In December 1991, in response to Germany's declaration that Bonn was determined to recognize Bosnia-Herzegovina as well, Vance once more cautioned against hasty recognition. Germany's refusal greatly undercut his efforts. Interestingly, Bosnia's and Macedonia's leaders had earlier pleaded with Western capitals to withhold recognition of Slovenia and Croatia, fearing that such actions would provoke the Serbs.

Before Vance's appointment, EC representative Lord Carrington made an error at the outset of his mission by presenting the Yugoslav parties a document that declared the existing Yugoslav state at an end and proposed that negotiations begin on the creation of a new one. His action was viewed unfavorably by the Serbs, who did not want a breakup of the country, but played into the hands of the Slovenes and Croats, who did.

Soon thereafter it became evident that the EC countries were not interested in evenhandedness. The EC countries, as well as the United States, had said that they would respect the wishes of the Yugoslav peoples. It soon was evident that they meant that they would respect the wishes of the republics that wanted to secede but not those of the republics that wanted to remain a part of Yugoslavia. They did this by asserting that the boundaries between the republics could not be changed except by peaceful means. Ironically, they had already aided and abetted Slovenia and Croatia in their violation of the Helsinki Accords through the use of force to change Yugoslavia's borders. At the same time, they knew, or should have known, that the republic that suffered the greatest injustice when Tito carved up the country into republics and autonomous provinces was Serbia.

The action of the West encouraged the secessionist republics to believe that they could hold onto every inch of territory bequeathed to them by Tito and had no need to compromise. Moreover, this EC action enabled Serbia's president, recycled Communist Slobodan Milosevic, to pose as the only defender of Serbian interests, and declare that his answer to the EC would be to recognize as separate nations the Serb-inhabited areas of Croatia and Bosnia-Herzegovina.

It is important to note that at its meeting in Lisbon in February 1992, the EC proposed a cantonal solution for Bosnia-Herzegovina, i.e., dividing it into Serbian, Croatian, and Muslim units. About mid-March, all three Bosnian parties agreed to this solution in principle. Soon after returning to Sarajevo, however, the Muslim president,

Izetbegovic, reneged. The available evidence indicates that it was the United States that advised him to go back on his commitment, while the Europeans had reservations. The United States urged the EC to recognize Bosnia-Herzegovina, promising that the United States would follow suit and would also recognize Slovenia and Croatia, which is what happened. Hence a promising solution, before the fighting began, went by the boards.

Not having learned any lesson from the fact that the hasty recognition of Slovenia and, especially, Croatia had undesirable consequences, the EC and the United States extended recognition to Bosnia-Herzegovina in April 1992. Western policy-makers seemingly again did not weigh the possible consequences of their acts or did not care. They had ample warning when the Serbs of Bosnia-Herzegovina, numbering about a third of the population but occupying more than sixty percent of the area,[1] boycotted the independence referendum and openly declared that if the republic proclaimed its independence, they would form their own republic.

Nevertheless, the Bosnian Muslim leaders seemingly had no worries. In a trip to Washington, the president and his secretary for foreign affairs personally assured Secretary Baker that "no one can divide us." They insisted that they were building a democratic state. Perhaps the Americans were influenced by the success of earlier Croatian propaganda in portraying the conflict in Yugoslavia as one of democracy and communism, which of course was not the case. The regimes in all of the republics continued to be run by Communists or former Communists. Ironically, there was much more freedom for the opposition in Serbia than in the other republics.

Astute observers predicted that diplomatic recognition of Bosnia-Herzegovina would be followed by more bloodshed than had been experienced in Croatia. And they were proved right. Some spokesmen for the EC had justified recognition on the grounds that this would prevent serious strife. Actually, it did the exact opposite. It was a formula for disaster. As an American scholar with no ethnic roots in Yugoslavia said at an academic gathering in November 1992, "The West came to Yugoslavia as fire fighters and ended up being pyromaniacs."

While U.S. State Department diplomats at the working level did not show outward displeasure with policy decisions, they knew that these came down from the highest levels -- Bush-Baker. The best proof is to be found in the fact that just before the denial of landing rights to the Yugoslav airline, Yugoslav experts in the State Department were privately assuring one and all that the United States would not take such an action.

While it cannot be confirmed, there are strong reasons to believe that the president and his secretary of state, determined to achieve peace in the Middle East, were being pressured by Saudi Arabia to recognize Bosnia-Herzegovina. The Saudis, so the story goes, stressed to the United States that the Muslim leaders in Sarajevo were moderates, the type of Muslims that America was relying upon in the Middle East. It is also important to note, as Secretary Baker did for some of us who went to see him in July 1992, that he had been under great pressure from members of Congress who had Croatian, Slovenian, and Muslim constituents.

In any case, we need to stress that as bloodshed in Bosnia increased, the Western powers, instead of reflecting on their failed policies, have since that time concentrated on dealing with the consequences of those policies. The event that triggered Secretary Baker's going to the United Nations to ask for sanctions against Yugoslavia (i.e., Serbia and Montenegro) was the killing of a number of Sarajevo residents who were lined up in front of a bakery to buy bread, for which Serb gunners were blamed. Subsequently, it was determined that the victims were killed by anti-personnel mines laid by anti-Serb elements. Some observers had introduced doubts at the time because of the fact that TV cameras were on hand to record the tragic event and because none of the victims had wounds above the waist. In addition, subsequent terrorist acts initially blamed on Serbs were discovered to have been done by others.

Moreover, an hour after the sanctions were voted, the previous day's report by the UN secretary general surfaced, pointing out that Croatia had a sizable military presence in Bosnia, but there was no explanation why the report was not available to the Security Council when it voted. Some members were quoted as saying that their votes would have been different if the report had been available at the time. In any case, it should be noted that not only was Croatia's military presence significant but also that Croats were using the Croatian flag and Croatian currency and not those of Bosnia-Herzegovina.

The underlying assumption, unspoken but clearly conveyed, was that the Serbs and Serbia had no business being concerned with Bosnia or Croatia. Yet, aside from the fact that Serbs have lived in those areas for centuries, Serbia's right to those territories was recognized in at least two international agreements, to which reference will be made below.

Moreover, no one seems to have remembered that in the Balkan wars of 1912-13 and in the First World War, the Serbs of Serbia and Montenegro fought to liberate Serbian lands, including those in Bosnia-Herzegovina and Croatia, as well as liberating Slovenian, Croatian, and other South Slav lands. Nor was there any recollection that at the end of World War I, the Slovenes and Croats implored Serbia to accept them as parts of a common Yugoslav state.

And when the common state was dissolving in 1990-1991, the West proceeded on the assumption that Serbia and Montenegro should forget their enormous sacrifices in those wars and be satisfied to have nearly three million of their compatriots remain under the rule of others. We can imagine how this would be seen by Serbs, who, having lived in one state since 1918 after their ancestors had fought to get out from under foreign rule, especially from under the Muslim Turks, now should be asked to have a large number of them go back to Muslim masters.

Tragically, the print and electronic media in Europe and in the United States have dealt with day-to-day developments, and showed no desire to inquire into the basic issues that resulted in the conflict, nor did they engage in critical examination of the policies of the Western powers that not only failed to deal with those issues but also engaged in a violation of the Helsinki Accords, to which they were signatories. An Op-Ed column suggested that what was needed, if the divorce involving six parties was to be resolved amicably, was a peace conference steered by the major powers. That conference would tackle such issues as internal boundaries, allocation of responsibilities for the repayment of Yugoslavia's foreign debt of some 22 billion dollars, division of common properties, and other matters.

In August 1992, pursuant to a British call, a conference was held in London that the various Yugoslav parties attended. While it called upon the participants in the civil war to cease military action, most of the blame was heaped upon Serbia. All of the parties promised to be cooperative, but the attitude of the Western powers that Bosnia-Herzegovina could not be organized along the example of the Swiss cantons was not promising. Interestingly, the cantonal principle, apparently first suggested by Lord Carrington, had earlier been accepted by the three Bosnian groups but was soon thereafter rejected by the Muslims.

An important document guiding the Muslims was the "Islamic Declaration," authored by their leader, Alija Izetbegovic, in 1970 and circulated secretly, but published openly in 1990. It is revealing in that its basic goal is stated to be "the renewal of Islamic religious thought and the creation of a united Islamic community from Morocco to Indonesia." Moreover, it says that the Islamic movement should take power once it is "morally and numerically strong enough," and that "there can be neither peace nor coexistence between the Islamic religion and non-Islamic social and political institutions."

The declaration did not provide comfort to the Serbs and Croats of Bosnia, particularly when it openly stated that the "upbringing of the people, and particularly means of mass influence - the press, radio, television and film - should be in the hands of people whose Islamic moral and intellectual authority is indisputable. The media should not be allowed - as so often happens - to fall into the hands of perverted and degenerate people who then transmit the aimlessness and emptiness of their own lives to others."

This document explains the reluctance of the Muslims to accept the Vance-Owen Plan or any other plan that would postpone indefinitely their dream of an Islamic Bosnian state. The Croats, on the other hand, were glad to accept the Vance-Owen Plan because it gave them more territory than they could have hoped for, including a narrow strip of land that would prevent the Serbs of Croatia from having a geographic link with Serbia, while their part of Bosnia is adjacent to Croatia, to which they want to be annexed.

The Serbs, who would like to join Serbia, were also unhappy with the plan, not only because under it they would have less territory than they had before any fighting began (about 43 percent instead of over 60 percent), but also for two other important reasons: (1) the plan scattered them among several units and denied them a geographic connection between Serbia and the Serbian enclaves (Krajina) in Croatia, and (2) it gave to the Muslims the factories and coal mines and to the Croats the hydroelectric facilities and the munitions industry. A Serb negotiator reportedly said, "we get rocks and rattlesnakes."

Viewed from afar, the plan had a serious drawback in that it assumed that multi-ethnic Bosnia-Herzegovina was possible, whereas a multi-ethnic Yugoslavia was not. In addition, it dispersed the Serbs within Bosnia-Herzegovina just as Tito's scheme did in Yugoslavia. On the other hand, it did recognize that in a multi-ethnic society basic decisions should be reached by consensus instead of by majority vote. Hence, it gave most of the governmental powers to the several units and made the central government weak, so that it could not impose its will on those units.

In mid-March 1993, Vance and Owen were desperate to get the Muslims and Serbs to accept their plan. In order to get the signature of the Muslim president, they made changes in the plan that were vehemently opposed by the Bosnian Serb representative. And yet they hoped that in this way they could force the Serbs to sign. At a special meeting in Athens, Greece, the Bosnian Serb president signed, mainly because the plan was endorsed by Serbia's president, Slobodan Milosevic, but said that his signature would be valid only if his parliament agreed. The latter called for a referendum in which the plan was overwhelmingly rejected by the Bosnian Serb voters.

At the same time, Britain, France, and the United States prepared a new list of sanctions against Yugoslavia (i.e., Serbia and Montenegro), as well as enforcement of a "no fly zone" over Bosnia. Ironically, these actions came at a time when new information confirmed that the existing sanctions had proved counterproductive - that they had actually solidified domestic support for Serbia's president. Even his political opponents conceded that the United Nations sanctions, and the idea of tightening them, evoked universal criticism in Belgrade, even among those who detested Milosevic.

Not long after the rejection of the Vance-Owen Plan by the Bosnian Serbs, the presidents of Croatia and Serbia put forth a plan to divide Bosnia-Herzegovina into three units along ethnic lines. The Muslims' immediate reaction was negative. Ironically, they could have had much more under an EC plan proposed in early 1992, before the fighting began, a plan initially accepted by all three sides, but soon thereafter rejected by the Muslims.

In July 1993, all three parties agreed to a three-way division with a weak central government whose competence would be mainly in foreign affairs and trade. Almost immediately, however, the Muslim president walked out because, in the interim, the Serbs had captured two mountain peaks overlooking Sarajevo. He was encouraged in his walk-out by the U.S. threat of military air strikes unless the Serbs withdrew. When they withdrew in August, the talks resumed and the three-way division agreement was reinstituted. The parties also agreed that for a period of up to two years Sarajevo would be demilitarized and put under UN jurisdiction. Still to be worked out was the problem of where the borders of the three units would be drawn on maps.

In the meantime, while it may be futile to speculate as to the future, it is difficult to avoid the question: Why did not Serbia's allies in the two world wars (Britain, France, and the United States) go to the Serbs, the largest ethnic group and the strongest supporter of the Yugoslav state (which the West favored), to seek their cooperation in a solution when that state began to disintegrate? Or, at least, to assure the Serbs that, while recognition of Slovenia and Croatia seemed justified, in any final settlement Serbian grievances would also be addressed?

If the West had done that instead of condemning the Serbs for wanting precisely what the secession forces wanted -- self-determination -- would it have found a need to talk about ethnic cleansing and about seeking to frame rules of war for an ongoing civil war? Where was the statesmanship?

After all, the West had some examples from the past that might have guided its actions. The U.S. Civil War comes to mind, when a part of Virginia did not want to secede from the Union and formed its own independent state of West Virginia. This is almost exactly the situation with the Serbian-Krajina region of Croatia. And the British have Northern Ireland.

Some aspects of the West's intervention in Yugoslavia's civil war would be amusing if the situation was not so tragic. It should be recalled that one of Lincoln's great worries was Britain's contemplated recognition of the Confederacy. If that had come, he was prepared for war with the British. In the case of the Yugoslav conflict, Western nations have openly taken sides against the side that was winning - the Serbs. Moreover, in their efforts to get aid to the losing side, the West has expected the Serbs to cooperate!

There would seem to be a moral issue of the highest order in encouraging the losing side to continue resistance and thereby perpetuate the carnage. Paradoxically, the West has blamed only the Serbs, totally ignoring the fact that historically hostilities end when the losing side surrenders. What kind of perverse logic holds that the winning side should stop while opponents continue shooting? How are so-called humanitarian concerns advanced by policies that have the effect of promoting killing?

Wars generally end when the losing side recognized that it can no longer expect its supporters to make additional sacrifices. In the American Civil War, General Robert E. Lee at one point realized that the cause was lost, that he could no longer ask for sacrifices that would be futile, and asked for an armistice. Ironically, the West, by its intervention in the Yugoslav conflict, has not promoted its ending but rather its continuance.

Again, reflecting on our Civil War, we know that the warship *Alabama* was built in England and was permitted sail to join the Confederate navy. And two ironclad ships were being constructed for the Confederacy, but the project was stopped at the last moment. Had the British been more determined (alas, there was not a powerful media to push them), and if the technology for delivering food to the Confederates had been available, perhaps the Civil War would have lasted another four years!

We should also note that the West's intervention in Yugoslavia's civil war poses some interesting questions in the field of international law. First of all, there are at least two historic international acts that need to be mentioned. The signers of the Treaty of London in 1915 agreed that after the war Bosnia-Herzegovina, a large part of Dalmatia, and a large part of present day Croatia should go to their ally, Serbia. Another ally, Montenegro, was promised a part of the Dalmatian coast, including the city of Dubrovnik. With the creation of the Yugoslav state, these and other one-time Austro-Hungarian areas went to that state. Moreover, following the First World War, the Versailles treaties of Trianon and St. Germain treated the Kingdom of the Serbs, Croats, and Slovenes (i.e., Yugoslavia) as the successor state of Serbia. All international agreements to which Serbia was a party were transferred to the Yugoslav state. These two international acts gave to Serbia more than Serbia's Milosevic ever dreamed of claiming.

Another aspect of the international law questions concerns the action of several sovereign European nations acting to assist in the destruction of another sovereign European state. They did not wait for the outcome of the civil war but worked actively to determine the outcome. They sought to provide a fig leaf of legitimacy by the hasty recognition of secessionist republics. The question as to whether this was consistent with the basic principles of the international system and the Charter of the United Nations cannot be avoided. Moreover, there certainly will be questions about efforts to create laws of war for a civil war in the midst of it, and even to suggest the names of persons who might be brought to trial for war crimes.

As we know, civil wars are the most tragic of all wars, in which many atrocities are committed. Witness the Confederate prison of Andersonville, where tens of thousands of Union soldiers were held and where over 12,000 died.

Past atrocities do not, of course, excuse those that have been happening in Bosnia, where all three sides have been guilty. Serbian shelling of Sarajevo with its helpless civilian population has been the most obvious, but the Croatian and Muslim shelling of smaller cities has been equally repugnant, if on a smaller scale. Similarly, Serbs, Croats, Muslims, and Albanians have all been guilty of ethnic cleansing. But where has there been a civil war without atrocities?

In the final analysis, the question of the culpability of the Western leaders for what has happened cannot be avoided. They sought to justify their actions on the ground that Serbia's Communist leader, Slobodan Milosevic, was primarily responsible for the civil war in Bosnia. This position ignored several key elements: (1) the Bosnian civil war was part and parcel of the Yugoslav civil war, which began with the secessions of Slovenia and Croatia; (2) the Bosnian Serbs, whose forebears had lived there for centuries, fought for the defense of their lives and homes; (3) in anticipation of defense needs, Communist dictator Tito had made Bosnia-Herzegovina the Yugoslav army's arsenal, so that the Bosnian Serbs had no need of importing arms from Serbia; (4) the sizable military units from Croatia were a significant factor in the Bosnian conflict; (5) the Bosnian Muslims' rejection of an EC proposal in early 1992 for a three-way division of Bosnia-Herzegovina, after originally having joined the Serbs and Croats in accepting it. Seemingly, the West ignored all of these factors.

What can be said about the responsibility of powerful great powers that engaged in punishing only one of the three parties involved in the dispute, especially when there was ample evidence that the other two parties were very much implicated in bringing that dispute about? Who is to be held accountable for the horrendous harm that has been visited upon the Serbian people and Serbian nation as a result of the lack of evenhandedness on the part of the West? There would seem to be no way that the Serbian people can be compensated for the damage done as a result of the denial to them of vital medical care, or the general setback to the society as a result of the costly and irreparable brain drain resulting from the UN sanctions, to mention but two specific areas.

Without any attempt to exculpate Serbia's Milosevic for his contribution to the Yugoslav tragedy, it certainly appears that the West's determination to lay sole blame on him is but a lame effort to justify a one-sided policy. At the same time, any objective effort to assign responsibility for the Yugoslav civil war and its consequences must include all Yugoslav leaders - Serbs, Croats, Slovenes, Muslims, Macedonians, and Albanians - as well as the media in the West, which battled unashamedly to make foreign policy but with no corresponding responsibility.

In terms of the future, it seems appropriate to ask what can be learned from the West's mismanagement of the Yugoslav crisis. We need not wait until the Yugoslav tragedy plays itself out, however, before setting forth a few basic principles as guides for the United States and other great powers. In sum, they are: (1) Do not take lightly getting involved in the destruction of an existing internationally recognized nation state; (2) Avoid taking sides in civil wars, particularly when the issues are not clear; (3) Offer advice, and perhaps even facilitate the formation of arbitration tribunals, but insist that the parties reach political settlements before considering diplomatic recognition; (4) Clearly define the issues of national interest; (5) Encourage allies to act on the basis of the foregoing principles. Other observers may suggest additional or modified sensible guides to action as a way of avoiding similar tragedies in the future.

NOTE

1. It is interesting to note that in all census figures from 1910 to 1971 the Serbs were the largest ethnic group in Bosnia-Herzegovina. In the census of 1971, the category "Muslim" as an ethnic concept was officially introduced for the first time. Prior to that time, Muslims who thought of themselves as Serbs reported that they were Serbs; some said that they were Croats; some said that they were Yugoslavs. Consequently, we find that in the 1991 census the Muslims were approximately 44 percent, the Serbs 34 percent, and the Croats 17 percent.

THE ANATOMY OF A MYTH: SERBIAN HEGEMONY*

The old myth of Serbian hegemony has recently been resurrected following disturbances in Yugoslavia in the last years of the past decade. These protests were sparked by a variety of Serbian grievances, the most immediate of which was the seeming inability of the Yugoslav authorities to protect the Serbian minority in the autonomous province of Kosovo from persecution by the provincial Albanian majority. The myth, some would call it a canard, of Serbian hegemony has an old and interesting history. It bears examination, especially in view of recent events in Yugoslavia.

Two English publicists were in the main responsible for spreading the myth. They are Wickham Steed and R.W. Seton-Watson, mainly the latter. Both had been critics of the Austro-Hungarian Empire and strong proponents of a south Slav state. They, however, had some preconceived notions of what that state should be, or perhaps what it should not be. Seton-Watson, writing in 1911, concluded, "the triumph of the Pan-Serb idea would mean the triumph of the Eastern over Western culture, and would be a fatal blow to progress and modern development throughout the Balkans."[1] Moreover, he even denied the importance of Serbs in Croatia by quoting the position of the party of Pure Right, led by Joseph Frank, which saw the Serbs in Croatia as not really Serbs but as "merely Orthodox Croats."[2]

After the new state, first called the Kingdom of the Serbs, Croats, and Slovenes, came into being in 1918, and especially when it became evident that it would not be an instant success, Steed and Seton-Watson began an assiduous search for the reasons. The easiest solution was to settle on the Serbs as culprits, that is of seeking to dominate the other south Slavs. The two Englishmen had identified the prime minister of Serbia, Nikola Pašić, as one who, they believed, was not really in favor of a Yugoslav state, even before World War I was over.[3] It seemed to matter little to them that at that very time the western allies were offering Pašić a Great Serbia on a

---

* *Slavic Review*, Fall, 1991, pp. 659-662. Reprinted with permission of the American Association for Advancement of Slavic Studies.

silver platter, as a way of being able to fulfill their promise in the 1915 Secret Treaty of London, which compensated Italy with territory populated by south Slavs, mainly Slovenes and Croats, in return for Italy's fighting on the side of the Allies. Serbia, for her part, was to get Bosnia-Hercegovina and a part of the Dalmatian coast. Serbia rejected the offer and stood by its 1914 statement of war aims - a south Slav state that would include Serbs, Croats, and Slovenes.

Seton-Watson and his friends seemed to see little consequence in the possibility that the difficult early years for Yugoslavia might not have been the fault of the Serbs - that there had never been a Yugoslav state, that varied religious convictions created suspicions, that past political experiences of the ethnic groups had been totally different, that the ravages of war seriously impeded economic recovery, or that the fear of Serbian dominance had been employed by Austria-Hungary to scare the south Slav inhabitants of the empire who might be attracted to union with Serbia.

Seton-Watson, as well as many other English journalists and scholars, traveled to Yugoslavia in the 1920s and 1930s to survey the situation. They found that the Serbs, joined by Slovene leaders and the principal Moslem leader from Bosnia, were largely in charge. The king was a Serb, in accordance with an agreement signed in 1917 on the island of Corfu between Pašić and the leaders of the wartime Yugoslav Committee, headed by the Croat Ante Trumbić. The cabinet of the new sate was headed by Pašić. The Croats, represented by Stjepan Radić, the leader of the largest Croatian political party, the Croatian Peasant Party, had decided not to recognize the Yugoslav state and refused to participate in its governing. When Seton-Watson and his friends took trips to Yugoslavia they spent much more time in talking with the opposition - Serbs as well as Croats - than with government ministers. Moreover, they carried on an extensive correspondence with opposition leaders. The efforts of the British minister to Belgrade, Sir Neville Henderson, to disabuse them of their anti-Serb view, particularly their hatred for King Alexander, apparently had little effect.[4]

Their investigations spread the concept of Serbian hegemony. On the surface, one can see how they might have come to their conclusions, but their failure to dig below the surface had untoward consequences. When United States scholars began to write about Yugoslav matters they simply borrowed the expression *Serbian hegemony* and entered it into their books and articles as a given. No proof was needed, and none was offered, except for glib references to the "Serbian King" and "Serbian ministers."

Seton-Watson and his British friends found themselves strange bedfellows of the Comintern, which in the 1920s and early 1930s condemned Yugoslavia as a "Versailles creation" (itself a myth). The Comintern, including its Serbian component, condemned what they depicted as the "hegemony of the Serbian bourgeoisie" and called for Yugoslavia's dismemberment and the creation of several states in its place.

A more recent study in Yugoslavia asserts that as a result of the Comintern position, all Yugoslav ills were explained in terms of the so-called Serbian hegemony. This notion was found "not only in propaganda, but also in literature with scientific pretensions" and was bought in influential British circles. This thesis, Veselin Djuretić notes, was also used to win over non-Slav elements (especially leftists) in the West.[5]

The Croat leaders, for their part, recognized the monarchy and the constitutional system in 1925 and began participating in the government. Unfortunately, Radić and several other members of parliament were shot during one of its sessions in 1928 by a hothead from Montenegro, who was a Serb. Thereafter the Croats boycotted parliament. Radić died several months later, and in 1929 King Alexander proclaimed a temporary dictatorship, which in 1931 he replaced with a modified constitutional system. the aim of the latter was to bring the Croats back into the government. This aim was accomplished in 1939, five years after a plot by extremist Croats led to Alexander's assassination during a state visit to France.

In 1938, an influential Croat spokesman, Rudolf Bićanić, wrote a brief book, published by Vladko Maček, Radić's successor as leader of the Croatian Peasant Party. The book sought to show, in statistical tables and text, that Croatia had been unfairly treated and even exploited to the advantage of the Serbian areas.[6] The book was enormously influential, even in Serbian regions. Practically forgotten was a little volume by Bogdan Prica, published in Belgrade in 1937 which had used statistical tables to demonstrate that Croatian areas were neither neglected nor exploited.[7] In 1939 a Serbian periodical began publishing a series of articles, mainly by economists, which were collected and published as a book in 1940.[8] The series of articles sought to answer Bićanić point by point. In my book, *The First Yugoslavia*, I attempted to summarize the positions of the Croatian and Serbian sides and concluded that the evidence did not support the Croatian charges.[9]

After World war II studies of Yugoslavia confirmed the essence of the prewar answers to Bićanić. They pointed out that at the time of the creation of Yugoslavia, Slovenia and Croatia had far greater investment capital per capita than did Serbia and that in the two decades of the common state much more had been invested in Slovenia and in Croatia than in Serbia.[10]

Bićanić, in an English-language book, *Economic Policy in Socialist Economic Policy in Socialist Yugoslavia*, seemed totally oblivious to the conclusions of his earlier work. He pointed out that the prewar Yugoslav economy as a whole was beset by similar problems and admitted that Croatia was "one of the most developed parts of the new [state].... The capital concentrated in the banks of Croatia [in 1921] amounted to 50 percent of the total bank capital of Yugoslavia." Zagreb, the capital of Croatia, "became the strongest financial centre as well as the biggest industrial and commercial centre."[11]

The Serbs may be blamed for much, but as the above suggests, they have not been guilty of economic exploitation of any group or groups. If anything, they exploited themselves for the benefit of the nation as a whole. True, in the prewar Yugoslavia there was corruption, largely in terms of conflicts of interest and the purveying of privileged information, but this corruption benefited only a small circle of people and they were not exclusively Serbs.

In the first Yugoslavia the Serbs also held most of the key positions in the central government, but Slovenes participated in every cabinet and once held the prime ministership. The predominance of the Serbs was in large degree forced on them by circumstances in the country in its early years: lack of self-governing experience outside of Serbia, the initial refusal of elected Croatian representatives to participate in the governing of the country and their subsequent obstructionist tactics, and the myriad of problems (economic, religious, cultural, social) that accompanied the newly created state. If it can be said that the result was Serbian hegemony, it was the least planned, the least conscious, and the least profitable kind of hegemony.

One of the sharpest critics of Serbian-led cabinets and a close collaborator with the Croats, Dragoljub Jovanović, reflecting on events many years later, concluded that "Serbia is neither Great Serbian nor hegemonistic, it is not against the Croats ... neither revengeful nor capricious."[12] Jovanović is not alone among erstwhile critics of the Serbs in refuting charges that Serbia exploited its political position for material enrichment or the subjugation of other peoples.

Perhaps those who held responsible political positions were seeking to realize the virtually unrealizable - a Yugoslavia in which the various peoples would be free and equal and satisfied. The Serbs themselves, reflecting on pre-1918 Serbia, can by comparison reach only negative conclusions about their experience in Yugoslavia.

Some observers have made much of the fact that King Alexander was a Serb, but no evidence shows that he favored one nationality. On the contrary, all the available evidence indicates that he was a sincere Yugoslav. He believed that it was necessary for citizens to think of themselves first as Yugoslavs and only secondly as Serbs, Croats, and Slovenes, a belief that turned out to be unrealistic. He gave his three sons Serbian, Croatian, and Slovene first names. He used a variety of means to achieve unity - the stick and the carrot, idealism, changing the name of the Kingdom of the Serbs, Croats, and Slovenes to Yugoslavia, and even dictatorship. Ironically, in using dictatorial rule in an effort to impose a consensus, he did not win over the Croats but increasingly divided the Serbs. As Jacob Hoptner has put it, "the flat refusal of a substantial minority [the Croats] to participate in the government except on their own terms forced the crown to resort to controlled elections and coercion, rather than consensus, to administer the state."[13]

I hope that these brief observations will lead scholars and others who are tempted to use the term *Serbian hegemony* to spell out exactly what they mean by it and to replace simplistic jargon with a more critical scholarly methodology.

NOTES

1. R.W. Seton-Watson, *The Southern Slav Question and the Habsburg Empire* (London: Constable, 1911), 336-337.

2. *Ibid.*, 339.

3. Alex N. Dragnich, *Serbia, Nikola Pašić, and Yugoslavia* (New Brunswick, NJ: Rutgers University Press, 1974), chapter 7, especially pp. 119 and 127.

4. Neville Henderson, *Water under the Bridges* (London: Hodder and Stoughton, 1945), 181.

5. Veselin Djuretić, *Saveznici i Jugoslovenska ratna drama* (Belgrade: Balkanološki Institut, 1985), 1: 23; 2: 55ff.

6. Rudolf Bićanić, *Ekonomska podloga hrvatskog pitanja* (Zagreb: Dr. Vladko Maček, 1938).

7. Bogdan Prica, *Hrvatsko pitanje i brojke* (Belgrade: n.p., 1937).

8. Slobodan Drašković, *Istina o ekonomskoj podlozi hrvatskog pitanja* (Belgrade: Sloboda, 1940).

9. Alex N. Dragnich, *The First Yugoslavia: Search for a Viable Political System* (Stanford, CA: Hoover Institution Press, 1983), chapter 7.

10. Kosta Mihailović et al., *Proizvodna snaga N.R. Srbije* (Belgrade: Ekonomski Institut N.R. Srbije, 1953), 54-55; Miodrag Jelić and Radoslav Cvetković, *Razvoj privrede FNRJ* (Belgrade: Nolit, 1956), 52-53; Ivan Božić et al., *Istorija Jugoslavije*, 2nd ed. (Belgrade: Prosveta, 1973), 424-426.

11. Rudolf Bićanić, *Economic Policy in Socialist Yugoslavia* (Cambridge: Cambridge University Press, 1973), 4.

12. Dragoljub Jovanović, *Ljudi, Ljudi* (Belgrade: Author, 1973), 1: 403.

13. J.B. Hoptner, *Yugoslavia in Crisis, 1934-1941* (New York: Columbia University Press, 1962), 293.

THE BELGRADE STUDENT DEMONSTRATIONS OF 1968[*]

Several Western European nations witnessed large-scale student demonstrations in the 1960s. No one really expected to see their equivalent in Communist states. Yet in June 1968, Yugoslav Communists discovered that they were not immune to student power. During one hectic week, Tito's Yugoslav regime was badly shaken by student demonstrations at Belgrade University, when such slogans as "Down with the Red Bourgeoisie" made their appearance.

This was the first known serious challenge to a Communist regime. There was at least one case of earlier student demonstrations at the University of Belgrade in October 1954, but this was hushed up and went unreported until 1991.[1]

Belgrade University was the scene of many student demonstrations in the pre-Communist years. It was the place where many of Tito's comrades had cut their political teeth. During the years of Communist rule, however, it had been, as other institutions in such regimes, a dull and docile place.

The events of early June not only surprised and frightened the government, but also embarrassed it. The Yugoslav press, which had been giving extensive and favorable coverage to student demonstrations elsewhere, particularly those in France, found itself anything but sympathetic with the Yugoslav student actions.

Tito's government was not only shocked by the student demonstrations but also by the instantaneous and open support they received from several quarters, including the vocal or tacit support of most of the professors. They also received open support from academies, institutes, actors, artists, writers, as well as initially favorable treatment from two newspapers. Less open assistance came from workers of some enterprises. As we shall see later, the government was pathologically fearful that the students and workers might make common cause, which could mean the end of the regime.

---

[*] *Serbian Studies*, Spring 1992, pp. 29-39.

I

It is by no means clear whether the demonstrations were spontaneous or whether they had been more or less planned. There is evidence on both sides. Of one thing there can be do doubt: the students had been discussing and thinking about the problems that found eloquent, if sometimes ambivalent, expression in their public demands and actions during that critical week in early June.

The student actions were triggered by an incident at the dormitories in New Belgrade, which are just across the Sava River from Belgrade proper. An evening's entertainment, entitled "Friendship Caravan," had been prepared in honor of the members of certain work brigades. Originally, through some error, it had been announced as an open-air performance. When it became evident that, because of space limitations, it would be open only to a select audience, a large body of students attempted to enter, and a fight ensued. The police were called, which further aggravated the situation. Some of the students began to march into Belgrade, but were prevented from doing so by the police and forced to return to their dormitories.

That evening and a part of the next day were apparently spent in organizing and discussing. The students invited all of the deans to attend at least one of their proceedings. Many professors also came. After the meeting with the deans and professors, the students began to march into Belgrade, with the idea of demonstrating at Marx and Engels Square (which is surrounded by university buildings) and there to ask for a special session of the *Skupština* (parliament) to consider their demands.

This time they were met by some of the top Communist leaders of the republic of Serbia (who were backed by some detachments of the "people's militia"), seeking to dissuade them from marching into the city. The students were seemingly not in a receptive mood. After about twenty minutes some one shouted, "Beat," and a beating of students by the police began. Truncheons, night sticks, and tear gas were used unmercifully. Some shots were also fired. Several eye-witnesses as well as injured students were quoted in the student newspaper to the effect that police brutality was barbaric. One professor was quoted as having said that he participated in student demonstrations before the war and had come into conflict with the police, but that he had never expected to live to see anything such as that which took place in New Belgrade.[2]

Some professors who were with the students were also hit, as was Miloš Minić, the president of the government of Serbia, apparently not recognized by an eager militiaman.

Following these events, special meetings of the various faculties were called, with students invited to present their demands and to join in the discussion. Despite government efforts, the professors for the most part decided to support the students.

The students, for their part, managed to occupy most of the university buildings, where many of them stayed day and night during that eventful week.

The regime threw a cordon of police around all university buildings, although they apparently did not interfere with the goings and comings of students and professors. The students, however, established their own watch at the entrances of all buildings, requiring the showing of identity cards so as to prevent entrance by anyone except students and professors.

For a little over a week all normal university activities stopped. Students and professors discussed, and students formulated their demands and their program, producing five special numbers of their newspaper, *Student*. The first and second of these were banned by the authorities, but the ban was subsequently lifted. When students began to distribute the June 4 issue in the night of June 6-7, militiamen beat one of the students and seized about 600 copies, tore them up and proceeded to burn them in the street. The fifth number of *Student* was banned and never released for distribution. Leaflets and other irregular publications were also put out. Posters with slogans on them hung from university buildings. Loudspeakers inside were turned up so that passers-by on the street could hear some of the discussion.

II

The students' program was broadly political, although they sought to present their demands as being consistent with the program of the Communist party (officially known as the League of Communists of Yugoslavia, or LCY). First in their program was the demand that the government take immediate action to reduce the great social (read income) inequalities in the nation. This was an allusion to what Milovan Djilas had more than a decade earlier called the "New Class," although the students did not want any association with Djilas, in name or person, for it would have made it easier for the regime to discredit them. For most of the students, Djilas was an "unperson" in any case. In Yugoslavia he had not been heard from for more than a dozen years, and his books were not available there.

The layer of relatively well-to-do party and government bureaucrats and their families had, under the liberalization program of those years, become larger and more opulent. Moreover, this group was augmented by an indeterminate number of non-party people. Consequently, differences in material wealth had become more evident.

A request that the government solve the unemployment problem (with over 600,000 officially unemployed) was second on the list of student demands. Many Yugoslav workers were at that time employed in Western European countries. The problem of unemployment was also clearly related to the problem of finding jobs for new university graduates.

Moreover, the students attacked the bureaucracy for its failure to carry out the avowed program of the party, and for being insensitive to the needs of the people. The bureaucrats, especially the upper layer where the Mercedes-Benz seemed to be *the* status symbol, were told (in a poem in a student paper) that "The wheel of the Mercedes is not the wheel of history."[3]

The official press sought to depict the problems of the students at the university as their main concern, suggesting that the students were motivated by selfish and personal interests. In point of fact, the students had two categories of demands, and only in Part II was there mention of the need for reform in the educational system.[4]

Once the police had acted against them, the students demanded the dismissal of everyone who was directly responsible for police brutality. They asked for the release of arrested students and a lifting of the police blockade around the university buildings. Moreover, because the press had allegedly misinformed the public about their program, they demanded the dismissal of editors of the daily newspapers, radio Belgrade, and the head of the official news agency, *Tanjug*.[5]

As the week moved on, the students increasingly emphasized certain basic freedoms in their demands. They wanted freedom of assembly and freedom to demonstrate. Even within the League of Yugoslav Communists they sought the realization of "real democratic relations, democratic and argumentative discussion and the solving of given problems in the same way."

The flavor of many of the student demands can best be appreciated by quoting a number of slogans from their newspapers[6]:

"Freedom, truth, justice"
"We have had enough of the red bourgeoisie"
"We don't want democracy in helmets"
"Down with the princes of socialism"
"Freedom of assembly and demonstration"
"Free means of information"
"We don't want false promises"
"As long as amateurs govern the proletarians will
        suffer"
"Democratization of all socio-political
        organizations and especially the League of
        Communists"

There were many other slogans in leaflets and posters, but it is difficult to know how representative they were of student opinion. Among these: "Don't believe the press," "Down with the pipe and poodle" (a reference to a picture of Tito smoking a pipe and leading a poodle), and a poster caricature of Tito's wife wearing a crown.

The students said that they wanted "to put an end to the conspiracy of silence. To look truth in the eye." Admitting that "truth can be alarming," they asserted that it must not be forbidden. "In this illogical time, we will permit ourselves at least one logical question: if, for example, a house is burning, is it permissible to awaken the dwellers?"[7]

III

The students were clearly in an angry mood, and the attempts in the press to misrepresent their program and demands only served to heighten this mood. The support, open or tacit, of most of the professors and deans encouraged them. The support of most non-university intellectual circles in Belgrade was heady wine, as was the support from workers, despite systematic government efforts to prevent it. Anonymous help was also forthcoming - envelopes with money arrived; bread, milk, chocolate, and other foods were delivered in the early morning hours to the students of occupied university buildings.

A few professors who attempted to say that the movement had an anarchistic and hooliganistic character were whistled down. Even the Rector of the University received the same treatment when he sought to say something favorable about Bugarčić, the Belgrade head of the ministry of interior who had apparently ordered the beating of the students.

Their newspaper, *Student*, carried a column entitled, "Pillar of Shame," as a way of damning those who misrepresented them. *Borba* and *Večernje novosti*, the Communist party organs, were singled out as having "carried the least enlightening and least accurate comments and reports about the student movement." The editors of *Borba* were referred to as those "grey eminencies in that dark publishing house," and their writing was characterized as a "blind attack upon the student movement."[8]

After the period of demonstrations was over, one of the student newspapers asserted that their greatest reason for bitterness was the writing of *Mladost*, organ of the League of Youth in Yugoslavia.[9] "Even though it is supposed to be concerned with the problems of youth, the editorship has no idea of what is happening in the city in which it finds itself...." *Mladost* had referred to the students as "anarchistically inclined" and as "enemies of socialism and self-management," who were "using the intervention of the militia to raise the temperature and to raise a hue and cry against organs of the government."

At one of the student meetings, the greatest applause followed quotations from Karl Marx, read by one of the student speakers, about how helpless one feels in the absence of a free press.

One of the student publications (*Vidici*) engaged in some levity. It reported that in the night some policemen had entered the Academy of Arts and Sculpture, and in the dark began beating the alive and the dead. "One of the militiamen beat a statue. It is not known if it was the statue of liberty."

The students, however, received some press support. The principal organ of Yugoslav writers, the "Literary News," was full of praise for the students, "their revolutionary socialist consciousness," and "their great sense of responsibility, self-denial, and self-discipline."[10] It asserted that it was primarily up to the political system whether this revolutionary energy would be turned into positive or negative channels. The official organ of the party, *Borba*, attacked the stand of the "Literary News" as neither objective nor responsible. The "Literary News" was soon looking for a new editor! *Borba* also criticized the editorial board of the trade union paper, *Rad*, for its treatment of the student demonstrations.

Aside from the fact that they had made a shambles of the hall where the performance of "Friendship Caravan" was to have been held (the incident that ignited the demonstrations), the students were by and large not destructive of buildings or their contents.

Moreover, they exhibited marks of political astuteness. They knew that their program had to be broadly consistent with the avowed goals of the existing system and said so. They carried and displayed pictures of Tito, but significantly these were pictures of his Partisan warfare days - the ones with the lean and hungry look.

Tactically, also, they displayed brilliance. They set up an "Action Committee" of students and professors, but lest regime actions be taken against a few, the composition of that committee was reportedly changed every 48 hours, with a few hold-overs each time, although not the same ones.

IV

Apparently caught by surprise, the government was unprepared to deal with the situation. Obviously, it was a serious matter, particularly in view of the extent to which instantaneous support for the students materialized. There is some evidence, too, that the leadership was divided, some leaders being so frightened that they were willing to agree to all of the student demands.

Two actions were taken quickly to prevent disorder. The one was to augment the police forces by bringing in reinforcements from the interior, and the other was to ban all street demonstrations and meetings in public places.

Equally important, the government was quick to grasp the threat to its very existence if the students succeeded in making common cause with the workers. Consequently, it engineered criticism from the workers, not so much of the student goals as their methods. It arranged for telegrams to be sent to Belgrade, protesting the student actions. Some of these, although coming from different parts of the country, were identically worded.[11]

Some of the students attempted to visit factories, with the aim of convincing workers that their respective causes were the same. But the workers had been told not to talk with the students, or certain workers were designated to talk with the students in an effort to convince them of the wrongfulness of their ways. Workers in some plants (or parts thereof) were forbidden from signing statements endorsing the student program. In other plants workers were told that they would be fired if they went to any of the student meetings.

Publicly, the government sought to convey certain impressions about the student actions, which were often contradictory. On the one hand, there was an attempt to show that what the students wanted was consistent with the party program. On the other hand, there was an effort to label those behind the demonstrations as hooligans, demagogues, and provocateurs. In addition, there was an effort to convince the public that the basic student demands concerned problems associated with the University, such as unsatisfactory material conditions, and the lack of a student role in the management of university affairs, and in this way diverting attention away from the political aspects of the students' demands.

Taking another tack, the authorities attempted to create the impression that certain professors had unrealized political ambitions and were using the student unrest as a personal vendetta against the government. In this way, the suggestion was conveyed that the professors were to blame for the poor ideological preparation of the students.

Also, the party sought to admit new members to its ranks from "reliable" students. It should be noted parenthetically that the percentage of young people (under 25) in the party had dropped in the years 1958-1968. It should also be observed that some weeks after the student actions, the primary units (at one time called cells) in the Philosophy and Sociology faculties were disbanded, affecting students and professors. Presumably, the party was seeking to rebuild its base anew in those parts of the University. Significantly, few reapplied for party membership. On the contrary, some 150 signed a complaint charging that the dissolution of the party units was improper, but the complaint was turned down by the Congress of the Serbian party. This decision was subsequently upheld by the Congress of the LCY.

Capping the regime's response to the student actions was Marshall Tito's radio and TV speech on the evening of June 9th, seven days after the beginning of the student demonstrations.[12] Those who saw him on TV reported that he appeared visibly shaken by the events.

He said that he understood the student dissatisfactions. He believed that the demonstrations were spontaneous, and that he did not believe that they were influenced by similar actions of French and German students. He did indicate that he believed that elements hostile to socialism had infiltrated student ranks.

Moreover, he admitted that the party and government had not moved fast enough to resolve certain serious domestic problems, and promised action, the direction of which would be made clear by a series of guidelines.

In the matter of the police clash with the students, Tito promised that if an investigation proved that anyone had violated the law, he would be called to account no matter who he might be.

He concluded by saying that if he was incapable of solving these problems he would no longer remain in the position that he occupied. Finally, he urged the students to get back to their studies and their exams.

Parenthetically, it should be noted that in an address to the trade unions a few days later, Tito took a considerably tougher line, emphasizing the "infiltration" line. A *Borba* correspondent echoed this line in a conversation with the author when he said that he thought the NKVD (Soviet secret police) was implicated.

V

In the end, the students got promises and went back to their studies, but many Yugoslavs began asking what the new school year would bring. Many students, those wishing to push things to the end, were disappointed. They felt let down by the faculty, most of whom were for cooling things off for tactical reasons. The students were reportedly going to continue their Action Committee, particularly in view of the fact that the commission appointed to investigate the police clash with the students reported that it had not been able to agree on the facts.[13] In addition, there was little to suggest that conditions at the University were improving or that the students would be given a voice in university affairs.

Moreover, it was not clear if the students realized that what they were asking for would logically lead to the question of alternatives if Tito and his comrades were inadequate to the task. In their publications at the heat of the controversy, the students indicated that they were aware that whatever democracy existed in Yugoslavia was a purely formal type. But there was no solid evidence that they had thought about the question of political parties. There was evidence, however, that at that time the students were not easily frightened. They did not seem to know the psychology of fear that their fathers and mothers had experienced. And they received some sympathy from students at other Yugoslav universities.[14]

VI

The reaction among a large number of Belgrade citizens was epitomized by the remarks of a young professor when he said: "The important thing is that it could happen - that people could hear things said that they had thought and felt for twenty years, but could not say them."

A pre-World War II socialist politician, Dragoljub Jovanović, whom the Communists once praised to the skies (and with whom he once thought he could cooperate), noted that several things should be said of the demonstrations. First of all, he contended, was the fact that they took place in a Communist country. Secondly, he observed, the youth in whom most people had lost confidence, proved to be virulent, intelligent, and tactically brilliant. He emphasized the latter point by saying that they had committed no excesses which might have been used by the regime as a pretext to take severe actions against them. Thirdly, it is important to note, he added, that the demonstrations took place in Serbia, recalling that Serbia had a strong tradition of struggle for democracy, especially the insistence upon freedom of expression. Finally, he pointed out that the students were not an amorphic mass, that they had the support of most of the professors as well as other independent-minded people.[15]

"This is only the beginning," observed another, perhaps overly-optimistic professor. Speculation among most Yugoslavs with whom I talked was not prefaced by "if" but by "when." Some believed that the students would not wait long, while others said it might be a year or two.

When the new academic year opened, however, Soviet troops had occupied Czechoslovakia. While that Moscow action was interpreted by some as an implied threat to Yugoslavia, it did serve a purpose in Belgrade. Future student demonstrations could be depicted as playing into the hands of the Soviets. Ironically, Moscow seemed to have provided Tito and his associates a reprieve from student unrest.

Just to be sure, the regime saw to it that student meetings in June 1969 did not commemorate or glorify the June 1968 events, or produce any new confrontations.[16] In addition, the student publication, *Susret*, ceased coming out in mid-May 1969, amidst allegations that the regime had taken another step to prevent further trouble on the student front.[17]

AFTERWARD

The foregoing is based largely on materials (including conversations) that I gathered almost immediately after the student demonstrations during a research trip to Belgrade. I have not had access to studies in Yugoslavia concerning those events. I am sure that there are differing interpretations. I was, however, struck by the recent observation of one who had participated in the student demonstrations. He now views that movement as the last gasp of those who still believed that the Marxian promises of the future society could be realized.

NOTES

1. *Borba*, June 5 and 6, 1991. In the years prior to 1968, dissatisfaction had been building: see special edition of the student newspaper *Susret*, June 11, 1968, for excerpts from its editions of March 20, April 3, May 1, May 15, and June 1 of the same year. This special edition contains a comprehensive summary of events during the critical week. Unfortunately, the pages are not numbered, but marginal headlines help to locate items.

2. *Student* (special edition), June 4, 1968, p. 3. For quotes from several students, see *Student*, June 8, 1968, and *Susret*, June 11, 1968.

3. See poem by Milovan Vitezović, *Susret*, June 11, 1968.

4. *Student*, June 8, 1968.

5. *Ibid.*, June 4, 1968, p. 3, and *Susret*, June 18,1968.

6. See special edition of another student publication, *Vidici*, June 1968.

7. *Student*, June 18,1968, p. 4.

8. *Ibid.*

9. *Susret*, June 11, 1968.

10. *Književne novine*, June 6, 1968,

11. *Susret*, June 11, 1968.

12. For text of Tito's speech, see special edition of *Susret*, June 11, 1968.

13. The commission appointed to investigate could not agree on the facts, *Borba*, June 12, 1969, p. 4.

14. See *Borba*, June 9, 1968, p. 16, and *Politika*, June 19, 1968, p. 6.

15. Conversation with author, July 1968.

16. See *Politika*, May 28 and 29, 1968.

17. *Student*, May 20, 1969, p. 2.

BOSNIA-HERZEGOVINA:
A CASE STUDY OF ANARCHY
IN THE THIRD WORLD*

I. Introduction

The conflict in Bosnia-Herzegovina [hereinafter Bosnia] cannot be adequately considered except in the context of the Yugoslav civil war, especially when considering that Bosnian soil has been the scene of the greatest bloodshed in that war. The primary intention of this essay is to analyze the issues that led to the present conflict in Yugoslavia, and in Bosnia in particular, and the efforts expended by the international community in attempting to resolve them.

In order to understand the underlying causes of the current bloodshed, some elementary knowledge of Bosnia's history is essential; specifically how and why it became a constituent part of the former Yugoslavia. The geographical area known as Bosnia never existed as an independent or recognized nation-state.[1] Under Roman rule it had neither a separate name nor an individual history. However, following the Slavic migrations in the seventh century, the name Bosnia was accepted for the valley of the Bosna River. Over the next few centuries, regional clan leaders fought to become viceroys of various European rulers who were in control of the Bosnian region. Bosnia found itself mainly under direct rule of either Hungary or Croatian princes who were vassals of Hungary. In the fourteenth century, Bosnia became part of the Serbian empire, headed by Tsar Dušan. However, after Dušan's death in 1356, Serbia's grip over Bosnia weakened, and provided the opportunity for a local leader, Stefan Tvrtko, a Serb related to the historic ruling family of Serbia, the Nemanićes, to aspire to be Dušan's successor. While Bosnia was still under the rule of Serbia's Prince Lazar from 1372 to 1389, Tvrtko (although in theory a subservient ally of Lazar) pronounced himself to be "Stefan I, King of Bosnia, Serbia, and all the Seacoast." However, his claim was short-lived.

* *Cardozo Journal of International and Comparative Law*, Spring 1995, pp. 163-179. This article is based on a paper presented at the Conference on Anarchy in the Third World, sponsored by the American Bar Association, June 3, 1993. Reprinted with permission.

Lazar's eventual defeat by the Ottomans at Kosovo in 1389 led to Turkish domination and control over Bosnia. Following the fall of Constantinople in 1453, Turkish sultans looked upon Bosnia as the gateway to Hungary and the rest of Europe. Conversion of the magnates of the Bogomils[2] to Islam allowed them to become Turkish surrogates and achieve important military and administrative positions in the Ottoman Empire. These developments were followed by the conversion to Islam, both religiously and culturally, of a large portion of the people in the Bosnian region, mainly Serbs and Croats. Those in the Bosnian region who remained Christian were then forced to become serfs.

Following the resurrection of the Serbian state in the nineteenth century, the dreams of independence for Bosnian Serbs were rekindled. In 1875, people of Serbian descent in the region engaged in an insurrection against Ottoman rule.[3] This event prompted Serbia and Montenegro to join Russia in the 1876-77 wars against Turkey, in the hope of gaining Russian aid in the liberation of Bosnian Serbs. However, Russia soon betrayed her Orthodox allies at the Congress of Berlin in 1878 by agreeing to the occupation of Bosnia by the Austro-Hungarian Empire.[4] The Austro-Hungarians believed that an implicit understanding had been reached at the Congress permitting them to annex Bosnia at a future date. In 1908, they did so unilaterally.[5] Serbia could do little but protest, and Russia, weakened by its recent war with Japan, was powerless as well.

While fighting on the Allied side during the First World War, Serbia pronounced its intention to undertake the liberation and unification of all Serbs, Croats, and Slovenes.[6] During the war, in representative meetings of various South Slav nationality groups from Austro-Hungary and Serbian government members, preparations were made for the creation of a common state.[7] In November 1918, with the impending defeat of the Central Powers, forty-two out of fifty-two Bosnian districts requested unification with Serbia.[8] In the same month, Slovenian, Croatian, and Serbian delegates from the crumbling Austro-Hungarian empire traveled to Belgrade, requesting unification as well. On December 1, 1918, the Kingdom of the Serbs, Croats, and Slovenes came into existence.

The new state was organized on the unitary principle and thus was not divided into ethnic units. Even so, Bosnian Muslims obtained a separate political identity when they created their own party, the Yugoslav Muslim Organization, led by Mehmed Spaho, until his death in 1939.[9] The party voted for the first Yugoslav Constitution in

1921, contested most elections, and participated in most of the governing cabinets.

During World War II, most of Bosnia became part of the Nazi-Fascist state of Croatia, responsible for the massacre of hundreds of thousands of Serbs, along with Jews and Gypsies. Bosnian Muslims took part in these massacres and, moreover, under the inspiration of the Grand Mufti of Jerusalem, formed the dreaded Handjar Division to fight alongside the Nazis.[10]

After World War II, the Communists who gained power in the Yugoslav civil war (1941-1945) established the Second Yugoslavia based on the principle of federalism, albeit with a Soviet variation.[11] Thereafter, Yugoslavia was divided into six republics and two autonomous provinces in the Republic of Serbia. The Communist dictator and leader of the ruling party, Josip Broz Tito, averred that this division was the appropriate method of solving the nationality problem in Yugoslavia. In actuality, Tito was determined to weaken his perceived primary enemy, the Serbs, then the largest ethnic group in Yugoslavia and the strongest supporters of the common state. Tito accomplished this by dispersing Serbs, leaving one-third of them in other republics - the largest numbers being in Croatia (between 600,000 and one million) and Bosnia (about 1.5 million), with others in Macedonia and Montenegro.

Tito's creation of the Bosnian Republic was motivated by a desire to prevent dominance by Serbs, the largest ethnic group - twice as numerous as the Croats, who were the second largest ethnic group. He also desired to win favor among the Muslims, who although ethnically Croat or Serb (mainly the latter), had converted to Islam during centuries of Turkish rule. In the Bosnian Republic, Muslims would not be a part of Croatia or Serbia. By 1971, Tito had gone even further by creating a new ethnic category, ironically for a Communist state, based on religion - Muslim.

II. THE BEGINNING OF YUGOSLAVIA'S BREAKUP

At the federal level, Tito's strong dictatorship preserved the unity of the state. However, policy changes in the National Communist Party, the League of Yugoslav Communists, led to the increasing prominence of the communist parties in the republics. These developments stemmed from Tito's drive toward greater decentralization in a "trial and error" effort to deal with the country's problems. Therefore, for all practical purposes, by the late 1970s, Yugoslavia had six (some argue eight if the two autonomous provinces are included) Communist parties instead of one.[12] Following Tito's death in 1980, differences among the republics grew, increasingly taking on nationalist overtones. Bickering among the republics became more visible in the late 1980s, as the national government seemed unable to handle the mounting economic challenges.

By January 1990, it became apparent that the country was in the middle of an alarming crisis, when the Extraordinary Congress of the National Party broke up, unable to agree on how to modify the political system. These arguments were prompted in part by the downfall of communism in other East European countries. While there was agreement that the Communist Party should no longer have a monopoly of political power, strong disagreement remained on what precise changes needed to be made. The Serbs believed that Yugoslavia's ills were the result of excessive decentralization, and pointed to the divisiveness of trade wars between the republics as an example.[13] They wanted to strengthen the Yugoslav Federation. Conversely, Slovenia and Croatia desired the further weakening of the central authority of the federation. A *New York Times* reporter compared Yugoslavia's main political conflict to "the states' rights clash of pre-Civil War America."[14] The chasm between the ethnic groups seemed unbridgeable, confirmed by the fact that elections in 1990 in Slovenia and Croatia were won by recycled communists posing as nationalists. In December 1990, a referendum in Slovenia favored independence; a May 1991 referendum in Croatia voiced the same sentiment.[15]

On June 25, 1991, Slovenia and Croatia declared their independence by seceding from Yugoslavia. Yugoslavia's Parliament saw this as a direct attack on the sovereignty and territorial integrity of the federal union, and the same day declared the secessions null and void.[16] These actions were subsequently nullified as well by the Yugoslav Constitutional Court. In addition, the Yugoslav Parliament authorized the Federal Executive Council[17] to take immediate action to quell the secessions. In defiance, Slovene authorities quickly took over border and customs posts, and replaced Yugoslav signs and flags with those of the Republic of Slovenia. These actions had been anticipated by the Executive Council, which on the previous day had issued an order, signed by Prime Minister Ante Marković, forbidding such acts.[18]

The Slovenes then blocked numerous heavy vehicles that were in international transit near the Austrian border, using them to render the highway useless to units of the Yugoslav Army which had been ordered to assist in reclaiming federal authority at approximately thirty-five border crossings. On the same day, Slovenian forces attacked Yugoslav Army units, which having been ordered to retaliate only in the case of dire necessity, sustained over forty casualties.[19]

The European Community [hereinafter EC] engineered a meeting on July 7, 1991 between the leaders of the Yugoslav republics and three EC ministers on the Yugoslav island of Brioni. This meeting secured a three-month suspension of the Slovene and Croatian acts of secession.[20] During the interim, the status of the borders was to return to the pre-June 25 period, and the Yugoslav Army was to return to its barracks. Although the Slovenes made half-hearted efforts to share border authority, they refused to remove the Slovene flags and signs. The EC halted aid and assistance to the republics during the suspension period, and by the end of the three-month period, the situation had regressed to the pre-June 25 conditions. The Yugoslav Army did little except retreat from Slovenia, a retreat which was not made easy by the Slovenes.[21]

The secession of Croatia led its Serbian minority to revolt and create the Krajina Serb Republic. This resulted in an armed conflict with Croatian authorities. The units of the Yugoslav Army in Krajina allied themselves with the Serb rebels, and the civil war intensified. The Slovenes and Croats insisted that the Yugoslav Constitution gave them the right to secede. While the preamble to the Constitution discussed the right to self-determination,[22] including the right of secession, the text failed to delineate actual procedures for secession. In fact, at least two articles in the Yugoslav Constitution suggested that unilateral secession was unconstitutional. Article 5 stated that the frontiers of Yugoslavia could not be altered without the consent of all the republics and autonomous provinces and stipulated that boundaries between republics could be altered only by mutual consent.[23] Article 240 stated that the Yugoslav armed forces were to protect the independence, sovereignty, and territorial integrity of Yugoslavia.[24] Moreover, several articles in the federal constitution, as well as in the constitutions of the republics, outlined the responsibilities of the republics to the federation.[25]

The disastrous slide into chaos for the peoples of Yugoslavia began with the secessions of Slovenia and Croatia, which paved the way for the secession of Bosnia. On October 14, 1991, the Bosnian Parliament ordered a referendum on independence from Yugoslavia.[26] The validity of such a referendum was contested by the

Serbian deputies in the Bosnian Parliament, partly because the vote was taken after the President of the Parliament had declared the session adjourned, but primarily because the Serbs wanted Bosnia to remain part of the Yugoslav federation. Bosnian Serbs refused to participate in the referendum which they considered unlawful. Furthermore, they declared that in the event of the passage of such a referendum, they would form an independent Bosnian Serb republic. In the Bosnian referendum, held in February 1992, Muslims and Croatians voted for independence.[27] Despite efforts of the European Community to prevent a conflict, by late March 1992, the Yugoslav civil war, which began in Slovenia and Croatia, spread to Bosnia. The earliest acts of violence in Bosnia's main city, Sarajevo, erupted with an armed attack on a Serbian wedding party. Total civil war soon followed.

III. THE BASIS OF SERBIAN ACTS AND FEARS

The Serbs living in Croatia and Bosnia fought against secession because of the fear of living as a minority. This fear stemmed largely from the experiences of their predecessors during World War II. The destruction of the First Yugoslavia by Germany in April 1941 was accompanied by the creation of an Axis-satellite state, the Independent State of Croatia. That state, ruled by the extremist Croatian movement known as the Ustashi,[28] controlled Croatia and most of Bosnia, with approximately two million Serbs in those regions.

An influential figure in the Ustashi movement, Mile Budak, created a formula to disempower the large Serbian population: one-third to be killed; one-third forced to flee; one-third to be converted to Roman Catholicism. Estimates vary, but most historians on the subject agree that approximately 700,000 Serbs were brutally massacred in Croatia and Bosnia by the minions of the Ustashi regime.[29] Some of the harshest atrocities committed against the Serbs took place in Bosnia by the Ustashi regime and Muslims such as the Handjar Division. In addition to the Serbs, other victims of these atrocities included approximately 60,000 Jews and 20,000 Gypsies.[30]

The present Croatian regime, headed by Tito's former partisan general Franjo Tudjman, added to Serbian fears of persecution in both Bosnia and Croatia. Prior to the outbreak of hostilities, the Croatian republic engaged in discriminatory acts in employment and civil rights against its Serbian minority. Serbs were victimized by hostile tactics such as nocturnal shootings, bias attacks, and vandalism.[31] In addition, the Tudjman regime adopted some of the symbols and trappings of the hated Ustashi state.[32] Furthermore, while Croatia's pre-independence constitution viewed the Croats and Serbs as equals, the new text created after the secession reduced the Serbs to minority status.

In Bosnia, the "Islamic Declaration,"[33] authored in 1970 by Muslim leader Alija Izetbegović, the current president of Bosnia, and re-issued in 1990, also gave Bosnian Serbs, as well as Croats, reason for alarm. The declaration stated that the Islamic movement should seize power once it is "morally and numerically strong enough,"[34] and that "there can be neither peace nor co-existence between the Islamic religion and non-Islamic social and political institutions."[35] The Declaration further states that:

> [the] upbringing of the people, and particularly means of mass influence - the press, radio, television, and film - should be in the hands of people whose Islamic moral and intellectual authority is indisputable. The media should not be allowed - as so often happens - to fall into the hands of perverted and degenerate people who then transmit the aimlessness and emptiness of their lives to others.[36]

These declarations were in sharp contrast to the Muslim assertions during the civil war that they wished to live in peace and harmony with Serbs, Croats, Jews, and other Bosnians.

IV. WESTERN RESPONSE TO YUGOSLAVIA'S BREAKUP

After the 1991 secessions and ensuing hostilities, the EC's initial response was to organize a mission to Yugoslavia led by former British Foreign Secretary Lord Carrington. Almost immediately differences between the EC and the United States emerged on the proper Western response to the crisis in the former Yugoslavia. Lord Carrington proceeded on the presumption that the Yugoslav state had ceased to exist, and proposed the initiation of negotiations for the creation of a new state. This proposition was viewed unfavorably by the Serbs, who did not want Yugoslavia to disintegrate. However, it naturally gained the praise of the Slovenes and Croats, who eagerly sought the break. The United States, however, continued to adhere to the position it had expressed prior to the 1991 secessions. Then, Secretary of State, James Baker, declared that if Yugoslavia were to break apart, Washington would wait until the various factions had resolved their differences through political settlements before deciding on the question of diplomatic recognition. Simultaneously, Baker personally advised the Slovenian and Croatian leaders that a unilateral secession would result in civil war.[37]

Although Great Britain and France indicated their reservations about unilateral secessions, the EC, incited by Germany and Austria, did not share that position. Both the UN envoy, former U.S. Secretary of State Cyrus Vance, who was seeking a cease fire between the fighting parties in Croatia, and then UN Secretary General Javier Perez de Cuellar, warned Hans-Dietrich Genscher, Germany's foreign minister, that premature recognition of Slovenia and Croatia could intensify and widen the war.[38] Vance's warning was in part motivated by the fact that, during the summer of 1991, Germany had displayed its willingness to recognize the independence of the former Yugoslav republics, including Bosnia. Genscher had been in frequent contact with Croatian leaders, conveying the notion that Germany would acquiesce to a Croatian declaration of independence. In fact, some well-informed individuals insist that he even encouraged such conduct. In contrast, Bosnian and Macedonian leaders had pleaded with Western leaders to withhold the recognition of Slovenia and Croatia, fearing Serbian retaliation.

In January 1992, despite such reservations, the EC recognized Slovenia and Croatia as independent nations.[39] The United States followed suit, and by early April it, too, recognized the independence of Slovenia, Croatia, as well as Bosnia.[40]

It immediately became clear that the West would respect the wishes of the republics who desired secession but not of the republics who desired Yugoslavia to remain intact. This policy was reflected by the declaration that boundaries between the republics could be altered only by peaceful means.[41] In contrast, the West, through recognition of Croatia and Slovenia, in effect aided and abetted them in their violation of the Helsinki Accords proviso against altering internationally recognized boundaries by force. Western leaders knew, or should have known, that Serbia was the republic which suffered the greatest injustices when Tito carved the country into separate independent republics and autonomous provinces.

Western policy-makers seemingly did not weigh the consequences of their acts or they simply did not care. They may have been influenced by effective Croatian propaganda in fallaciously defining the conflict in terms of democracy versus communism.

Western leaders disregarded recent European history by not recalling that in the Balkan wars of 1912-13, as well as in World War I, the Serbs fought to liberate Serbian lands as well as other South Slav regions. Additionally, the Serbs were barbarically persecuted by Croatians and Muslims during World War II. Instead, the West proceeded on the assumption that the Serbs ought to forget their enormous past sacrifices and abuse, and simply be satisfied to have nearly three million of their compatriots revert once again to foreign rule. The Serbs pointed out that their objective was not the creation of a mystical empire of the Middle Ages, as the Western media often portrayed, but only to safeguard the rights of Serbs who had lived in a common state since 1918. The Western response to the current Yugoslav conflict was succinctly summarized at an academic gathering in November 1992: "The West came to Yugoslavia as fire fighters and ended up being pyromaniacs."[42]

Rather than admit a mistake in its policies, the West attempted to confront the consequences of failed policies. In this endeavor, the print and electronic media of Europe and the United States assisted, reporting daily developments without showing the slightest interest in questioning the basic historical, cultural, or economic origins of the civil war. The media did not engage in any critical examination of the policies of the Western powers, but rather spread misinformation.[43]

For example. television broadcasts reported that Serbian forces shelled and killed a number of people standing on line to buy bread in Sarajevo.[44] The graphic reporting of this story prompted the United States to request that the United Nations impose economic sanctions on Yugoslavia (i.e., Serbia and Montenegro). Several months later, it was determined that Muslims, not Serbians, were most likely responsible for the attack. Another example was the failure of the Western media to report that 40,000 to 60,000 Croatian troops were stationed in Bosnia, with no sanctions imposed on Croatia for this violation.[45]

Throughout the months of violence, blame for the death and destruction was placed almost entirely upon Serbs and Serbia. Discussion continually focused on the "Serb-dominated Yugoslavia." It must be noted that prior to the secessions, key positions in the Yugoslav government were held by non-Serbs: Prime Minister Ante Marković and Foreign Minister Budimir Lončar were Croats; Minister of Defense and Supreme Commander General Kadijević was the son of a Serbian-Croatian marriage; Deputy Commander of the armed forces, Stane Brovet, was a Slovene; and Chief of the Air

Force, Zvonko Jurjević, was also a Croat. While the army's officer corps was predominantly Serbian, the high command was 38% Croatian and 33% Serbian.[46]

In the months following the breakup of the former Yugoslavia, the EC sponsored a number of conferences to address the ongoing violence and hostilities. A February 1992 meeting in Lisbon generated a promising recommendation: that Bosnia, on the verge of hostilities since the October 1991 referendum on independence, should be divided into three constituent units, a proposal accepted by all three Bosnian leaders (Radovan Karadzić for the Serbs; Mate Boban for the Croats; Alija Izetbegović for the Muslims).[47] Soon after, however, Izetbegović repudiated his acceptance of the agreement, on a recommendation by the United States,[48] and moved toward independence despite the stated Serbian position that such a course was unacceptable. The resulting civil war led to negotiations that produced the Vance-Owen Plan.

V. THE VANCE-OWEN PLAN

In January 1993, Cyrus Vance, acting as United Nations negotiator, and one-time British Foreign Secretary Lord David Owen, who had replaced Lord Carrington as European Community negotiator, introduced a plan to solve the Bosnian dilemma. Their plan, known as the Vance-Owen plan, proposed the division of Bosnia into ten districts - three with Serbian majorities, three with Muslim majorities, and three with Croatian majorities. The tenth district was to encompass Sarajevo and its surrounding suburbs. Sarajevo was to become the capital of the country, where the three ethnic groups would presumably be represented equally.[49]

Vance and Owen recognized that in a multi-ethnic society, fundamental decisions should be arrived at through consensus rather than majority vote. Accordingly, they proposed vesting most governmental powers in the nine districts while a weak central government was to concentrate its resources on building and nurturing consensus among the diverse ethnic groups. Their goal was to make Bosnia a viable, multi-ethnic state. Many observers believed this to be unattainable, reasoning that if Yugoslavia could not succeed as a multi-ethnic country, Bosnia had even less of a chance to do so.

Vance and Owen knew that Bosnian Serbs sought a union with Serbia, and that the Bosnian Croats wanted to merge with Croatia. Although they were aware of the Bosnian Muslims' long-term goal of an Islamic state, they reasoned that in the short-run they would accept a multi-ethnic state if given a favorable territorial agreement. The real obstacle was convincing Bosnian Serbs to agree to the recommended solution. Because of intense Western pressure on the Serbs, Vance and Owen were seemingly confident that the Serbs could be forced to accede to an agreement that was satisfactory to the Muslims and the Croats. Assuming Serb acceptance of such an arrangement, there remained the additional issue of how to avert a future breach, i.e., how to deter Bosnian Serbs from attempting to unite with Serbia in the future.

In confronting the latter possibility, Vance and Owen formulated the following ingenious solution: arranging the Serbian units so that they were not contiguous to one another or to Serbia,[50] and inserting a Croatian district so as to prevent a geographic link between Serbia and the Serbian Krajina region of Croatia.

The concept was clever, but assured to be rejected by Bosnian Serbs. Surprisingly, the Bosnian Serbs deliberated somewhat before publicly rejecting the plan. The only explanation for this hesitation was expressed in their acceptance of the plan in principle. Specifically, they announced that the "maps" would need to be altered,[51] an indication that they were not adverse to the idea of having separate districts. Some observers close to the Bosnian Serbs believe that had it not been for the denial of a geographic link to Krajina, the Serbs would have signed the agreement under the assumption that at some future date a better deal with the Muslims and Croats could have been negotiated.

There are other reasons why Serbs found the plan unacceptable. The proposed division of land gave the Croats more territory than they could have expected. Additionally, the proposed Croatian districts were rich in natural resources and included hydroelectric facilities. Meanwhile, the areas allocated to the Muslims contained the major industries. This left the Serbs, in the words of one Serbian negotiator, with "rocks and rattlesnakes."[52]

In March 1993, Vance and Owen took a further step that made the plan even less palatable to the Serbs. In a desperate move to obtain Muslim acceptance of the plan (particularly in view of the Clinton Administration's desire to secure a better arrangement for the Muslims), changes were made in the provincial boundaries around Sarajevo and neighboring areas so that a Muslim majority could be created. The terms of the plan regarding the creation of an interim central government were also revised, reflecting a favored status towards Muslims. Bosnia's Muslim president signed the plan, but Serbian negotiators objected vehemently.

A desperate effort was made to salvage the plan at a May 1993 meeting in Greece.[53] Under intense international pressure, the Bosnian Serb leader Radovan Karadzić signed the agreement but stipulated that it would be valid only after formal recognition by the Serbian Parliament in Bosnia. The Serbian Parliament decided that the decision should be submitted to the Serbs in a referendum. The plan was overwhelmingly rejected by Bosnian Serbs in the referendum, and the Vance-Owen plan came to an end.

VI. IMPLICATIONS FOR INTERNATIONAL LAW

The conflict in Bosnia, as well as Slovenia and Croatia, raises interesting questions regarding diplomacy and international law. One question is whether the EC had a legal right to determine the collapse of Yugoslavia at a time when Yugoslavia remained a member of international organizations such as the United Nations and the Conference on Cooperation and Security in Europe (CCSE), especially when no country had either broken diplomatic relations with Yugoslavia or ceased to recognize its existence.[54] Several sovereign European nations, such as Germany and Austria, actively assisted in the destruction of another sovereign European state. They did not wait for the civil war to end, but instead worked actively to determine its outcome. They sought to provide a fig leaf of legitimacy to their actions by the hasty recognition of the secessionist republics.

The question of whether the actions of the EC, and the United States, were consistent with the basic principles of international diplomacy and the Charter of the United Nations cannot be avoided. Clause IV of the Helsinki Agreement, entitled the Declaration of Principles Guiding Relations Between Participating States, pronounces that "[t]he participating States will respect the territorial integrity of each of the participating States. Accordingly, they will refrain from any action ... against the territorial integrity, political independence, or the unity of any participating State, and in particular from any such action constituting a threat or use of force."[55]

By recognizing the secessionist republics, the West arguably aided and abetted the secessionist republics in overt violation of the Helsinki principles. Also questionable are efforts to create, in effect, laws of war for a civil war still in progress, and simultaneously suggesting names of individuals who might be brought to trial for violation of such laws. On December 16, 1992, then United States

Secretary of State, Lawrence Eagleburger, accused four Serbs and two Croats of committing war crimes. He also asserted that Slobodan Milošević, President of Serbia, and two Bosnian Serbs, Radovan Karadzić and General Ratko Mladić, could be held responsible for failing to prevent atrocities.[56]

Additionally, the question of Serbia's legal rights to some disputed lands seems to have been totally ignored. There are at least two international treaties which cannot be ignored in the analysis. First, the signatories of the Treaty of London[57] in 1915 agreed that after World War I, Bosnia, a large section of Dalmatia, and a large portion of present day Croatia should be set aside for their ally Serbia. Another ally, Montenegro, was promised parts of the Dalmatian coast, including the city of Dubrovnik. With the creation of the Yugoslav state, these and other areas became part of Yugoslavia. Second, following World War I, the Versailles Treaties of Trianon and St. Germain[58] treated the Kingdom of the Serbs, Croats, and Slovenes (i.e., Yugoslavia) as the successor state of Serbia. All international agreements to which Serbia was a party were transferred to the Yugoslav state. It remains to be seen whether present day Yugoslavia (Third Yugoslavia -- Serbia-Montenegro) will take these issues to the Court of International Justice.

VII. CONCLUSIONS

The primary conclusion to be drawn from this essay is that the West, particularly Germany and Austria, mismanaged the Yugoslav crisis, first by failing to discourage secessionist-minded republics from declaring their independence, and second by extending hasty, ill-advised recognitions once the premature secessions were proclaimed, thereby contributing significantly to the actual outbreak of the civil war.

The second and related conclusion is that expertise concerning the complicated Yugoslav situation was either lacking, ignored, or both. Clearly there was little or no appreciation in the West of valid Serbian interests in the conflict and of their determination to defend what they considered to be vital interests. Such myopia enabled Germany and Austria, even against the advice of their ambassadors in Belgrade, to persuade other European countries to quickly recognize Slovenia, Croatia, and Bosnia.

Finally, Western leaders perceived six to eight months ago that the Bosnian Serbs had won the civil war, and yet led the losers in the conflict (i.e., the Muslims) to believe in a possible rescue through

Western intervention. That policy compounded the tragedy, resulting in the continuation of the carnage still gripping Bosnia-Herzegovina today.

VIII. APPENDIX[59]

BOSNIA-HERZEGOVINA POPULATION STATISTICS IN PERCENTAGES

	1879	1910	1921	1931	1948	1953	1961	1971	1981	1991
Serbs	43	43	44	44	44	44	43	37	34	34
Muslims	39	32	31	31	31	31	26	39	40	44
Croats	18	23	23	24	24	23	22	21	17	17
Yugoslavs							9	2	8	?

NOTES

1. For a good general background on the topics in the following pages, see Rebecca West, *Black Lamb and Grey Falcon* (1982), pp. 271-444.

2. One of the schismatic branches of Christianity that the Ottomans found less hostile than the Catholics or the Orthodox.

3. See David MacKenzie, *The Serbs and Russian Pan-Slavism, 1875-1878* (1967).

4. The best work on the rivalry of the Great Powers and Bosnia is Wayne S. Vucinich, *Serbia Between East and West: The Events of 1903-1908* (1954). See also MacKenzie, *supra* note 3; Bernadotte Schmitt, *The Annexation Crisis, 1908-1909* (1937).

5. Vucinich, *supra* note 4.

6. See Alex Dragnich, *Serbia, Nikola Pašić, and Yugoslavia* (1974), pp. 111-33.

7. For concrete details of their agreement, known as the Corfu Declaration of July 1917, on the organization of the Yugoslav state, see Dragnich, *supra* note 6.

8. Milan P. Djordjević, *Srbia i Jugosloveni za vreme rata 1914-1918* [Serbia and the Yugoslavs During the War 1914-1918] (1922), pp. 39-47.

9. See *supra* note 8, at pp. 24, 46, 48, 103.

10. For a critical treatment, see Enver Redzić, *Muslimansko autonomastvo i 13 SS divizija: autonomije Bosne i Hercegovine i treći rajh* [Muslim Autonomism and the 13th SS Division: The Autonomy of Bosnia and Herzegovina and the Third Reich] (1987).

11. Soviet federalism was not federalism as we know it, because the units of the federation did not have powers that the central government could not take away. One hardly expects to find federalism in a dictatorship.

12. This point of view was expressed by Milovan Djilas, a one-time close associate of Tito's (and later a leading dissident), in interviews with the author.

13. See Alex Dragnich, *Serbs and Croats: The Struggle in Yugoslavia* (1992), pp. 158-161.

14. Chuck Sudetic, "Ethnic Rivalries Push Yugoslavia to Edge," *New York Times*, October 14, 1990, at A14. It is important to note that Slovenia in September 1989 had already struck the first blow to Yugoslav unity when it passed amendments to its constitution depriving the federal center of its vital prerogatives.

15. Brenda Fowler, "Slovenes Vote Decisively for Independence From Yugoslavia," *New York Times*, December 24, 1990, at A6. Chuck Sudetic, "Croatia Votes for Sovereignty and Confederation," *New York Times*, May 20, 1991, at A8. For some background information, see Blaine Harden, "Yugoslav Area Rejects Communists; Slovenia Seeks Sovereign Status," *Washington Post*, April 14, 1990, at A1; "Croatians Vote in Final Round as Independence Party Leads," *New York Times*, May 7, 1990, at A8. See also Blaine Harden, "Croatian President-Elect Plans 'Sovereign State'; Nationalists Seek a Redefined Yugoslavia," *Washington Post*, April 30, 1990, at A13; Chuck Sudetic, "As Croatia Goes, Will All Yugoslavia," *New York Times*, May 5, 1990, at A4.

16. See *Istina o oružanom sukobu u Sloveniji* [The Truth about the Armed Conflict in Slovenia] (Ivan Matović, ed., 1991).

17. *Ibid.*

18. *Ibid.*

19. *Ibid.*, p. 22.

20. *Ibid.*, p. 19.

21. The Yugoslav authorities documented in considerable detail violations by members of Slovenian armed units of international law concerning human rights, laws of war (especially breaches of the rights of the wounded and of the medical corps), and the rights of civilians. See *ibid.*, pp. 30-62. The authorities also documented an instance of the Yugoslav Army's movement of persons released from prison and of an instance of Yugoslav government negotiators being transported in helicopters with Red Cross markings. See *ibid.*, p. 63.

22. *Ustav SFRJ; ustavi socialističkih republika i porkrajina* [Constitution of Socialist Federative Republic of Yugoslavia; Constitutions of the Socialist Republics and Provinces].

23. *Ibid.*

24. *Ibid.*

25. *Ibid.*, Arts. 280 and 281. For rights and duties of the republics, see *ibid.*, arts. 303-312.

26. For an excellent treatment of this issue, see Robert M. Hayden, *The Partition of Bosnia and Herzegovina, 1990-1993*, 2 Radio Free Europe and Lib. Res. Rep. 1 (1993).

27. *Ibid.*

28. For an objective and informative description of the Croatian Ustashi movement and its followers' acts of genocide, see Aleksa Djilas, *The Contested Country: Yugoslav Unity and Communist Revolution, 1919-1953*, pp. 103-27 (1991).

29. *Ibid.*, pp. 125-126. The most frequently cited number of Serbs killed is between 700,000 and 800,000. Djilas reports that Hermann Neubacher, a high-ranking Nazi official, estimated that civilian victims numbered 750,000. He additionally says that German general Lothar Rendulic claimed that there were 500,000 victims in the first months of the existence of the Ustashi regime.

30. *Encyclopedia of the Holocaust*, Vol. I, p. 323; Vol. IV, p. 1552 (Israel Gutman, ed., 1990).

31. Gregory Copley, "Hidden Genocide," *1992 Def. & Foreign Aff. Strategic Policy 5.*

32. *Ibid.*; see also Blaine Harden, "Croats Field Militant Militia; Nationalist Party Fighters Invoke Images of Fascist Past," *Washington Post*, October 10, 1991, at A31; Stephen Kinzer, "Pro-Nazi Rulers Legacy Still Lingers for Croatia," *New York Times*, October 31, 1993, at A10.

33. *The Islamic Declaration: A Programme for the Islamization of Muslims and the Muslim Peoples* (1990). This was initially an unofficial publication, written and illegally circulated in 1970.

34. *Ibid.*, p. 5.

35. *Ibid.*, p. 30.

36. *Ibid.*, pp. 42-43.

37. Interview with James Baker, Secretary of State, in Washington, D.C. (July 28, 1992).

38. A.M. Rosenthal, "Preventing More Bosnias," *New York Times*, May 25, 1993, at A23.

39. "Croatia, Slovenia Get EC Recognition; U.S. Takes Wary Stand; Yugoslavia Loses Rebel Republics," *Facts on File*, January 15, 1992, p. 26. The Vatican recognized Slovenia and Croatia on January 13.

40. David Binder, "U.S. Recognizes Three Yugoslav Republics as Independent," *New York Times*, April 8, 1992, at A10.

41. Stressed by Secretary Baker, *supra* note 37.

42. American Association for Advancement of Slavic Studies, Bridging Ethnic Cleavages: Soviet and Yugoslav Lessons, Phoenix, AZ, November 20, 1992.

43. See Peter Brock, "Dateline Yugoslavia: The Partisan Press," 94 *Foreign Policy*, p. 152. See also Jacques Merlino, *Les Vérités Yuogoslaves ne sont pas toutes bonnes à dire* (1993).

44. The story, based on a UN report, was first broken by a London newspaper. See Leonard Doyle, "Muslims 'Slaughter their Own People'," *The Independent*, August 22, 1992, p. 1. See also Warren Strobel, "Bosnians Accused of Bloody Deceit," *Washington Times*, August 23, 1992, at A1. The essence of the story was confirmed by Lewis MacKenzie, *Peacekeeper: The Road to Sarajevo* (1993), p. 194.

45. See Copley, *supra* note 31, p. 2. See also *Report of the Secretary-General Pursuant to Paragraph 4 of Security Council Resolution 752 (1992)*, 47th Session, Plenary meeting, May 30, 1992, p. 5, UN Document S/24049 (1992).

46. James Gow, "The Yugoslav Crisis and the Role of the Military: In Search of Authority," *The South Slav Journal*, 54 (1990).

47. David Binder, "U.S. Policy Makers on Bosnia Admit Errors in Opposing Partition in 1992," *New York Times*, August 29, 1933, at A10.

48. *Ibid.*

49. David Binder, "Balkan Factions Begin New Talks," *New York Times*, January 3, 1993, at A1 and A6.

50. A fair number of Muslims and Croats would in either case be mixed in with the Serbs.

51. Paul Lewis, "Bosnian Muslims Join Croats in Accepting Peace Pact," *New York Times*, March 26, 1993, at A12.

52. Peter Brock lists eight specific reasons why the Vance-Owen Plan was unacceptable to the Serbs. These, he says, were not reported in the Western press. Brock, *supra* note 43.

53. "Bosnian Serbs Again Reject Peace Plan Despite U.S. Military Threat; Appeals by Yugoslav Leader Ignored," *Facts on File*, May 6, 1993, at A1.

54. For a more detailed treatment, see Alex N. Dragnich, "The West's Mismanagement of the Yugoslav Crisis," 156 *World Affairs*, p. 63.

55. For text of the agreement, see Charles E. Timberlake, *Detente: A Documentary Record*, (1978), pp. 154-81.

56. Elaine Sciolino, "U.S. Names Figures it Wants Charged with War Crimes," *New York Times*, December 17, 1992, at A1 and A22.

57. Dragovan Sepić, *Italija, saveznici i jugoslavensko pitanje, 1914-1918* [Italy, the Allies, and the Yugoslav Question] (1970), p. 139.

58. *The Treaties of Peace* (1924), pp. 267, 461.

59. Milena Spasovski, Dragica Živković and Milomir Stepić, *Etnički sastav stanovništva bosne i hercegovina* [Ethnic Composition of the Population of Bosnia-Herzegovina] (1992). Prior to 1948, the categories were based primarily on religious affiliation.

THE UNKNOWN CIVIL WAR*

The use of NATO military strikes against the Bosnian Serbs, at the urgings of the Clinton administration, camouflages for the moment a rift that has occurred in the Western alliance. Sooner or later recriminations over "who lost Yugoslavia?" are certain to come. And though it may be a while before historians render a verdict, there are already some indications that the answer will be "the Western European powers with the complicity of the United States." The reason: a failure to understand the basic issues in the Yugoslav crisis.

Since the Western media failed - or simply refused - to state or explain the issues in that civil war, particularly as seen by the largest ethnic group (the Serbs), I elicited information from Serbian friends and acquaintances who were visiting the United States or who were writing or phoning in an effort to be heard. What follows is a summary of those conversations.

"For nearly 50 years we were forced to suffer under communism, which we did not choose, and yet nary a word of concern from you. As a matter of fact, after 1948, your Presidents and Secretaries of State praised our dictator Tito, whom you know was a Croat and not a Serb. Communism was not our doing; you betrayed us near the end of World War II, when you abandoned our guerrilla leader, General Mihajlovitch, and supported the communists. We were your allies in the two world wars, and yet now you heap all sorts of evil upon our heads and blame us for everything in Yugoslavia."

The voice was that of an intelligent, well-educated, and well-traveled Serbian woman at least 20 years my junior. The allegations and imputations were obviously not personal, but as was to be the case in nearly every one of my encounters, there was the inescapable question: "Why?"

The torrent seemed unending, but I had to listen. These were friends. More than that, I wanted to learn more about the agitated Serbian psyche in the present tragic situation. I was eager to ask about Sarajevo, Dubrovnik, and ethnic cleansing, among other

* *Chronicles: A Magazine of American Culture*, October, 1994, pp. 27-31. Reprinted with permission.

things. But I quickly sensed that each conversationalist wanted to be sure that I viewed everything in the appropriate historical context.

In all of our conversations there was much harking back to Serbia's past, and no end of repetition. I cannot even estimate how often I heard the same plaintive voice that expected me to understand. Although American in every way - birth, education, profession, family - I am of Serbian parentage, which they believed would enable me to put myself in their shoes and to grasp the enormity of their psychological as well as material burdens.

These were friends with whom I spent many an enjoyable and interesting hour when I served as cultural attaché and public affairs officer in the American Embassy in Belgrade right after World War II, as well as many years later when I was doing research in Serbian and Yugoslav history. Many had read some of my books, most had not. They were aware that I was familiar with what they were telling me, but this did not diminish their determination to make sure.

I lost count of the times I was asked: "Are you Americans totally blind?" "Has foreign propaganda so hoodwinked you that you have lost your critical faculties?" "Are American Presidents and senators so mesmerized by TV pictures that they cannot think rationally; don't you have people in your State Department who know Yugoslavia and Yugoslav history?" These rhetorical questions I could handle with a shrug of the shoulders, a shaking of the head, or some other vague gesture. The substantive ones were more difficult. Many a time, I had to come back to my Serbian friends and acquaintances with the question: "Was there a way to avoid civil war?"

A Serb friend, whose family is from Croatia and whose university degree is in engineering, was quick to tell that although Slovenia fired the first shots in the civil war, that in itself was not critical because there were no appreciable minorities in Slovenia. Hence Slovenian independence came without much bloodshed. Croatia was different, he said, because of the large Serbian minority, which did not want to be in a Croatian state. "That situation might have been resolved," he continued, "if the Tudjman regime [in Croatia] had been willing to treat the Serbs as equals. Instead it reduced them to minority status and then engaged in all sorts of discrimination against them. In addition, there were anonymous telephone threats, ugly signs painted on Serbian homes, and the like.

And there was no chance that the Serbs would be given autonomy." When I asked him to amplify, he replied that the worst part of the regime was its "adopting of symbols and other trappings of the hated World War II Ustasha fascist state."

A Serb doctor from Zagreb pointed out that under the circumstances many of Croatia's Kraina Serbs fled to Serbia but that most of them stayed, organized, and resisted. "Yugoslav army units in the area," he added, "came to their defense, and the civil war in Croatia began." After several months, during which Serbian forces occupied a significant chunk of territory, there was a cease-fire and a United Nations peacekeeping force was brought in.

***

All of this was familiar to me, so I eagerly moved on to a discussion of Bosnia-Herzegovina (which I will simply call Bosnia), a highly complex and complicated subject. When the moment seemed appropriate, I usually began with the question: "How did it all begin?"

"As you know, communism was a failure here as in Russia and everywhere else," was most frequently the opening response. "When the Yugoslav Communist Party began to split up into many communist parties along nationality lines, what we had known but could not say publicly was out in the open - Tito and his comrades had not solved the nationality problem; they had made it worse. They swept it under the rug, where bitterness accumulated until the dam was ready to burst."

"You mean...," I started to say. "Yes, I mean Tito's vintage was where the grapes of wrath were stored," he replied, letting me know that he was familiar with some Americana.

"Yes," I said, "but how did the breakup of Yugoslavia begin?"

"As far as we Serbs are concerned, you know that we have always been the strongest supporters of the common state, but when we saw that others - especially the Croats - were not happy with Yugoslavia, we began to doubt the wisdom of our own position, particularly when we saw that under communism we got the short end of the stick."

"But," added a colleague, "we were not the ones that started to destroy Yugoslavia; we still wanted to save it."

"You know, Professor, a few years ago some of our intellectuals in the Academy of Arts and Sciences began drafting a statement about the problems and difficulties facing Yugoslavia and suggesting ways to deal with them, and you know what happened? Someone got a draft copy of what was called *The Memorandum*, and without the text being published anywhere, our communist press viciously attacked it as an expression of Serbian nationalism."

"Strange, isn't it," another friend added, "that now in the West they call it Miloshevitch's platform of Serbian nationalism!"

"Yes," declared his colleague. "When Miloshevitch became head of the Serbian party, he may have taken some ideas from it. You recall he went to Kosovo in April 1987, and in a huge meeting that lasted at least 12 hours he heard the sorrowful woes of many Serbs and how they had been persecuted by the Albanians and even by some of their Serbian colleagues in the government of the province - all of them communist party hacks."

"And," I broke in, "that experience made Miloshevitch a Serbian nationalist?"

"Well," my friend volunteered, "that is when he made the statement heard round the world," again seeking to impress me with his knowledge of Americana. "At that meeting in Kosovo, many Serbs seeking to get into the crowded hall were beaten by the police. When Miloshevitch, in response to a disturbance, was told what had happened, he ordered that more Serbs be allowed to enter and assured them with: 'No one will ever beat you again!'"

"Wait a minute," I interrupted, "there were other Serbian communists who defended Serbian interests - Rankovic, Nikezic, Perovic."

"But none of them survived politically," my friend hurried to say, "and maybe they were not really defending Serbian interests, and anyway they were all purged! Miloshevitch is the first, not only to survive but to rise to the top."

"And therein lies the tragedy," a retired university professor told me on another occasion, "because so many of my intellectuals hoped that he would launch Serbia on a democratic path, but their trust was misplaced."

A young professional who grew up in Kosovo and whom I had just met for the first time sought to emphasize the importance of Kosovo to Serbs, calling it "Serbia's Jerusalem" and "the cradle of the Serbian nation," as well as the area of Serbia's sacred monuments - Christian churches and monasteries.

"And you know," he added, "during the entire Tito period, the Kosovo Albanians were systematically persecuting the Serbs - setting haystacks on fire, cutting down fruit trees, raping young girls on their way from school - and desecrating their monuments, and yet there was not a word about it in our or the world's press. Several years after Tito's death we learned that the Serbian Orthodox Church in Belgrade in 1969 had sent a protest to Tito, but the public heard nothing of it at the time. Tito gave some assurances, but nothing changed."

I was eager to leave Kosovo and to move on, but another friend told me not to forget that during the Tito years Kosovo Albanians had not only persecuted Serbs and forced them to flee, while countless thousands of Albanians were immigrating to Kosovo, but had also "brought hundreds of teachers and textbooks from Albania."

When I turned my attention to Bosnia, the immediate response was: "Bosnia is Serbian; Sarajevo is Serbian." Subsequently, the response was qualified - I could not understand the problem of Bosnia-Herzegovina except in the context of the Yugoslav civil war, which began with the secessions of Slovenia and Croatia. "Had it not been for the hasty recognition of them by the West," I was told, "Bosnia-Herzegovina would not have sought independence, and there would not have been this bloodshed." "Once Western Europe followed Germany's decision to recognize Slovenia and Croatia, there was no way that the Yugoslav state could be saved," was a familiar refrain that I heard over and over again. "And," my friends kept repeating, "when the West recognized the rights of Slovenes and Croats to self-determination, we Serbs believed that the same principle should apply to us, but we soon found out that such was not the case."

"Yes," chimed in another friend, "the West told Slovenia and Croatia that it was OK for them to violate the Helsinki Accords with respect to changing international boundaries by force but told us we could not do that even after they aided Slovenia and Croatia in those violations. Our grievances did not matter!" The lack of evenhandedness in the West's approach to the Yugoslavs was pounded into me on countless occasions, and there was always the "Why?"

"You know, Professor, there were nearly a million Serbs in Croatia, and they did not want to live in a Croatian state, especially in view of the fact that hundreds of thousands of their forebears were massacred by the Croats when the latter were last independent as a satellite of Germany in World War II." To this I could only nod.

"And, Professor, you know we could not abandon our brothers in Bosnia. There are over a million and a half of them. At the time of the Turkish conquest in the 15th century Bosnia was Serbian. And once Serbia regained her independence in the 19th century, we fought to regain Bosnia, but the Great Powers gave it to Austria-Hungary, from which we finally got it in World War I. And then we all formed Yugoslavia."

Here I was again listening to a lot of history I already knew, but I was at least partially helpless to stop the prose. "But what happened under communism?" I interjected.

"Professor, it is a long story. In the 1920s and 1930s we did not divide up into republics, but Tito split us up. And when the Muslims and Croats in Bosnia wanted to follow Croatia and Slovenia by seeking independence, our brothers who had lived there for centuries did not want to be separated from Serbia."

"And you know what is so tragic," added another friend, "is that the Muslims bet on the wrong horse twice - in World War II, when they joined pro-Nazi Croatia in the extermination of Serbs, and now in this try to form a nation that never existed before."

More than once my friends reminded me that the Muslims were mainly the descendants of Serbs who had converted to Islam under the Turks. "Would you want to live under such people?" I was asked. "What would you think of citizens in your country who, if you were occupied by a foreign power, would accept the foreign religion of your conqueror and then serve him, and now you are asked to live under the rule of such people?" Again and again there was a return to the question: If self-determination was good for the Croats and Slovenes, why not the Serbs?

I pointed out that in 1992 the Serbs were but 34 percent of the population of Bosnia-Herzegovina even though they held more than 60 percent of the territory before the fighting began, but I was promptly given official statistics showing that between 1878 and 1971 the Serbs were the largest group. In 1971, Tito introduced the ethnic category "Muslim," and that reduced the number of persons listing themselves as Serbs. According to the 1991 Yugoslav census, the population distribution was: Muslims, 44 percent; Serbs, 34 percent; Croats, 17 percent; and various other minorities, 5 percent.

***

So much for history. I wanted my friends to talk about the ongoing war and recent atrocities. "What about the shelling of Sarajevo's skyline buildings?" I asked a Serb economist born and reared in Sarajevo. "I cannot defend the shelling of civilian areas," he said, "but let's look at it from the point of view of the Bosnian Serb authorities. First, you know that Serbian money built much of modern Sarajevo, that the Yugoslav National Army built the Olympic Village and other facilities in connection with the Olympics. So Serbs are reacting like the boy who builds something for his playmates, who then kick him off the field. He, in turn, seeks to destroy what he built. Irrational reaction to ingratitude? Maybe, but...."

"In addition," he continued, "many of the tall buildings were being used as observation towers by the Muslim forces." Part of the problem, he added, is "Serbian frustration - not knowing how to deal with fellow-citizens with whom you thought you were building a better country, only to find out that they wanted to go their separate way once they got as much as they could from the common effort."

"What of ethnic cleansing, prison camps, atrocities?" I asked another Serb from Bosnia, as well as several Serbs from outside it. All of the answers were similar. "As you know," said one, "civil wars are the most tragic of wars, but in all wars there are people who are displaced from their homes, there are prison camps, and many people are killed, some in battle, some accidentally, and others in fits of anger resulting from a variety of circumstances."

"But what about charges of genocide?" I asked. "There was no genocide," was the universal answer. "It is true that in many densely populated places many Muslims were killed, but so were many Serbs as well as Croats. Some massacres were awful and cannot be defended, but all three parties have been guilty."

"Muslims were not killed because they were Muslims," another friend was quick to add. "It is true that in some areas of Bosnia that Serbs occupied, many Muslims were dispossessed - but not killed, unless they refused to obey the occupying forces. In many such areas, they were not disturbed if they did not constitute a threat to the occupation army." Another friend was anxious to tell me that, of course, rapes were committed by all sides, but, he said, "there was not a shred of evidence that rape was ordered by anyone in authority, and certainly not as policy."

A Serbian writer from Belgrade, who had been with Serbian forces in Bosnia and Kraina, wanted to tell me of Muslim prisons for Serbs in Sarajevo, as well as of Sarajevo Muslims killing Serbs so that they could take their apartments. "Your press talks about harmony in Sarajevo and Bosnia generally, but, you know, a Serb apartment dweller in Sarajevo does not dare show his face on his balcony for fear of being shot, on the grounds that he is signaling Serb forces." "But," he shouted, "you won't read about these matters in your press, even though American newsmen know about them. After all, they are reporting from Sarajevo, and if they reported these things they would soon be on their way out. That's like getting your news of World War II happenings from Berlin," he said, with emphasis and a note of bitterness in his voice.

Another Serbian friend wanted to know why the American media were concentrating all of their attention on Sarajevo. "Why don't they tell your people about the long Croat shelling of Trebinje, or the Muslim and Croat shelling of Mostar, as well as many smaller places?" And, he added, "why no mention of the Croats placing guns alongside the cathedral in Sibenik?"

This prompted me to ask about the shelling of Dubrovnik. "The fighting around Dubrovnik," said a Serb who was born in that area, "was prompted by the Croatian forces' attack on our naval facilities at the base of the Prevlaka peninsula, not far from Dubrovnik." In addition, he continued, "the Croats had placed their troops in the hotels around the old city, so that they spied on our signal station on top of the mountain, so some of the building and boats by the old city were hit. But Serbian forces did not destroy Dubrovnik. At least one American professor, and Roman Catholic at that, visited the old city and confirmed that there was only minor damage inside the old city. The major damage was to the Serbian church library." He asked me if I had seen any pictures showing the destruction of Dubrovnik, and I had to admit that I had not - and neither had any of my friends.

On one occasion I turned to an old acquaintance - I could not call him a friend, because when I first knew him most of my friends viewed him as close to the regime - and asked what the situation was like in 1991, when it seemed that Slovenia and Croatia were about to secede. I got a learned lecture. "You know," he began, "we thought that the government could handle the situation. We had become accustomed to viewing the dictatorship as all-powerful. And there was the Yugoslav National Army, which Tito always told us could be counted upon to save Yugoslavia in any emergency."

"But," I asked, "who was in charge?"

"Well, maybe if we Serbs had been in charge," he noted with a tone of resignation, "things might have been different."

"Where were the Serbs?" I demanded. "The American media almost always speaks of the 'Serb-dominated Yugoslavia,'" I asserted.

"Your media is absolutely wrong. When Slovenia seceded, the Yugoslav government was mainly in the hands of non-Serbs. Just look who was prime minister, Ante Markovic, a Croat. And who was minister of foreign affairs, Budimir Loncar, another Croat. The minister of defense and supreme commander was General Veljko Kadijevic, son of a Serb-Croat marriage, and his deputy was Stane Brovet, a Slovene. The chief of the air force was Zvonko Jurjevic, another Croat. Does that look like a Serb-dominated Yugoslavia?!"

"And," my friend continued, "it was Ante Markovic who signed the order to have the army take over frontier posts on Slovenia's border, as he was ordered to do by the Federal Executive Council."

"What puzzles us," he went on to say, "is why your leaders were in such a hurry to help those who wanted to destroy Yugoslavia. And after the dismemberment began, why were they so determined to perpetuate Tito's greatest injustice to us Serbs? Instead of seeking to resolve disagreements here, they were willing to have communist Miloshevitch be the only defender of Serbian interests. Why?"

***

Another friend took up the question of sanctions. "You went to the U.N. and got sanctions against us and against no one else. Why? You knew that there were 50,000 Croatian troops in Bosnia, but no sanctions against Croatia. Is this what you call a fair and impartial policy?"

The wife of a Serbian doctor, recently on a visit to Belgrade, told me of the suffering that the Serbian people are enduring. "My friends asked me," she said, "if you Americans realize who the sanctions were hurting. Don't they know that the rulers here are not hurting, but the common people?"

"And," her companion chimed in, "it is the children who are suffering the most. They tell you that medicine and medical supplies are exempt from the sanctions, but those at the U.N. who write the sanctions rules and procedures have made life impossible; they keep changing the rules. Our doctors are desperate, but do you care?"

"Your press," observed a professor friend of mine while visiting relatives in the United States, "keeps talking about refugees from Bosnia in Western Europe, but not a word about Serbian refugees. And what about all the refugees we have here? Don't you Americans know that we have over a half-million refugees in Serbia? And thousands are Muslims, who would rather come here than go to Croatia. And we have Croats, too. Somehow, we think you know but just don't care." I admitted that I do not have any answers.

The same professor wondered out loud, while we were having our after-dinner coffee: "Where are your intellectuals, your professors and specialists on Eastern Europe? They must know what is going on. Are they not outraged by the lies being purveyed by your media? You know, we had our weak-kneed intellectuals, but under a communist dictatorship what could you expect? But you pride yourself on being a democracy, a place where independent inquiry and dissent does not send you to jail. What has frozen the mouths of your intellectuals?"

"A few have spoken up," I responded, "usually in letters to the editor, but for the most part major media channels have not been open to them, certainly not the columns of such influential newspapers as the *New York Times*, *Wall Street Journal*, *Los Angeles Times*, or *Washington Post*." I did not like to admit this, but I knew it to be true. I was glad he did not ask about the major network TV newscasts.

We returned to the topic a few days later, and I was able to show him an article from *Foreign Policy*, written by Peter Brock, a politics editor of the *El Paso Herald-Post*, entitled "Dateline

Yugoslavia: The Partisan Press," wherein he detailed the distortions, and even fabrications, of certain correspondents and their editors. Some had unashamedly engaged in "Serb-bashing." I was also able to show him translated excerpts from a 1993 book by the Frenchman Jacques Merlino, the title of which (in English) reads *The Truth From Yugoslavia Is Not Being Reported Honestly*. Among other things, Merlino reports that an official of a public relations firm in Washington told him that their greatest success was in having, in effect, led the major American Jewish organizations by the nose over to the pro-Croatian side.

A friend of mine had already given the professor a few copies of *Chronicles*, with informative articles by Thomas Fleming and Momcilo Selic. Earlier, I had mailed him a few of my op-ed pieces that had appeared in papers in Philadelphia and Nashville, as well as a few articles written by university faculty friends of mine. "Yes," he said, "the truth is breaking through in a limited way, but your major news sources are very much like a broken record." I could not disagree.

At another time I was talking with a lawyer friend who lives in Belgrade. He told me of a friend who in 1992 had long talks with a non-Serb American attorney who had held important positions in the United States government. The Serb told the American: "Look, we believed that only you Americans could be trusted to help, to be fair. What of Britain, we asked? Well, we knew that Britain was over the hill. France? Incapable and not really trustworthy. Russia? Russia has too many problems of her own. That only left you, but what did you do? You turned us over to the Germans, our bitter enemies in two world wars."

When I asked another Belgrade friend if Serbs had any contact with the American Embassy, she spoke matter-of-factly: "They don't really want to see us, and you know when a friend of mine came to Belgrade from Bosnia, she went to the American Embassy and told a young American officer there that she wanted to report on atrocities. When he asked what atrocities, she said they were atrocities against Serbs, and you know what he told her? They were only interested in those committed *by* Serbs!"

When I began a conversation with a retired professor of sociology, a woman, she cut me off before I could put forth a question: "You Americans have lost Serbia's trust and friendship forever." The bitterness in her voice left me with a feeling of sadness. It all seemed so unnecessary. Were we really so inept in handling foreign relations, especially in dealing with people who in the past had been such faithful allies? At least I had heard voices about the Yugoslav civil war that are almost never heard in our media.

SERBIA'S TRAGEDIES IN THE TWENTIETH CENTURY: SOME REFLECTIONS*

Serbia journeyed from relatively monumental achievements and great expectations at the beginning of the twentieth century to chaos and catastrophe at the present. A people that in the past century fought successfully against the Ottomans to regain their independence and established a democratic political system, and a people who in this century sacrificed every third male in their wars of liberation and struggle for Yugoslavia, were merely told by the Western powers in the last few years that they should accept a situation where a third of them would live under foreign governments.

It is my aim, in this essay, to record briefly the major developments that have affected the Serbs and Serbia in the twentieth century, with some of my considered reflections. What I write here should not be interpreted as in any way minimizing the tragedies of other peoples of former Yugoslavia.

For the benefit of the reader, I want at the outset to record how I became interested in Serbia and the South Slavs. My interest in Yugoslavia was incremental and cumulative. My illiterate parents, Serbs from Montenegro, came to the United States some nine decades ago. I learned the rudiments of the language from them - my first language - but little of the people or their history. It was not until my university years that I gained a bit of the history of my forebears.

At graduate school I began doing some background reading, wondering if I could do a Ph.D. thesis on Serbian or Yugoslav history and politics. One of the books I read was that of the English historian, Harold Temperley, and a particular passage caught my eye: "There is no race which has shown a more heroic desire for freedom than the Serbs, and achieved it with less aid from others - or at more sacrifice to itself." [1] Moreover, the tales of the Serbs' bravery in their historic struggle for freedom from Ottoman rule, further piqued my curiosity.

In 1939, at the end of my first graduate year, I borrowed money for a summer trip to Europe, most of it spent in Yugoslavia, including my parents' birthplace. A few years later, during World

---

* *Serbian Studies*, Vol. VII, 1993, pp. 1-15. Reprint permission not needed.

War II, I began dealing with Yugoslav affairs, as part of my first government job in Washington. After an interlude of two years' university teaching following the war, I went to the American Embassy in Belgrade as Cultural Attaché, where I spent two and a half years. During those years I saw much of the country, met many of its peoples, learned more of its history, and observed the Communist system in action.

After having returned to university life in 1950, I spent the summer months of 1952 in Yugoslavia, completing research for my first book, *Tito's Promised Land: Yugoslavia.* After that I observed Yugoslav developments from afar until 1966. In that and following summers, I spent many months in Yugoslavia doing research on studies that resulted in several books and articles on Serbian and Yugoslav history and politics.

Serbia's History

Serbia has a long history. In the Middle Ages for over 100 years, it was the strongest empire in the Balkans. But in 1389, the Serbs were defeated by the Ottoman Turks at Kosovo, the cradle of the Serbian nation, and were to remain under Turkish colonial rule for nearly 500 years.

Revolts in 1804 and 1815 led to *de facto* independence by mid-century (*de jure* in 1878), to be sure over a relatively small area. As soon as the Ottomans agreed to grant autonomy to the Serbs under a Serbian prince, his absolute authority was challenged. From then on a twofold struggle, side by side, dominated the national affairs. One was to gain complete independence from the Turks and the other to achieve a constitutional democratic system. Victory in the first came sooner and with less effort. The second was more difficult and took longer; there were victories and setbacks.

By 1903, however, Serbia achieved a constitutional monarchy with a functioning parliamentary system. The press was free and political parties contested in free elections, and the monarch accepted the results. Cabinets were responsible to the elected parliament. The country was basically rural, but some modest economic development had begun in the last decades of the previous century. Prior to the First World War, there was progress on the cultural and social fronts. Moreover, Serbia was a state with a balanced budget.

There were troubles, however, on the foreign front, mainly the determination of Austria-Hungary to expand her power and influence in the Balkans. One sign of Vienna's success was the failure of the

Serbian uprising in Bosnia-Herzegovina in 1878, where Turkish power was on the wane. Instead of Serbia getting the largely Serbian provinces, the great powers of Europe gave Austria-Hungary permission to occupy it, with an implied understanding that Vienna could subsequently annex it, which it did in 1908. Serbia was in no position to challenge the annexation, and neither was Russia, Serbia's patron, which had met defeat by Japan in 1905.

Serbian leaders, smarting from weakness and the knowledge that large Serbian areas remained outside Serbia, in 1911 organized an alliance of the small Balkan nations - Greece, Romania, Bulgaria, and Montenegro - dedicated to throwing the Turks out of the Balkans. In 1912 they launched a war against the Turks, which was phenomenally successful, much to the chagrin of Vienna and the surprise of the other European great powers. Because of a disagreement between Serbia and Bulgaria over some areas, Bulgaria in 1913 launched a surprise war against Serbia, which the Serbs won, with the support of the other Balkan powers, which were offended by Bulgaria's failure to have the Russian tsar resolve the issue, as provided in the Balkan alliance.

The great powers, however, forced Serbia and Montenegro to give up some of the lands that they had gained, and then proceeded to create an Albanian state. Nevertheless, Serbia doubled its territory and increased its population from about two million in 1878 to four million in 1913. But Serbia was greatly weakened. This did not satisfy Vienna, which could not forget that Serbia's aim was to liberate other Serbian lands, especially in Croatia and Bosnia-Herzegovina. The Habsburg dynasty was also troubled by Serbia's democratic political system, which was attractive to the Slavic peoples of those lands.

The First World War and the Creation of Yugoslavia

The assassination of the heir to the Habsburg throne on June 28, 1914, in Sarajevo provided Vienna with a pretext for crushing Serbia. With the backing of its ally, Germany, it presented Serbia with an ultimatum that no independent country could accept, and then declared war. The Serbs fought valiantly. Furthermore, at the end of the first year of the war they had driven the Austro-Hungarian army off their soil. But the arrival of German troops in 1915 forced the Serbs to retreat, resulting in heavy losses in lives and matériel, especially as the army and government laboriously fought their way over the Albanian mountains in the winter of 1915-1916, ultimately reaching the Greek island of Corfu. Within a year they were to return to battle on the Salonika front, from where they, with the help of the allies, fought their way back to Belgrade near the end of the war.

Soon thereafter, on December 1, 1918, a Yugoslav (South Slav) state was established, known at that time as the Kingdom of the Serbs, Croats, and Slovenes. Ideas for the formation of a common state had been widely discussed among intellectuals but not among the peasantry, which made up the bulk of the populace. Among the leading advocates was the Croat, Bishop Strossmayer.

Moves toward the realization of the idea came early in the war. Forced to withdraw to the interior by the Austro-Hungarian attack, the Serbian government in December 1914 nevertheless found time to declare its war aims. The most important - next to victory - was the liberation and unification of all Serbs, Croats, and Slovenes.

In 1915, this objective conflicted with the Entente's determination to entice Italy, a member of the Triple Alliance, to join Britain, France, and Russia in the war against Germany and Austria-Hungary. To achieve that, they concluded the Treaty of London (which was kept secret), promising Italy certain Austro-Hungarian areas along the northern Adriatic with a large South Slav population. In an effort to get the Serbs to drop the idea of a Yugoslav state, they promised Serbia all of Bosnia-Herzegovina, parts of present-day Croatia, and a large part of Dalmatia. Montenegro was to get a small part of Dalmatia, including the city of Dubrovnik. In effect, a large or Great Serbia on the proverbial silver platter! The Serbs, however, were not appeased and continued to work toward the establishment of a Yugoslav state. This proved to be an ominous decision, certainly not realized by Serbian leaders at the time.

Despite Serbia's open commitment to the formation of a common Yugoslav state, Serbian motives came into question among some South Slavs, primarily Croats in the Yugoslav Committee, formed after the war began and made up mostly of Serbs, Croats, and Slovenes who were subjects of Austria-Hungary. Ostensibly, the Committee's main task, in cooperation with the Serbian government, was to work in Allied circles to promote the establishment of the common state. The discord that developed between it and the Serbian government led to a meeting of representatives of the two groups on the island of Corfu in July 1917, where an agreement was reached on the formation of the common state.

The Corfu Declaration, as the agreement came to be called, was quite precise. The new state was to be called the Kingdom of the Serbs, Croats, and Slovenes. It was to be a parliamentary constitu-

tional monarchy headed by the Serbian monarch. It was to be a
unitary state. It was to have a new constitution, framed by a
constituent majority, adopted by a "numerically qualified majority."
This phrase was not otherwise defined and was to be a bone of
contention. When the constituent assembly met, which the Croat
delegates boycotted, the Serbs defined it as an absolute majority of
the delegates, while some delegates thought that it should be two-
thirds. The Serbian view prevailed, and the constitution was adopted
in June 1921.

The First Yugoslavia

The First Yugoslavia took off to a shaky start. While the
Croats continued their boycott, the Serbs undertook the enterprise of
the new state with enthusiasm, aided by the Slovenes, the Yugoslav
Muslim Organization, and other smaller parties. The Serbs assumed
that the Croats would come along; after all, they had already
demonstrated eagerness to be part of the common state. Even when
the Croats boycotted the making of the constitution and engaged in
other acts of non-cooperation, the Serbs viewed these as passing
phenomena, convinced that as the system began to function more or
less normally, Croatian attitudes would change. And indeed they did
change when in 1925 the Croats accepted the constitution and the
monarchy, and joined the parliament and the cabinet. But this change
of attitude was to prove short-lived.

The Serbs seemingly did not notice and obviously did not pay
much attention to the writings of some Croatian nationalists who had
been quite explicit in their anti-Serbian campaign. Nevertheless, the
Serbs were optimists. Serbia gave up her flag, coat of arms, and her
democratic constitution, confident of the future. Knowing that the
other ethnic groups had joined the common venture, the Serbs
quickly overcame all doubts and thus embraced a new faith in the
undertaking. Moreover, Serbia's past achievements and the size of her
population, twice that of the next largest group, the Croats, endowed
them with a feeling of strength.

In retrospect, it can be seen that the commitment to a Yugoslav
state among the non-Serb nationalities, especially among the Croats,
was less enthusiastic. The Slovenes appeared satisfied, having gained
important concessions, among them posts in every cabinet and even a
prime ministership in one. And the Yugoslav Muslim Organization
also obtained significant privileges. The Croats, however, never
seemed to feel at home in Yugoslavia and never praised it as their

own country. When their yearning for an independent Croatia seemed unrealistic, they opted for Yugoslavia, knowing that the Serbs would always welcome them.

The Serbs, on the other hand, did not sufficiently appreciate the Croats' fears and reservations, nor their feelings of inferiority and even inadequacy when dealing with the much more numerous and politically experienced Serbs. Some critics have also faulted the Serbs for stopping to think as Serbs and for thinking exclusively as Yugoslavs. They failed, say these critics, to balance the interests of Serbia with those of the new state. While other ethnic groups were looking out for their respective interests, the Serbs were subordinating theirs to the common, i.e., Yugoslav, interest and hence to the detriment of the Serbs.

As mentioned above, the recognition of the existing political institutions by the Croats and their return to the parliament, as well as their taking positions in the cabinet, all seemed to bode well for the future. Unfortunately, within a brief period of time obstructionism in the parliament became the order of the day, made possible in part by the liberal parliamentary rules, but most of all by the fact that no political party possessed a majority of the seats. In the midst of the obstructionism and the emotional fireworks it engendered, several Croatian deputies were shot in the parliament in June 1928 by a Serbian deputy from Montenegro. The Croatian deputies left the parliament.

For several months, King Alexander sought coalitions that could govern at least provisionally. Not satisfied with the results, he assumed personal power on January 1, 1929, dissolved the parliament and abolished all political parties. He did this, he said, to save the state.

Parliamentary democracy had failed. What was he to do? Some political leaders - Serb, Croat, and Slovene - advised him to turn to temporary dictatorship. Some suggested federalism and some recommended "amputation," i.e., ridding Yugoslavia of Croatia. We know that for a time he toyed with the latter. But like so many Serbs, and being the biggest Yugoslav of them all, he could not admit that the common state had been a mistake. And he believed that federalism would gradually tear the country apart. Consequently, he opted for temporary personal rule. He hoped that by changing the name of the country to the Kingdom of Yugoslavia, dividing it into nine administrative units (named after waterways) that could not be identified with ethnic groups, and by subsequently introducing "guided democracy," he would win loyalty for the country among those who had been disaffected.

Since he was assassinated in October 1934, it is futile to speculate as to the chances of his dream being realized. On the basis of more than a half century of hindsight, and especially in view of the countless tragedies that befell the Serbs during the past six decades, it is difficult to escape the conclusion that he should have opted for "amputation."

Before leaving Alexander, we should note that he was much concerned about foreign dangers to the new state. The main threats he perceived were Mussolini's Italy, Bulgaria, and Hungary. Under King Alexander's leadership and under French auspices, the Little Entente (Yugoslavia, Czechoslovakia, and Romania) came into existence as a mutual defense pact. It was during Alexander's visit to France that he was assassinated by terrorists of Bulgarian background, who had been instructed by extremist Croats (*Ustashe*) and trained in camps in Hungary.

The Serbs have also been faulted, again with the benefit of much hindsight, for their treatment of the Kosovo area with benign neglect, to say the least. The cradle of the Serbian nation, Kosovo was liberated in the Balkan wars of 1912-1913, after nearly 500 years of Turkish occupation. Soon thereafter Kosovo again was under foreign rule - Bulgarian - during World War I. In 1917, the victorious Serbian army once again brought Kosovo into Serbia's fold. The benign neglect was all the more tragic in that the Serbs had a relatively free hand in the early years of the First Yugoslavia when the Croats were boycotting the governing process. Considering what happened in Kosovo over the next several decades, it is easy to conclude that from a purely Serbian national point of view, Kosovo should have had a high priority.

Trying to accelerate the economic development of the new country, the government's benign neglect of Kosovo is easily under-stood. Two South Slav areas of the Austro-Hungarian empire that had some industry were Slovenia and Croatia. So it was logical to put major investment capital there. Ironically, Serbia did not get credit for this policy, hence no tradeoff resulted from neglect of other areas. On the contrary, Croatia and Slovenia seemed to take their more rapid economic development for granted, and subsequently began complaining that they were paying more than their share into the national treasury.

Some observers also argue that the Serbs made a serious error when Alexander's first cousin, Prince Regent Paul, signed the agreement (*Sporazum*) in August 1939 with Croatian leader Vladko Maček. That agreement created a large Croatian unit that went a long way toward establishing a federal system.

From the Serbian side there were three major objections to the agreement. The first questioned legality: the Yugoslav constitution forbade amendments during times when the monarch was not of age. The second objected to the piecemeal changes, arguing that if there were to be changes they should include all regions, notably Serbia and Slovenia. The third objection centered on the fact that the agreement gave the Croats non-Croatian territory, pointing out that close to a third of the total population in the new Croatian unit were Serbs.

Prince Paul and his ministers replied: (1) that legal authority for what they did was found in the Constitution's emergency article; (2) that commissions had already been appointed to work on the creation of Serbian and Slovenian autonomous units; and (3) that the agreement provided that the boundaries of autonomous Croatia were provisional and that the definitive boundaries would be determined at the time of the reorganization of the state, at which time some counties and even villages might be added and others subtracted. Moreover, the agreement was subject to ratification by the parliament.

When World War II broke out within a month after the signing of the agreement, all of the foregoing were shelved. Hence we shall never know if the steps initiated by Prince Paul would have paved the way to a viable political system.

In all fairness to Paul and his government, it should be noted that they were under enormous pressure to reach some agreement with the Croats, as a way of keeping Yugoslavia out of the coming war. The people around Paul were aware of the fact that Maček's intermediaries were talking with the Italians about possible scenarios in the event of war.

A second step that Paul took in an effort to keep Yugoslavia out of war was to sign an agreement with Hitler, clearly unwilling, to preserve Yugoslav neutrality. Hitler had reached agreement with the leaders of Hungary, Bulgaria, and Romania for them to adhere to the Tri-Partite Pact (Germany, Italy, and Japan). The Yugoslavs were under similar pressure, but resisted for a number of months, and finally signed a watered-down accord that promised respect for Yugoslav neutrality and security without any obligation to assist the Axis, a fact not generally known to the public at the time.

A few days later (March 1941), much to the detriment of Serbia and the Serbs, Yugoslav (Serb) generals overthrew the Regency and the cabinet. This act was popular in Serbia, where opinion was widespread that Paul had put Yugoslavia in the same pro-Axis boat as Hungary, Romania, and Bulgaria. When the coup leaders read the document, however, they concluded that there was nothing there that could not be accepted. But it was too late; Hitler was not going to let these Balkan upstarts get away with insulting Germany. In the first weeks of April he launched a massive attack, aimed mainly at Serbia.

Again, with the benefit of hindsight, we can see what an enormously tragic mistake the coup turned out to be. Yugoslavia was quickly dismembered, a pro-fascist regime was formed in Croatia under *Ustashe* leader Ante Pavelić, which proceeded to massacre some 700,000 Serbian inhabitants of that state, along with some 60,000 Jews and 20,000 Gypsies. Other parts of Yugoslavia came under Italian and German occupation, with some lands being turned over to the Balkan satellite regimes. While under German occupation, Serbia had the equivalent of France's Marshall Petain in General Milan Nedić, who sought to keep order so as to save as many Serbian lives as possible. He was never trusted by the Germans, because they knew that he was not really a friend of Hitler's regime. After the war, it was learned that he had provided some secret help to the Serbian guerrillas under Draža Mihailović.

The War, the Civil War, and Communist Rule

In the next several years a civil war raged, pitting two guerrilla movements, Mihailović's Četniks and Tito's Communist-led Partisans, against each other. The former, the first European underground uprising under the occupation, was so firm in Serbia that the latter had little support there, partly because the latter became active only after the Nazi invasion of the Soviet Union in June 1941. Furthermore, it demonstrated early enough that their movement was aimed at a Communist seizure of power. Ultimately, as we know, the Partisans were victorious, with no small amount of Western and, at the end, Soviet assistance.

So, step by step, the Serbs moved from independence to war, to Nazi reprisals, to massacres in Croatia, to slavery under Communism. During the next half century, after the conclusion of the Second World War, for the first time in her thousand-year history, Serbia's fate and the welfare of the Serbian people were to be determined by a man of a different faith and nationality, Josip Broz Tito.

Carving up Yugoslavia into republics, plus two autonomous provinces in Serbia, Tito dispersed the Serbs so that one-third of them found themselves in republics other than their own. One of the worst aspects of Tito's action was what happened in the autonomous province of Kosovo-Metohija (usually referred to in the media as just Kosovo), the cradle of the Serbian nation and the location of its historic religious monuments.

Once ethnically Serbian, with the Ottoman occupation of Serbia after 1389, Kosovo was flooded by Albanians who were brought into the region as surrogates under the Ottoman Turks. While they accepted Islam and with the approval of the Porte, the Albanians persecuted the Serbs on a large scale, many of whom fled to Hungary in sizable numbers. Despite this and the high birthrate among the Albanians, the Serbs were still a majority when Kosovo was liberated in the Balkan wars of 1912-1913. During the interwar Yugoslav state, the percentage of Albanians grew, but on the eve of World War II, the Serbs were just short of a majority.

The Second World War brought tragedy. Italy aided in the creation of a Great Albania, which included Kosovo, and the Bulgarians received their share of Serbian territory. Again, many Serbs were forced to flee. At the end of the war, however, Tito formally forbade their return. In the course of the war, he made many promises to the Albanians in the hope of getting their help in his war against the Mihailović Četniks, including their right to be annexed by Albania. He got practically no help from them. And while he reneged on the promise of annexation, he made it an autonomous province and facilitated the immigration of some two to three hundred thousand Albanians from Albania.

For the next several decades, the Kosovo Albanian leaders, part and parcel of the Yugoslav Communist Party, engaged in ethnic cleansing of Serbs and their institutions in the region (rape, arson, theft of Serbian properties, desecration of Serbian churches and cemeteries were widely practiced). Countless thousands of Serbs were forced to flee to other parts of Serbia or Montenegro. Moreover, the Kosovo Albanians imported university professors and textbooks from Albania. Unpublicized protests by the Serbian Orthodox Church and others were to no avail. The net result of some 35 years of Communist rule in Kosovo was that the Serbian population was reduced to between twelve and fifteen percent; in 1993, perhaps only 10 percent.

Until dictator Tito died in 1980, not a word appeared about the ethnic cleansing in the Yugoslav media. Soon thereafter, however, news began to leak out, and before long even some Yugoslav Communists referred to the Albanian actions as genocide. In the mid-1980s, the Serbian Bar Association addressed a number of messages to high Yugoslav government bodies, pointing to the vast violation of human rights of Serbs in Kosovo, but no significant actions were ever taken.

When Slobodan Milošević became leader of the Serbian Communist Party in the late 1980s, he exploited the Albanian behavior, and made himself the defender of the Serbian interests. While he gained a good deal of popular support initially, his failure to launch Serbia on a democratic path resulted in the loss of much of that support.

Serbia also suffered economically under the Communists, as did other Yugoslavs. However, major industrial investments went to Slovenia and Croatia, and to some extent Bosnia-Herzegovina. This was also true in the first Yugoslavia, precisely because there was already an industrial base in Croatia and Slovenia. And while Tito may have been similarly motivated, he was also determined to punish Serbia, because he maintained that Serbia was responsible for all that went wrong in the interwar years. Ironically, in the post-Tito years Slovenia and Croatia were to complain that they were paying a disproportionate share into the national treasury. In view of that claim, it is noteworthy that in 1991, the average per capita income in Slovenia was $12,618, in Croatia it was $7,179, and in Serbia, the alleged "exploiter," it was only $4,870.

Serbia also suffered politically under Communism. Its only representation in the government were the Serbian Communists, who had been Tito's allies all along. Their position was extremely precarious. On the whole, they subordinated Serbian interests to regime policies. Only years later did some of them express astonishment that they were duped. The well-known novelist and a wartime political commissar in Serbian Communist ranks, Dobrica Ćosić, wondered out loud in 1987: "Why did we Partisans and revolutionaries for so long follow, praise, and worship those who deceived, subjugated, bribed, humiliated, and disgraced us in front of our children and the whole world?"[2] In 1968, he and Jovan Marjanović, at a meeting of the central committee of the Serbian party did warn against the escalation of Albanian nationalism. That led to their expulsion from that body.

It was evident to many that Tito did not fully trust Serbian Communists, and when he suspected that they were deviating from his line, he demoted them or even expelled them from the party. The few intellectual party stalwarts who became aware that Tito hated Serbs (Dobrica Ćosić, Mihailo Marković, and others) did little or nothing until after Tito's death. Even then they were still committed to an integral Yugoslav state. Only about 1988 did some of them suggest that if the other ethnic groups were not in favor of staying together on the basis of equality, perhaps the Serbs should also go their separate ways.

After Tito's death in 1980, all Communist Party leaders representing the various ethnic groups were seeking to follow "Tito's Path," or at least they said they were. In fact, however, the party soon began splitting along nationality lines. At that point the unraveling of the state fabric had already begun. Each republic's party started stressing regional interests, except the Serbian party. When Slobodan Milošević became head of the Serbian party in 1986, he concluded that the injustices to the Serbs in Kosovo could no longer be hidden. While continually taking a pro-Yugoslav stance, he insisted that Serbian interests must be protected.

As the crisis in the economy worsened and as political wrangling as to who was at fault intensified, leaders in the prestigious Serbian Academy of Sciences and Arts began a scholarly analysis of the crisis in the Yugoslav economy and society, and suggested remedies. While still in a draft form, a copy reached the Communist Party press, which labeled it "The Memorandum" and pilloried it as a statement of Serbian hegemonism. While the Memorandum stated how the Serbs suffered in both Yugoslavias, the Communist credentials of its main authors were such that no one could portray them as counter-revolutionaries or enemies of the Federal Republic of Yugoslavia. Yet in the course of the forthcoming civil war in 1991, Serbia's enemies were to call it the program for a Great Serbia, without ever mentioning that Serbian Communists were the first to criticize it.

At an extraordinary congress of the national party at the outset of 1990, representatives from the various republics concluded that agreement was no longer possible. The Slovene delegates were the first to walk out, followed by the Croats. The Tito party that promised "brotherhood and unity" came to an inglorious end.

The Civil War and the Deluge

When in 1991 the Second Yugoslavia began to fall apart, the Serbs, hitherto the strongest supporters of the common state, were willing to see the other republics go their separate ways, but in that case they were most concerned with the future of the Serbs in Croatia and those in Bosnia-Herzegovina. When the Serbs of those two republics sought self-determination for themselves, the Serbs of Serbia and Montenegro were willing to offer assistance.

The secession of Slovenia and Croatia involved the use of force - the Slovenes fired the first shots in this civil war. This was in violation of the Helsinki Accords proviso that the boundaries of internationally recognized states could not be altered by force. Moreover, the Slovenian and Croatian political moves were unilateral, and hence also in violation of the Yugoslav constitution. In a move designed to prevent any attempt on the part of the Serbs to redress their grievances, the Western great powers told them that they could not alter the Tito-imposed borders, which these powers sought to make international via the stroke of a diplomatic pen. There was not even a hint from the West that in any final resolution of the Yugoslav question Serbian grievances should also be addressed. Nor were there any references to the promises to Serbia of the Treaty of London, referred to above, or to the rights conferred by the Versailles Treaty on Yugoslavia as successor state of Serbia. This lack of evenhandedness in no small degree contributed to the civil war.

While the acts of secession by Slovenia and Croatia were viewed by the West as legitimate exercises in self-determination, any such efforts on the part of the million and one-half Serbs in Bosnia-Herzegovina or the three quarters of a million of them in Croatia were viewed as illegitimate. Nevertheless, the Serbs in Krajina (a region in Croatia) revolted. Similarly, when in early 1992, the Muslims and Croats agreed to secede, they were strongly opposed by the Serbs, and civil war spread to Bosnia.

Before the fighting began in Bosnia, the European Community proposed a three-way division of the former republic, to which all three parties agreed. Soon thereafter, the Muslim leader reneged, apparently on the advice of a highly placed United States diplomat.

In May 1993, a dozen or so residents of Sarajevo were killed while standing in line to buy bread at a bakery. Immediately, the Serbs were blamed, which led the United Nations to impose sanctions on Yugoslavia (i.e., Serbia Montenegro), allegedly because they were involved in fighting in Bosnia, although thousands of soldiers from Croatia were similarly involved. A few months later it was ascertained that Serbs were not responsible for the bread line massacre. But this did not have any impact on the UN sanctions.

In subsequent months the media in Europe and the United States, as well as nearly all political leaders, had a field day, labeling the Serbs as aggressors, comparing their actions to Iraq's invasion of Kuwait, etc., totally ignoring the fact that they "internationalized" former internal Yugoslav boundaries *after* the civil war had begun. I wonder how Abraham Lincoln would have reacted if the international community had taken a similar stance toward our Civil War?

The media ascribed all sorts of evil deeds to Serbs and Serbia, usually without proof of any kind. Serbian armed forces were said to have raped tens of thousands of Muslim women as a matter of "policy," but provided no confirmation. While all sides in such wars commit atrocities, those committed by the Croats and Muslims received little or no attention. Only when they massacred each other in late 1993 did the media report some, but vilification was still reserved for the Serbs.

Disinformation about the Serbs was endless. For example, the media constantly referred to the Serbs' "capturing," "seizing," "overrunning" two thirds or seventy percent of Bosnia, whereas they have lived there for centuries and *prior* to any fighting they inhabited more than sixty percent of it. Moreover, the media reported that some republics were seceding because they did not want to live in "Serb-dominated Yugoslavia." This is a canard, because at no time before the secessions were the Serbs dominant in Communist-ruled Yugoslavia.

It was often said that the Yugoslav Army was Serb-dominated. The Serbs may have had a disproportionate number of officers, but in the high command they were under-represented. It should also be noted that at the outset of the civil war in 1991, the key civil and military positions in the Yugoslav government were in the hands of Slovenes and Croats. In addition, it should be made clear that dictator Tito sought a united national army without ethnic coloration. He demonstrated his pride in that army in public, boasting that in times of trouble the army could be counted on to save Yugoslavia. There is reason to believe that in the course of the civil war, many army officers may have been motivated by their understanding of Tito's testament.

In any case, rarely, if ever, have a nation or a people been so mercilessly vilified and pilloried in the media, and their stands and motives so little understood as Serbia and the Serbian people. From day to day, week to week, month to month, the slanted news and commentaries failed to convey elemental facts or engaged in outright distortions. The misrepresentation of a nation's and a people's history was the order of the day. The Western leaders, proceeding on the simplistic notion that as Yugoslavia was breaking up, the republics that were seceding were democratically-oriented while those that wanted a Yugoslav state, notably Montenegro and Serbia, were determined to preserve Communism and were non-democratically oriented. Therefore, they condemned only the Serbs. This Western attitude became more and more fixed as Serbia and the Serbs sought to help their brothers in Croatia and Bosnia-Herzegovina. Ironically, self-determination was positive for all except the Serbs.

In the anti-Serb hysteria no responsible Western leader stepped forward to ask who else might be liable for the carnage taking place in what once was Yugoslavia. Even after the Serbs had won the civil war, the United States took the lead in the anti-Serb crusade, seeking to appropriate more for the losers, the Muslims, thus insuring a continuation of the bloodshed.

Moreover, it is also puzzling that no leading media outlet in the United States or in Western Europe pointed out that the Serbs of Serbia and Montenegro had a legitimate national interest in the Serb-populated areas of Croatia and Bosnia-Herzegovina. Serbia and Montenegro believe that they have a right, indeed a duty, to be concerned for those of their compatriots with whom they lived in one state for the past 75 years.

For this the Serbs have been lambasted as "aggressors," a charge that will not stand up to serious and objective scrutiny, just as the charge of Confederate newspapers that Lincoln's actions constituted a "war of Northern Aggression" could not stand. A civil war is a civil war!

In the meanwhile, the U.N. sanctions caused no end of harm to the Serbs. The damage to the economy is incalculable, and there is no way of measuring the brain drain that resulted from so many younger people leaving Serbia. Even medicine and food, which were supposed to be exempt from the sanctions, were effectively denied because of bureaucratic procedures. Innocent children died because Serbian hospitals did not have the needed drugs. Many older persons committed suicide. Many refugees from the war fronts fled to Serbia and Montenegro, but received little or no help from the outside, which provided relief to other countries with a refugee problem. The rulers in Serbia were not hurt. As a matter of fact, the people tended to see them as the sole defenders of Serbian interests.

In the end, history will condemn the brutalities of all the participants in the Yugoslav civil war - Serbs, Croats, Muslims, and others. It will also record that the Serbs, faithful allies to the Western democracies in two world wars (contrary to the Croats and the Muslims who sided with Hitler's government in WWII); and before Communism was imposed on them, dedicated to liberal-democratic values, were brutally and malevolently sacrificed on the altar of expediency by the Western leaders while they searched for solutions to the consequences of their own failure in managing the Yugoslav dismemberment.

NOTES

1. *History of Serbia* (London, 1919).
2. *Književne novine*, June 1, 1987.

THE FUTURE OF KOSOVO*

The fate of Kosovo, Serbia's troubled province, has in recent years received a good deal of attention in the world press, usually in connection with the actions of Serbia's president, Slobodan Milošević. A somewhat obscure communist until he became head of the Serbian Communist Party in 1986, Milošević went to Kosovo in April 1987 to assess personally the charges of the persecution of Serbs by the Kosovo Albanians, at which time he uttered the words heard round the world   - "No one will ever beat you again." Although spoken in a limited context, those words were frequently interpreted in the West as signifying the ascent of rampant Serbian nationalism.

The cradle of the Serbian nation and the site of its historic Christian monuments, Kosovo at the time of its capture by the Ottoman Turks in 1389 was ethnically almost entirely Serbian. At the time of its liberation in the Balkan wars of 1912, however, Kosovo's population was nearly 40 percent Albanian. By the end of World war II, it was close to 50 percent, by 1987 it was between 75 and 80 percent and at present it is around 90 percent.

With the inauguration of communist rule at the end of World War II, Kosovo was made an autonomous province within the republic of Serbia and was governed by the Kosovo Communist Party, part and parcel of the Yugoslav Communist Party. Although Milošević must have had at least a general awareness of what had transpired in Kosovo during the years of dictator Tito's rule as well as after his death in 1980, it is not clear what prompted him to go to Kosovo. Be that as it may, the critical question is: Why did Milošević, a disciplined communist who was nurtured in Tito's party, and who followed other Serbian communists in being a ruthless critic of Serbian nationalism decide to change Communist Party policy with respect to Kosovo? This question cannot be answered without first reviewing that policy and its consequences in Kosovo. And we should note that two years elapsed between his visit and his action to change the constitutional status of Kosovo.

When word got out that Milošević was coming to Kosovo, over 15,000 resident Serbs came to meet him, but only some 300 pre-

---

* *Chronicles: A Magazine of American Culture*, April 1995, pp. 14-17. Reprinted with permission.

selected ones could be accommodated because of the size of the building where the meeting was to be held. Many more were determined to get in but were forced back; some were beaten by the police, which resulted in considerable commotion. At one point, Milošević asked what the disturbance was about, and when informed, he ordered that more people be let in. And when told about the beatings, he delivered his now well-known words.

The meeting lasted 13 hours and 78 people spoke. The vast majority, apart from decrying their persecution by the Albanians, openly attacked the communist regime. Reports on the meeting were printed in the party press in Belgrade. A few sentences will suffice to give a taste of the proceedings:

> Serbian man: "I know why Germany was divided after the war, but why was Serbia divided?"
>
> Serbian man: "... heads will roll, because it is impossible to endure and to permit the beating of our children and women."
>
> Serbian man: "Serbs want to live together with the Albanians... but here counterrevolution is being financed by the federation."
>
> Serbian woman: "Either there will be some order in Kosovo, or by God we will take up arms again if need be."
>
> Serbian woman: "Since the establishment of Pristina University there has been a process of ethnic epuration of Kosovo and the process of cultural purity."
>
> Serbian man: "How is it that Yugoslavia protests one-language signs in Austria but agrees to them in Kosovo?"
>
> Serbian man: "How is that according to the 1974 constitution Serbo-Croatian is also an official language in Kosovo, while in the constitution of the province it is not obligatory?"

Another man asked about the erection of a monument to the Albanian Prizren League, which he characterized as a fascist organization that sought to tear Yugoslavia apart. He also asked why the program of the Albanian nationalist group, Balli Combetar, was being carried out in Kosovo. Others condemned Serbian communists in Kosovo who "served with the Albanians" in putting their personal interests ahead of the national interest. The complaints that Milošević heard were more personal and specific than what he may have heard while sitting in Belgrade, but they certainly could not have come as a surprise. He must have been aware of past efforts by other Yugoslav leaders to deal with the Kosovo problem.

During his struggle to seize power during World War II, the communist leader of the guerrilla movement, Josip Broz Tito, promised the Kosovo Albanians much in return for their assistance. The Albanians insist that he promised them the right of self-determination, including the right to be annexed to Albania, but Tito and his comrades denied that claim. In any case, in 1946 he made the Kosovo-Metohija area (now simply Kosovo) an autonomous province within the republic of Serbia. That autonomy was considerably augmented in 1963, 1969, and especially in 1974. Tito and his communist comrades proceeded on the assumption, erroneous as it turned out, that if given broad autonomy - perhaps more extensive than that granted to a minority in any other European state - the Kosovo Albanians would be loyal citizens of Yugoslavia.

Following the adoption of Yugoslavia's 1974 constitution, the Kosovo Albanians became, in effect, a law unto themselves. It is as if part of an American state, say New York City, gained such power that it could ignore New York state authorities, which could not intervene to stop the city from violating the state's laws and constitution or change any laws affecting the city without its consent.

Why, it might be asked, did the Serbs object to such power for Kosovo? For the same reason that a comparable situation would not be acceptable to the state of New York. More precisely, the Kosovo Albanians abused their enlarged autonomy to force the Serbian minority to leave Kosovo. Their attempt at "ethnic cleansing" was initially made by Tito's explicit order forbidding the return of Serbs who had fled the area during World War II to escape Albanian and Bulgarian persecution. Moreover, Tito, who had promised the Kosovo Albanians much in the hope that they would help him seize power, wittingly or unwittingly encouraged large-scale immigration from Albania as a way of changing the ethnic composition of Kosovo.

The Kosovo Albanian persecution of Serbs included the desecration of historic Orthodox Christian monasteries, churches, and cemeteries; the burning of barns and haystacks; the theft or mutilation of cattle and other livestock; the destruction of Serbian houses; pressure to force Serbs into selling their properties; as well as rape and other physical assaults. Prior to Tito's death in 1980, there was no public mention of these actions. There were unpublicized protests, locally as well as to high Communist Party circles, which were to no avail. Even the official protest to Tito by the Serbian Orthodox Church in 1969 brought only a statement declaring that he had ordered governmental authorities to apply the law. Following the demonstrations in 1981 by the Kosovo Albanians, demanding the status of a separate republic - which they had in all but name - and even the right to be annexed to Albania, the problem reached high party authorities more than once. And this was several years before Milošević came on the scene.

For example, the Bar Association of Serbia, in letters to the presidents of the Serbian and Yugoslav parliaments on July 3, 1985, called attention to the violation of the constitution and the laws in Kosovo. (Texts of letters and replies and speeches referred to herein can be found in the autobiography of Veljko Guberina, onetime president of the Serbian Bar Association.) The letter to the president of the Serbian parliament, Dušan Čkrebić, demanded answers to nine specific questions, including: "How many families who were forced to sell their properties under duress have returned to their land?" "What has happened to the lost court papers and was anyone held responsible?" The letter concluded with the statement that "Only one nullification of an agreement made under duress to purchase property and the return of that family to their land would contribute more than all the appeals and assurances concerning the settlement of the situation in Kosovo."

Čkrebić answered on July 29, claiming that a lot was being done but admitting that it was not enough. He added that "of special concern was the failure to achieve constitutional principles concerning the equality of nations and nationalities" whose consequences have led to Serbs leaving Kosovo, which he said was "the most difficult problem." He also said that the activities of Albanian irredentists and other enemies in Kosovo cannot be neutralized by governmental agencies alone. It is necessary, he argued, "to create a broad front of working people and citizens, belonging to all nations and nationalities against irredentist forces."

The letter to Miodrag Trifunović, president of the Federal Council of the parliament of Yugoslavia, complained that serious crimes were being treated as misdemeanors in Kosovo, that not one sale of property under duress had been nullified, and that the emigration of Serbs and Montenegrins continued. Trifunović's answer on July 18 cited specifics acts of parliament ordering governmental authorities to deal with abuses. He admitted that some of these were not carried out and said that parliament was asking the Constitutional Court to concern itself with these matters. He added that parliament would look into the execution of decisions by the Federal Council concerning the emigration of Serbs under pressure.

On July 6, 1985, a letter on behalf of the League of Republic and Province bar associations was sent to the president of the Federal Council of the Yugoslav parliament. Letters of similar content were sent to all other federal bodies. The letters spoke of violations of constitutional and legal rights, specifically of non-Albanian citizens, failure to nullify real estate sales that had been made under duress, the damaging of cultural-historical monuments and cemeteries, and policies that forced Serbs, Turks, Gypsies, and others to leave Kosovo.

The president of the Serbian Bar Association, Veljko Guberina, said in speeches in Serbia, Croatia, and Slovenia in 1988 that the violations of the rights of Serbs in Kosovo reminded him of the "dark days of the occupation when fascism ruled over the expanse of our country." In one speech he concluded, "Emigration continues and oppression has increased, as if the enemies of this country desired to demonstrate that they are afraid of no one and that they are stronger than the regular governmental authorities, or show publicly that those authorities are with them." The lawless seemed to be protected by "persons in the presidency of the Communist Party."

Guberina quoted from remarks by onetime minister of defense and close ally of Tito, General Nikola Ljubičić, to a joint meeting of the presidency of Serbia and the Party Central Committee of Serbia (September 5, 1988): "Some things which are happening are so drastic that I simply ask myself how can we tolerate that in a legal state." Ljubičić then proceeded to tell (with name of place and family) of an Albanian who moved into a Serbian house and moved the old lady out. When the son went to settle the matter, he found her sitting on a stump outside. He had to resort to legal action over a period of two to three years, and he won. But when an officer came to carry out the court order, the Albanian said that he had a machine gun and warned: "Whoever approaches will be mowed down!" The militiaman had to return with task unaccomplished. "What kind of state are we?" asked Ljubičić.

In another speech, Guberina said that Serbia's crippled constitution does not permit Serbia to exercise its governmental authority on the territory of the provinces, and that federal bodies which have that authority are quiet, while open enemies of

Yugoslavia escalate their evil deeds. It is clear, he said, that "the Serbian people has again found itself in a situation, as in 1941, to be or not to be!"

Concern about developments in Kosovo was also on the agenda of the Yugoslav Communist Party leadership, at a time when all Yugoslav ethnic groups were represented and before Slobodan Milošević became the principal actor. In June 1987, for example, the Central Committee and the Presidency of the Party (officially the League of Yugoslav Communists) took the position that "the most difficult part of the problem of Kosovo and the whole of Yugoslav society is to be found in that the policy of the [League] is not being implemented." Moreover, "the pressure on the Serbs and Montenegrins must be stopped with all the means of our socialist self-management system." (Belgrade newspaper *Politika*, June 11, 1987).

A month earlier, at an "ideological" plenum of the Central Committee, one member, Dušan Dragosavac, asserted: "If we cannot quickly overcome genocide ... then I see as the only way out an urgent convoking of an extraordinary Congress of the League of Yugoslav Communists and the calling of free elections with multiple candidates, so that men can come to the top who can bring an end to genocide." (Communist Party organ *Borba*, May 23, 1987.)

Some Yugoslav newspapers openly used the term "genocide" as early as May 1987, along with expressions of surprise that six years after the 1981 Kosovo Albanian demonstrations, there still had not been a single resignation in Kosovo or at the top in Yugoslavia that might suggest a feeling of responsibility. Instead, the authorities "continue with the same announcements in which they avoid naming criminals."

It was clear that the situation, instead of improving, was becoming worse. In the summer of 1987, a scandal - some referred to it as "administrative genocide" - came to light when Serbian Orthodox Church authorities in Peć discovered at the local cadastral office that many of their churches had legally disappeared. Someone had simply listed them as mosques. The ancient Serbian Patriarchate at Peć was listed as an ordinary "religious object." One church had been transformed into a cemetery. The pearl of medieval Serbian culture, the monastery at Gračanica, was listed as general public property. The equally well-known 650-year old Dečani monastery was listed as an "ordinary building." In some areas Serbian Orthodox churches had become pasture lands; in others, property of the state forestry enterprise. As might be expected, these actions against

Serbian history and culture evoked bitterness among the Serbs, particularly when no individual culprits were named.

Ironically, the Kosovo Serbs could not appeal to the minority rights provisions of Tito's 1974 constitution. By definition, all ethnic groups that had their own republics were classified as nations, while others were categorized as nationalities, meaning minorities. Hence, Albanians, Hungarians, and other minorities could call upon the minority rights provisions of the constitution, but those provisions could not be invoked to protect the rights of Serbs, Croats, and others who might be living in republics other than their own.

In the spring of 1989, two years after his 1987 visit to Kosovo, Slobodan Milošević tackled the Kosovo problem. He did so by engineering an amendment to the Serbian constitution, limiting Kosovo's autonomy. The police, the courts, and defense came under direct Serbian control. Though in all other spheres local autonomy was not curtailed, the Kosovo Albanians insisted nevertheless that "their autonomy" had been taken away, and they promptly refused to participate in any governmental activities. They refused to operate schools or health facilities and established their own schools and clinics in private homes. And they went on strike in government-operated economic enterprises. Their refusal to cooperate in any way led the Serbian government to establish a strong police and military presence. This in turn enabled the Kosovo Albanians to push their claim that they were forced to live under dictatorial rule. This was also the position taken by foreign supporters of the Albanians, such as United States Senator Robert Dole. The result has been a stalemate, one example of which was the issuing of diplomas stamped "Republic of Kosovo" or the "Independent Republic of Kosovo," which Serbian authorities refused to recognize.

Some of Milošević's critics have accused him of Great Serbian nationalism, and cite the so-called Memorandum of the Serbian Academy of Arts and Sciences as his political platform, arguing that Kosovo was merely a pretext. They seem to have overlooked the fact - if they ever knew it - that Milošević, along with other Serbian communists, criticized the memorandum. This is not the place for a detailed examination of the document, but a few things need to be said about it. In the first place, it was a draft of an internal academy document that was never circulated publicly. The draft somehow fell into the hands of the communist newspaper *Borba*, which did not publish the text but attacked it as a Serbian nationalist document. Second, its main authors, Antonije Isaković and Dobrica Ćosić, had such a solid party past that they could not be put in the camp of counterrevolutionaries or enemies of Yugoslavia. Third, the authors asserted that Yugoslavia could not come out of the critical crisis in which it found itself without fundamental changes in the economic and political systems.

The memorandum analyzed the many shortcomings of the economic system (e.g., ruinous competition among and between the republics, unprofitable enterprises, waste and general inefficiency). It also pointed to the unworkability and paralysis of the political system, which required unanimity among the republics on virtually all questions. The authors saw that under the system Tito bequeathed to his heirs, Serbia had fallen behind in many ways. They also realized that the 1974 constitution effectively denied Serbia the power to do anything about the advantages that had been conferred on other republics. It was obvious to them that the two most advanced republics, Slovenia and Croatia, would not agree to any changes that would adversely affect them. Consequently, the authors argued in favor of democratization of the political system. It was understandable, therefore, that Milošević's critics could, after the fact, point to things in the memorandum that seemed to have guided him, ignoring the fact that he had joined the party press in condemning the memorandum.

Milošević's critics in Slovenia and Croatia avowed that his assertion of control in Kosovo signaled that Serbia was out to dominate Yugoslavia. His critics in the West have attempted to explain the secessions of Slovenia and Croatia on the grounds that they did not want to live in a Serb-dominated Yugoslavia. This constitutes a grave failure to understand Titoist Yugoslavia, because at no time prior to the secessions could it be said that Yugoslavia was Serb-dominated. In fact, the most that can be said is that the Slovenes and Croats feared that at some time in the future Yugoslavia might be dominated by Serbs.

While many Slovenes and Croats saw Milošević's assertion of control as an internal Serbian matter, their communist leaders, fully aware that Serbia would seek the redress of other grievances, viewed it as the beginning of a process that would be detrimental to the achievements of their republics. Therefore, proceeding on the well-known principle that the best defense is a good offense, they charged that Serbia's action in Kosovo was proof that Serbia wanted to control Yugoslavia. They did not even want to hear Serb arguments in defense of their action in Kosovo. For example, when a group of

Serbs living in Slovenia attempted a peaceful demonstration, Slovene authorities used force to disband it.

While the international community's concern about Kosovo is understandable, failure to grasp the essence of the issues can lead to disastrous policies. The media have not helped. Commentators often speak of historical animosities. Historical perspective requires a reminder: prior to the Ottoman conquest of Kosovo, relations between Serbs and Albanians were good. That was when most of the Albanians were Christians. It was only after they became Turkish surrogates, and especially when large numbers of them accepted Islam, that hostilities developed. This was mainly in the 18th century, but large-scale persecutions of Serbs came in the 19th century. These persecutions are well documented in the reports of British, French, and Russian consuls who were stationed in the Kosovo area. After Kosovo was liberated by the Serbs in the Balkan wars (1912), Serbian policy was clearly stated: there would be no retribution against Kosovo Albanians for past actions. And the most that can be said about the policies of interwar Yugoslavia is that Kosovo was treated with benign neglect, which was more detrimental to its Serb inhabitants than to the Albanian ones.

It seems to me that Milošević was transformed not by a desire to establish or solidify a dictatorship - even if that could have been a motive - but by the compelling nature of events. As pointed out above, he was slow in taking up the cause of the Kosovo Serbs. Although he presumably recognized the seriousness of their plight after his visit to Kosovo in April 1987, he waited a full two years before taking concrete steps to change the situation. One thing is absolutely clear: prior to his action, Yugoslav communist authorities had utterly failed to solve the Kosovo problem.

Some columnists, in their blazing hatred for Milošević, have proclaimed in shrill tones that, as an extreme nationalist, he is the main threat to peace and security in the Balkans. An apt response might be to say of nationalists what Aldous Huxley once said of propagandists: "A propagandist canalizes an already existing stream; in a land where there is no water he digs in vain." One does not have be a defender of Milošević to observe that he does not function in a vacuum.

When in 1981 I asked Milovan Djilas, onetime Tito comrade and at that time Yugoslavia's best-known dissident, what the solution was to the Kosovo question, he said: "There is no solution." Just a few months prior to our conversation the Kosovo Albanians had staged demonstrations demanding the status of a republic and even the right to be annexed to Albania. From that year until Milošević took action in 1989, the government of Yugoslavia (not that of Serbia) had tried unsuccessfully to deal with the Kosovo problem.

Since Milošević's action, the attitude of the two sides can best be summarized in one sentence: the Serbian government has said that it is willing to discuss any and all questions with the Kosovo Albanians except secession, while the latter has said that it wants to discuss nothing short of secession. This would suggest an unqualified deadlock. However, two possible solutions have been advanced. One is a partition of Kosovo, letting one part join Albania. The Serbs would want to retain as many of their historic religious monuments as possible, as well as the mining complex of Trepće. By and large, this solution would not be acceptable to most Serbs, who look upon Kosovo as a holy place. But some Serbian intellectuals, including a former president of Yugoslavia, Dobrica Ćosić, support the idea. Albanian hard-liners would accept such an outcome only if they could get most of the territory. The one aspect of this proposal that would have some appeal in Serbia is an agreement that all Albanians on the Serbian side of the boundary line would have to leave. The principal reason why this would be popular with many Serbs is that the large number of Albanians who have settled in Serbia proper, well beyond Kosovo, are seen as a critical future problem, especially given the Albanians' extraordinarily high birthrate. Moving them as part of a settlement would be far easier now than later.

The second suggestion is for the Kosovo Albanians to accept autonomy without the attributes of statehood. The Serbs have indicated that is what they wanted all along. To the Albanian hard-liners, this would constitute capitulation. Recently, however, there has been some movement in this direction among the more moderate elements. At least two former Kosovo Albanian leaders have spoken out in favor of participating in elections and working in other ways toward viable arrangements that would let Kosovo Albanians manage their own affairs while remaining loyal citizens of the country in which they live. The second alternative seems to hold the best prospect for a peaceful resolution of this critical problem.

SERBIA'S AND THE WEST'S MISCALCULATIONS*

The Yugoslav tragedy has prompted me to reflect on my half-century long interest in that country and to ponder the miscalculations made by its strongest supporters, the Serbs, and those made by Western leaders when Yugoslavia showed signs of its impending disintegration. While there are many participants in and reasons for the failure of the Yugoslav state, it seems desirable to concentrate on the country's largest ethnic group, which subsequently was to get much of the blame for the failure. Many Serbs, viewing the resulting chaos, have asked themselves what mistakes they made. It is from that perspective that I, admittedly an outsider with the benefit of hindsight, seek to explore the problem, and, in subsequent pages, to look at the miscalculations of Western leaders.

It seems to me that the first mistake the Serbs made after the creation of Yugoslavia was to stop thinking as Serbs and to start thinking exclusively as Yugoslavs. They failed to balance the interests of Serbia with those of the new state. While other ethnic groups were looking out for their individual interests, the Serbs thought first of the common, i.e., Yugoslav, interests.[1]

The Serbs threw themselves into the enterprise with enthusiasm, assuming that the others would do likewise. After all, the Slovenes and the Croats eagerly joined Serbia and Montenegro in forming the state of Yugoslavia. This was not unexpected, first because the best known of pro-Yugoslav thinkers were to found among the Croats. Secondly, the Slovenes and Croats were aware that without a Yugoslav state they would be left as minorities in Austria, Italy, and Hungary. On the other hand, the Serbs seemingly failed to note that the Croats and Slovenes could have been acting as opportunists, and they apparently forgot the writings of a number of Croat nationalists who had been fairly explicit in their anti-Serbian statements.

The Serbs were optimists. Serbia gave up its flag, coat of arms, and democratic constitution, confident of the future. Knowing that the other ethnic groups had joined in the common venture, the Serbs quickly dispelled any doubts about their own loyalties and were given

---

* *Mediterranean Quarterly* (Summer 1995), pp. 74-90. Reprinted with permission.

added faith in the undertaking. Moreover, Serbia's past achievements and the size of her population, twice that of the next largest group, the Croats, endowed her with a feeling of strength.

When the Croats boycotted efforts to write a constitution and engaged in other acts of non-cooperation, the Serbs viewed these as passing phenomena, convinced that as the system began to function more or less normally, Croatian attitudes would change. Indeed, they did change when in 1925 the Croats accepted the constitution and the monarchy and entered parliament and the cabinet. But this cooperative attitude proved short-lived.

In retrospect, we can see that the commitment of non-Serb nationalists to a Yugoslav state was at best lukewarm, especially among the Croats. The Slovenes appeared satisfied, having gained important concessions, among them posts in every cabinet and even the prime ministership in one. The Croats, however, never felt at home in Yugoslavia and never praised it as their own. When their yearning for an independent Croatia seemed unrealistic, they opted for Yugoslavia, knowing that the Serbs would always welcome them. Conversely, the Serbs did not sufficiently appreciate either the Croats' fears and reservations nor their feelings of inferiority and even inadequacy when dealing with the much more numerous and politically experienced Serbs.

The Muslims in Bosnia-Herzegovina were not considered a separate nationality, as indeed they were not. In the interwar period, in fact, Yugoslavia was not divided into ethnic units. There was, however, the Yugoslav Muslim Organization, which for all practical purposes was a political party. It was headed by Mehmed Spaho, to whom important concessions were made concerning land ownership so that he would support the adoption of the first Yugoslav constitution in 1921. In subsequent years, he was a member of many cabinet coalitions.

The second critical misjudgment that the Serbs made came in 1929 when King Alexander assumed personal power in an effort to save the state. When parliamentary democracy failed, there were differences as to what should be done next. Some political leaders, Serb, Croat, and Slovene, advised him to turn to temporary dictatorship. Some suggested federalism, and some Serbs recommended amputation, i.e., letting the Croats go. We know that for a time he toyed with the latter idea. But like so many Serbs, and being the biggest Yugoslav proponent of them all, he could not admit that the common state had been a mistake. Further, he believed that federalism would gradually tear the country apart. Consequently, he opted for temporary personal rule, and by changing the name of the country from the Kingdom of the Serbs, Croats, and Slovenes to the Kingdom of Yugoslavia, by dividing it into administrative units that did not follow ethnic lines, and by introducing *guided democracy*, he hoped to win loyalty for the country among those who had been disaffected. Had he not been assassinated in 1934, it is barely possible that he might have been successful. Viewing it from the perspective of sixty years later, however, it seems more reasonable to conclude that he should have turned to federalism or amputation.

The next important mistake that the Serbs made, closely related to the second, was to treat the area of Kosovo with benign neglect.[2] The cradle of the Serbian nation, where its priceless cultural-religious monuments are located, Kosovo was liberated in the Balkan Wars of 1912-13 after nearly 500 years of Turkish occupation. Soon thereafter, during the First World War, Kosovo was again under foreign rule, this time Bulgarian. Then in 1918, the victorious Serbian army once more brought Kosovo into Serbia's fold. Considering what happened there over the next several decades, particularly under communist rule, it is easy to conclude that from a purely Serbian national point of view, Kosovo should have had first priority.

The benign neglect was all the more tragic in that the Serbs had a relatively free hand in the early years of Yugoslavia by virtue of the fact that the Croats were boycotting the governing process.

The results of the neglect have been nothing short of catastrophic. Not only was it allowed to lag behind other parts of Yugoslavia in economic development, but the high birthrate among Kosovo's Albanian inhabitants sharply increased their percentage of the population. When Tito's communist regime came to power, with its determined policy to weaken Serbia, additional Albanians were allowed (invited?) to come to Kosovo from Albania. This mass migration, numbering perhaps up to three hundred thousand people, encouraged Kosovo's Albanian inhabitants to persecute the Serbs, countless thousands being forced to flee their homes. Moreover, Tito explicitly forbade the return to Kosovo of those Serbs who had fled during the Second World War to escape the disasters of Bulgarian occupation.

A minority in Kosovo during Yugoslavia's formation, the Albanians had by 1991 attained a majority of nearly 90 percent. In all fairness to Tito and the communists, it should be pointed out that the increase of Albanians in Kosovo had been going on during their surrogate authority under the Ottomans, although at a slower pace.

From an almost nonexistent minority at the time of the Turkish conquest in 1389, the number of Albanians grew, especially in the 18th and 19th centuries, when they persecuted the Serbs on a large scale.

Looked at in the context of economic development on a national scale, the benign neglect of Kosovo is easily understood. Two South Slav areas of the Austro-Hungarian Empire that had some industry were Croatia and Slovenia; it was logical to put major investment capital there. Ironically, Serbia did not get credit for this policy, hence no trade-off resulted from neglect of other areas. Croatia and Slovenia, in fact, seemed to take their more rapid economic development for granted and subsequently began complaining that they were paying more than their share to the national treasury.

Similarly, under Tito's communist rule after the Second World War, major industrial investments went to Croatia and Slovenia, partly at least as a way of punishing Serbia. The ultimate reaction in Slovenia and Croatia was similar: they felt they were paying a disproportionate share to the national treasury. But how to square their contention with the fact that in 1991 the average per capita income in Slovenia was $12,618, in Croatia $7,179, and in "exploiting" Serbia only $4,870?

Further evidence of Serbia's concern for the new nation as a whole was to be found in steps taken to protect it from foreign dangers. Under King Alexander's leadership and under French auspices, the Little Entente (Yugoslavia, Czechoslovakia, and Romania) came into existence as a mutual defense pact. The main dangers were viewed as Mussolini's Italy, Bulgaria, and Hungary. It was during Alexander's state visit to France that he was assassinated by terrorists of Bulgarian background, who had been instructed by extremist Croats (*Ustashe*) and trained in camps in Hungary.

Some would argue that the Serbs made another mistake when Alexander's first cousin, Prince Regent Paul, signed the *Sporazum* (Agreement) in 1939 with Croatia's leader, Vladko Maček. That agreement created a large Croatian unit (*Banovina*), going a long way toward establishing a federal system.

At the time, three major objections to the *Sporazum* were voiced. The first was legal: the Yugoslav constitution forbade amendments during times when the monarch was not of age. The second argued that changes in the country's constitutional system should be all-inclusive, so as to deal with other regions, notably Serbia and Slovenia. The third objection charged that Croatia had been given large areas of non-Croatian territory, pointing out that of autonomous Croatia's population of 4.5 million, a little more than 1 million were Serbs.

Prince Paul and his ministers answered by saying (1) that they found legal authority for what they did in the constitution's emergency article; (2) that commissions had already been appointed to work on the creation of Serbian and Slovenian autonomous units; and (3) that the *Sporazum* provided that the borders of autonomous Croatia were provisional and that definitive boundaries would be determined at the time of the reorganization of the state, at which time some counties and even villages might be added and others subtracted. In addition, the *Sporazum* required ratification by parliament, which never acted on it.

When the Second World War broke out within a month after the signing of the *Sporazum*, plans for further reorganization of the state were shelved. Since the war intervened, we shall never know if the steps that Prince Paul initiated would have paved the way to a viable political system.

In all fairness to Paul and his ministers, it should be noted that they were under terrible pressure to reach some agreement with the Croats, as a way of trying to keep Yugoslavia out of the coming war. They knew that Maček's intermediaries were talking with the Italians about possible scenarios in the event of war that would lead to an independent Croatian state and thereby the destruction of Yugoslavia.

A second step that the prince regent took to keep Yugoslavia out of the Second World War was to sign an agreement with Hitler, clearly unwillingly, to preserve Yugoslav neutrality. Hitler had reached agreement with the leaders of Hungary, Romania, and Bulgaria for them to adhere to the Tri-Partite Pact (Germany, Italy, and Japan). The Yugoslavs were under similar pressure, resisted it for a number of months, but finally signed a watered-down agreement that promised neutrality and security without any obligation to assist the Axis.

Thereupon came perhaps the greatest error the Serbs made - more precisely the mistake that the Yugoslav (Serb) generals made in 1941 in overthrowing the regency and the cabinet. That act was popular in Serbia, where the opinion was widespread that Paul had put Yugoslavia in the same pro-Axis boat as Hungary, Romania, and Bulgaria. When after their act the coup leaders read the agreement with Hitler, they declared it acceptable. But Hitler was not going to let these Balkan upstarts get away with insulting Germany.

With the benefit of hindsight, we can see what an enormously tragic mistake the coup turned out to be. Yugoslavia was quickly dismembered, a pro-fascist quisling regime was formed in Croatia under *Ustashe* leader Ante Pavelić, with Bosnian Muslim participation, which proceeded to massacre some 700,000 Serbian inhabitants of that state, along with some 50,000 Jews, and 10,000 Gypsies. Other parts of Yugoslavia came under Italian and German occupation, with some lands being turned over to the Balkan satellite regimes.

Moreover, in the next several years a civil war raged, pitting two guerrilla movements, Mihailović's Chetniks and Tito's Partisans, against each other. Ultimately, as we know, the communist-led Partisans were victorious, with no small amount of Western and, near the end, Soviet assistance.

So, step by step, the Serbs went from independence to war, to massacres in Croatia, to slavery under communism, and to civil war. Did any other people experience a greater tragedy?

In the Second Yugoslavia, Tito's Serbian communist allies were Serbia's only voice, and a muted one at that. Whenever Tito suspected that they were not following his line, they were expelled from the party. On the whole, they subordinated Serbian interests to regime policies. The few Serbian intellectual party stalwarts who became aware that Tito hated the Serbs (Dobrica Ćosić, Mihailo Marković, and others) could do little until after Tito's death in 1980. Even then, they were still committed to an integral Yugoslav state. Only in about 1988 did some of them suggest that if other ethnic groups were not in favor of staying together on the basis of equality, perhaps they should go their separate ways.

After the secessions of June 1991, Marković engaged in a sort of collective self-criticism when he wrote that between 1918 and 1945, "we [Serbs] as a people flunked the test of historical maturity," when "contrary to our interests and without sufficient seriousness... in a state of euphoria, we entered into a common state."[3] In addition, he said that for the Croats, Yugoslavia was a "marriage of convenience." Be it noted that Marković had been in Tito's Partisan movement and was regarded as one of the intellectual stalwarts among the Serbian communists.

Tito demonstrated his distrust of the Serbs by narrowing the borders of the Serbian republic so that about one-third of the Serbs were left outside, and hence significant numbers of them were in each of the other republics, except Slovenia. In addition, he created two autonomous provinces inside the republic, Kosovo and Vojvodina, so as to placate the Albanians and Hungarians respectively, because during his struggle for power he had promised much to Yugoslav minorities. To satisfy the Muslims, and to prevent a struggle between Serbs and Croats in the region, he created a separate republic, Bosnia-Herzegovina.

During Tito's rule there were some warning signs of what lay ahead, coming mostly from Serbs abroad. One of them was the prewar Agrarian Party leader, Milan Gavrilović, who in a far-sighted statement in 1961 warned the Serbs that there were those who were waiting "for the moment of liberation from Communism," who would then start enslaving others, and warned the Serbs that they "must be ready for it before that moment arrives."[4]

In the same statement, Gavrilović told the Serbs "who are for Yugoslavia... that the only road to Yugoslavia leads through the defense of the Serbian people." He asserted that Serbs "have nothing against the unity of the Croatian people" but at the same time warned the Croats that hatred begets hatred.

After Tito's death in 1980, the leaders of the national communist party sought to follow "Tito's Road," or at least said that they did. In fact, however, the party soon began splitting along nationality lines. At that point, the unraveling of the state fabric began. Each republic's party began stressing republic interests, except the Serbian party. When Slobodan Milošević became head of the Serbian party in 1986, and the injustices to the Serbs in Kosovo could no longer be hidden, things began to change. While constantly maintaining a pro-Yugoslav stance, Milošević insisted that Serbian interests must be protected.

At an extraordinary congress of the national party in 1990, representatives from the various republics concluded that agreement was no longer possible. The Slovene delegates were the first to leave, followed by the Croats. The Tito Party that promised "brotherhood and unity" came to an inglorious end.

As the once powerful Yugoslav Communist Party breathed its last, recycled communists in the republics began styling themselves as democrats and/or socialists. Secessions were not far behind; Slovenia and Croatia declared theirs in June 1991, followed by Bosnia-Herzegovina in early 1992, and a little later by Macedonia. The Second Yugoslavia came to an end, and Serbia and Montenegro formed the Third Yugoslavia. At that point new miscalculations by the Serbs began, although there may be some disagreement over whether they can properly be so defined.

When Yugoslavia began to break up, the Serbs had every reason to believe that Western governments would be sympathetic to their position. After all, they had consistently been the strongest supporters of the common state, which the West favored. Even as secessions were in the air, U.S. Secretary of State James Baker III publicly expressed the hope that the Yugoslavs would stay together. Moreover, the Western leaders knew that after the Second World War, Tito had carved the country into federal and autonomous units, the most important impact of which, for the Serbs, was that about one-third of their people were left in other units, mainly in Croatia and in Bosnia-Herzegovina.

True, the West welcomed the fall of communists from power in Eastern Europe, and Serbia's president was communist Slobodan Milošević, but Croatia's Franjo Tudjman and Slovenia's Milan Kućan were also communists. Consequently, the Serbs could not imagine that they would be treated less fairly than the other ethnic groups. Moreover, the Serbs could not fathom why the West, which cheered the end of communism, should hold as sacrosanct Tito's geographic division of Yugoslavia.

Deep down in the Serb psyche was the awareness that among the South Slavs, the Serbs had been the West's allies in two world wars, while some of the others had actually sided with the enemy. The most prominent of the latter were the Croats, whose Nazi satellite regime had in 1941 declared war against the major Western states, including the United States, as well as against the Soviet Union.

While the Serbs knew that historically the Germans had no love for them, and had twice invaded them, they were confident that they could count on their traditional allies. They were distrustful of the British, who had acted against Serbian national interests at the Congress of Berlin in 1878 and who had played a dominant role in denying Serbia and Montenegro some of the fruits of their victories against the Turks in the Balkan wars, and who in the Second World War had deserted Serbia's General Mihailović. Nevertheless, the British knew about the massive massacre of Serbs in the pro-Nazi state of Croatia at the hands of Croats and Muslims. And when Britain's fortunes were at a low point in 1941, the overthrow by the Serbian generals of the Yugoslav government that had signed a pact with Hitler was hailed by Prime Minister Winston Churchill when he said, "Yugoslavia has found her soul!" The Serbs knew that France had been a consistent ally and friend, and the Americans had also been friends and allies. The Serbs were sure that among the great powers the United States would be the most fair.

In addition, they calculated that whether they were liked or not, the West was sure to appreciate the critical importance of Serbia in the Balkans. As the most numerous group and being strategically located, the Serbs could not be left out of any policy considerations. Moreover, the Serbs reasoned that if self-determination was legitimate for the Slovenes and the Croats, it would be no less recognized for the Serbs. As it turned out, they were naive.

Ironically, Western policy was in large part determined by Germany, whose military forces twice had invaded Serbia during wars in which the Serbs had been allied with Germany's enemies. Nevertheless, the Serbs knew that two international acts recognized Serbian interests in Bosnia-Herzegovina and Croatia. The first of these was the Treaty of London (1915), signed by Britain, France, and Russia. It had promised Serbia most of the areas of present-day Croatia, large parts of Dalmatia, and all of Bosnia-Herzegovina. In addition, the city of Dubrovnik and surrounding areas were promised to Montenegro. That treaty also promised Italy, in return for her changing sides and joining the Allies, areas in the northern Adriatic with large Croat and Slovene populations. The second international act was the Treaty of Versailles, which treated the new Yugoslav state as the successor state of Serbia.

The Serbs also relied on the 1975 Helsinki Accords. That agreement stated that the borders of an internationally recognized state could not be altered by force.[5] Yugoslavia was such a state. And Slovenia was the first to use force to change Yugoslavia's borders, followed immediately by Croatia and a little later by Bosnia-Herzegovina.

Yet what did the Western European signatories of the Helsinki Accords do? Instead of seeking to enforce the agreement, they aided and abetted the secessionist republics by extending diplomatic recognition to them. This surprised and upset the Yugoslav government in Belgrade, which was also a signatory of those accords. The government was most surprised by the stance of the United States, the author of the Stimson Doctrine (after former Secretary of State Henry Stimson), which declared that the U.S. would not recognize any international situation brought about by force.

The Serbs might also have thought that the 1932 Montevideo international convention on conditions for recognizing new states might have given Western leaders reason to pause, because aside from possibly Slovenia, none of the other secessionist Yugoslav republics met its conditions. But Western leaders seemingly gave no thought to their obligations under that convention.

THE WEST'S MISCALCULATIONS

Serbian errors were compounded by the miscalculations of Western leaders. When Yugoslavia began to fall apart in 1991, those leaders seemed to act largely in ignorance of history. As incredible as it may seem, they apparently thought that the Serbs would not fight for their rights, despite all of the historical evidence. They ignored the enormous sacrifices Serbs had made in liberating themselves from the Turkish yoke, when in 1911-12 Serbia organized the Balkan states (Bulgaria, Greece, Romania, Montenegro, and Serbia) into an alliance that drove the Turks from Europe and regained for Serbia the cradle of the Serbian nation, Kosovo, where the Serbs had been defeated by the Ottoman Turks in 1389.

Secondly, in 1914, the Serbs had stood up to the mighty Austro-Hungarian Empire, and in that war the Serbs of Montenegro and Serbia lost 40 percent of all mobilized men, losses that were three times those of their allies, Britain and France. It was in that war that Serbian lands in Bosnia-Herzegovina and Croatia were liberated, and Slovenes and Croats implored Serbia to form a common union - a Yugoslav state - which was done.

Thirdly, the Serbs in 1941 became allied with the West, when they again demonstrated their resolution in fighting for their rights, saying "no" to Nazi Germany at the height of Hitler's power. In that conflict and the resulting destruction of Yugoslavia, along with the civil war against the Yugoslav communists, Serbian losses exceeded 1 million.

In light of this historic Serbian persistence, determination, even stubbornness, in defense of national interests, it is beyond comprehension that Western leaders should in 1991 and 1992 have assumed that the Serbs would sit idly by and see their achievements go down the drain. It seems that persons in positions of responsibility in the West gave little thought to assessing Serbia's capabilities and intentions or to the related question of the future pivotal role of the Serbs in that region. If they did, it is patently evident that their judgments were wide of the mark.

Moreover, Western leaders seemingly did not contemplate the impact of their aiding in the demise of Yugoslavia, a charter member of the League of Nations and the United Nations, on the Serbs, the strongest supporters of the common state.[6] There is no evidence that

Western leaders were aware of the depth of determination of the Serbs of Bosnia-Herzegovina and Croatia not to live in Muslim or Croatian-dominated states.

And the United States apparently did not weigh the consequences of suggesting to the Bosnian Muslims that the European Community brokered agreement of dividing Bosnia-Herzegovina along ethnic lines, which the Muslim, Serb, and Croat leaders had agreed to in Lisbon in March 1992 (before the fighting broke out), was a bad one. We know that the Muslim leader, Izetbegović, reneged on the agreement soon after talking with American Ambassador Warren Zimmermann. While the latter has denied any complicity, there is some persuasive evidence to the contrary. In a long article in *Foreign Affairs* on the collapse of Yugoslavia, the former ambassador is strangely silent on the March agreement and on the consequences of its sabotage by the Muslims.[7]

Moreover, Zimmermann presents sufficient information, assuming that he reported it to the U.S. State Department, to show that others besides Serbs were responsible for the civil war. It "was the Slovenes," he writes, "who started the war," and who "bear considerable responsibility for the bloodbath that followed their secession." And it was Croatia's Tudjman who "presided over serious violations of the rights of Serbs." It was also Tudjman who was silent when in his and the ambassador's presence several of his ministers reviled "Serbs in the most racist terms." In addition, Tudjman warned him that the Muslims were "dangerous fundamentalists," a threat that the "civilized nations should join together to repel." And the Muslim leader, Izetbegović, played "a double game," and made a "disastrous political mistake."[8] Ironically, the United States subsequently forced the Bosnian Croats and Muslims to create a Bosnian federation to which Tudjman was forced to give his blessing.

It is difficult, therefore, to believe that Western leaders were not aware of the various considerations that I have set forth. To the extent that they were, they certainly underestimated them. In any case, it is necessary to ask what factors led the West to conclude that the Serbs would do nothing as they saw their hard-won achievements begin to disappear.

First of all, in the civil war during the Second World War and in the early years of Tito's communist dictatorship, the cream of Serbia's potential nationalist leadership was wiped out, had been put in prison, or had fled abroad.

Second, and a corollary of the above, the Serbs in the Yugoslav communist party were supine collaborators in Croat Tito's anti-Serb policies. Hence, there was little or no expectation that Serbian communists would defend Serbia's traditional national interests.

Third, it had been generally recognized that the Serbian cadre in the Yugoslav communist party was weak, and Serb communists who were suspected of the slightest independence were purged. In the post-Tito period, 1980 and later, the Serb cadre was still looked upon as weak, and initially Slobodan Milošević seemed to be no exception. After all, he came out of the same party structure.

Fourth, for years the Serbs in the national leadership did nothing about the persecution of their fellow Serbs at the hands of the Albanians in Kosovo. Pleas of Kosovo Serbs fell on deaf ears, even in the 1980s after Tito's death. Even after the Kosovo Albanian demonstrations of 1981, which were clearly anti-Yugoslav, the responsible communist party members in Kosovo (Albanians and even Serbs) did not lose their positions. From time to time, the Yugoslav communist party leadership issued declarations critical of separatist Albanian actions and insisted that party policies must be adhered to, but nothing really changed.

It is true that after Milošević became head of the Serbian party, he did in 1987 take a stand in defense of the Kosovo Serbs, but even then doubts remained as to his real commitment. Urgent and repeated pleas from the Serbian Bar Association for action on specific violations of laws and the constitution were more or less ignored.[9] And most of the Kosovo bureaucrats remained in their positions.

Fifth, another reason for the West's miscalculations concern the Yugoslav National Army, which Tito in frequent public statements had depicted as the ultimate guardian of Yugoslavia. When it failed to stop the secession of Slovenia, the West may have viewed Tito's assurances as empty boasts. We now know that while the Yugoslav National Army's officer corps was falling into disarray along national lies, it was far from impotent, as experience was to demonstrate.

It needs to be noted that at the time of the Slovenian and Croatian secessions in June 1991, as well as at the time of the bombardment of Vukovar and the so-called bombardment of Dubrovnik,[10] the key positions in the Yugoslav national government - prime minister, foreign affairs minister, and the heads of the air force and navy - were Croats and Slovenes. The minister of defense and supreme commander was General Veljko Kadijević, the product of a Serb-Croat marriage. While the cabinet acted promptly and forcefully in response to the secessions, it was generally viewed as weak.

One problem that to a degree handicapped the Yugoslav government was the dispute over the position of the president of the collective presidency. Under the constitution, this position was to rotate each year among the members, made up of representatives from each republic and autonomous provinces. It was Croatia's turn, but the constitution required a formal vote. For several months, the candidate (Stipe Mesić) could not get a majority, because Montenegro, Serbia, and the two autonomous provinces were opposed. The reason for their opposition was that Mesić had said openly that he would be the last Yugoslav president, and his prediction turned out to be correct.[11]

CONCLUSION

The foregoing raises a number of questions. The first is: what motivated the West in its lack of evenhandedness in the Yugoslav civil war? Ignorance of history is only a partial answer. Some observers point to Vatican pressure in support of the Catholic republics (Slovenia and Croatia). Others note the dependence of the West on Arab oil. In addition to the latter was the pressure from the moderate Muslim states, on whom the West (especially the U.S.) relied for help in promoting an Israeli-Arab peace, to secure Western help for the Bosnian Muslims.

The Western Europeans have been concerned with Washington's easy yielding to Middle East Arab pressure, because Europe has never wanted an Islamic state in the middle of the continent. Ironically, Yugoslavia was the best guarantee against such a state. Having helped to destroy it, the West sought the same guarantee in a multi-ethnic Bosnia. And in the end, when the Serbs refused to cooperate, the United States came up with the idea of a Muslim-Croat federation. Since the Serbs have refused to buckle under pressure and rejected joining that federation, its viability remains in question.

Another question concerns the role of publicity agencies. We know that publicity agents received considerable sums of money to publicize the cause of the secessionist republics, especially Croatia and Bosnia-Herzegovina. One such agency even bragged that their greatest success was to enlist the support of large Jewish organizations in the United States against the Serbs, historically the best friends of the Jews in the Balkans. The Serbs, on the other hand, believing that truth was on their side, refused to enlist the assistance of such agencies until much too late, when public opinion was well formed.

In addition, there is the question of the role of the media.[12] constantly fed anti-Serb materials by publicity agents. A number of persons have observed how journalists and various pundits have behaved as a flock of geese, repeating falsehoods uttered by their colleagues. The result has been a demonizing of Serbs to such an extent that one is led to ask: where is the critical inquiry that is supposed to be the hallmark of the journalistic profession? Why is the constant anti-Serb drumbeat in all of the TV newscasts and in the editorials of the major U.S. newspapers not been subject to critical analysis?

Further, no one in a position of influence has questioned the oft-repeated canard that Yugoslavia was "Serb-dominated." The evidence is to the contrary. In the Tito period, as well as in the post-Tito period prior to the secessions, the Serbs were in no way dominant. In all sorts of key Yugoslav government positions - prime minister, president (after Tito's death), and other offices, including diplomats - there was a rotation among Albanians, Muslims, Croats, Slovenes, Macedonians, and Serbs, with the Serbs often getting the less significant positions.

In addition, one must ask why policy makers in Western governments seemingly failed to seek verification of what was served up to them by publicity agents and the media. On a number of occasions, political leaders rushed to issue indictments of Serbs before any investigation into events could take place. The most notable of these was blaming Serbs for the explosion at a Sarajevo market in early February 1994, and then issuing an ultimatum to the Serbs to withdraw their heavy weapons to a certain distance. When none of several *subsequent* investigations could find any evidence that the Serbs were guilty, and that it was possible that the Muslims had done it,[13] the media and Western leaders continued to act as if the Serbs were guilty, and action against them stood.

Sad to say, Western European and American leaders seemed to have ignored the elementary definition of politics as the art of the possible, which holds that a stable solution cannot be based on a disregard of the interests of the major player in the region. Ironically, in this way they strengthened the position of the man they blamed for the war, Slobodan Milošević, who was thereby able to pose as the sole defender of Serbian interests.

NOTES

1. See Alex N. Dragnich, *The First Yugoslavia: Search for a Viable Political System* (Stanford, CA: Hoover Institution Press, 1983); and Alex N. Dragnich, "Yugoslavia in Historical Perspective," *Mediterranean Quarterly* 3 (Summer 1992): 5-19.

2. See Alex N. Dragnich and Slavko Todorovich, *Saga of Kosovo: Focus on Serbian-Albanian Relations* (Boulder, CO: East European Monographs, 1984).

3. *Politika* (Belgrade), August 30, 1991.

4. Milan Gavrilović, Series of 1960 lectures ["Serbs and Yugoslavia"] published in installments in *Glas Kanadskih Srba* (Voice of Canadian Serbs); see installment July 7, 1960.

5. For text, see Charles E. Timberlake, *Detente: A Documentary Record* (Westpoint, CT: Praeger, 1978): 154-81.

6. See Alex N. Dragnich, "The West's Mismanagement of the Yugoslav Crisis," *World Affairs* 156 (Fall 1993): 63-71. Also see Steven K. Pavlowitch, "Who is 'Balkanizing' Whom? The Misunderstanding between the Debris of Yugoslavia and an Unprepared West," *Daedalus* 6 (Spring 1994): 203-23.

7. Warren Zimmermann, "The Last Ambassador: A Memoir of the Collapse of Yugoslavia," *Foreign Affairs* 74 (March/April, 1995): 2-19.

8. *Ibid.*

9. See Alex N. Dragnich, "The Future of Kosovo," *Chronicles: A Magazine of American Culture*, April 1995: 14-17.

10. An American professor of Irish-Catholic background, John Peter Maher, visited Dubrovnik after the so-called bombardment and found that the historic walled city had not been hit, although surrounding areas had been. See Maher letter to the *Chicago Tribune*, January 17, 1993. Be it noted that some pictures of war damage in Vukovar were peddled to the American media as damaged Dubrovnik.

11. Stipe Mesić, *Kako smo srušili Jugoslaviju: politički memoari posljednjeg presednika presedništva FNRJ* [How we Destroyed Yugoslavia: Political Memoirs of the Last President of the Presidency of Federal Peoples Republic of Yugoslavia] (Zagreb: Globus, 1992).

12. Peter Brock, "Dateline Yugoslavia: The Partisan Press," *Foreign Policy* 93 (Winter 1993-1994): 152-72; Peter Brock, "'Greater Serbia' vs. the Greater Western Media," *Mediterranean Quarterly* 6 (Winter 1995): 49-68; and Jacques Merlino, *Les verités Yugoslaves ne sont pas toutes bonnes a dires* (Paris: Editions Albin Michel, 1993).

13. David Binder, "The Anatomy of a Massacre," *Foreign Policy* 97 (Winter 1995-1995): 70-78.

PART II

YUGOSLAVIA AT A CROSSROADS*

Daily reports out of Yugoslavia paint a somber picture of economic, political, and nationality problems facing the country. Capturing major attention, at least among foreign observers, is a nationality problem that appears to have no ready answer. Yet around it all other problems revolve.

It concerns the country's Albanian minority - about 2 million in a total population of about 23 million. Over 70 percent of the Yugoslav Albanians live in the province of Kosovo, where they are an overwhelming majority. Therein lies the problem.

Kosovo has several attributes. First, it borders Albania, for which Kosovo Albanians have a strong attraction. Despite the fact that economically and in some other ways they are better off in Yugoslavia, they have sought to Albanize Kosovo. They have imported teachers and textbooks from Albania. The Yugoslav authorities see subversion in some of this.

A second attribute of Kosovo is that the Kosovo Albanians have sought to make Kosovo ethnically pure. To that end they have engaged in brutal persecution of the Serbian minority (20 percent of the population) to force them to leave Kosovo.

The third attribute of Kosovo is that it is an autonomous province within the Republic of Serbia. Kosovo is the cradle of the Serbian nation, home of its cultural and religious monuments. In medieval times, Kosovo was ethnically Serbian. The few Albanians were mainly Christian and lived in harmony with the Serbs. For most Serbs, Kosovo is holy ground.

Fourth, in 1389 the Ottoman Turks fought for Kosovo - and stayed for nearly 500 years. Hence, the percentage of Serbs in Kosovo decreased. This was due in large part to the actions of Albanians who converted to Islam and who over the centuries acted in accord with Turkish occupiers.

A fifth attribute of Kosovo is that in the past 75 years it has passed through several historical phases. In the Balkan wars (1912), Kosovo was liberated from the Turks and returned to a by-then

---

* *Christian Science Monitor*, October 17, 1989. Reprinted with permission.

independent Serbia. But Serbia's presence in Kosovo was short-lived, because of her defeat by the central powers in World War I.

When the new Yugoslav state was created in 1918, the region was not given top priority. The government's agrarian reform - taking lands from the wealthy Turks and giving it to Albanians and to Serbian veterans - did not satisfy the Albanians.

When Mussolini conquered Albania in 1939, he allowed pro-Italian Albanians to form a Great Albania, including Kosovo, that forced thousands of Serbs to flee. The situation was aggravated by Kosovo Albanians who formed a pro-Nazi regiment.

In the meantime, the leader of the Yugoslav Communist Partisans, Josip Broz Tito, offered the Kosovo Albanians self-determination (meaning that they could join Albania) if they would assist him in his struggle for power. They did not take the bait, but in the end Tito gave them an autonomous province within the Republic of Serbia. Moreover, he allowed 100,000 Albanians to immigrate to Kosovo. He forbade, however, Serbs to return to their homes after the war.

The story of Kosovo in the Tito years was one of attempted Albanization. By 1981, however, the Kosovo Albanians began demonstrating for the status of a republic and the right to be annexed to Albania.

After the demonstrations were put down in some bloodshed, the details of Kosovo Albanian actions against the Serbian minority began to see the light of day - desecration of churches and cemeteries, pillaging and burning towns and farms, and killing livestock.

In 1987 the newly elected head of the Serbian communists, Slobodan Milosevic, made a trip to Kosovo and heard many of the Serbian complaints in person. Subsequently, he promised justice to the Serbian minority. To the Albanian majority he in effect said: Your rights will be fully respected, but we count on you to be constructive, loyal citizens of Yugoslavia.

During 1988, Milosevic, using his considerable oratorical skills, exploited the Kosovo issue to gain widespread popularity in his native Serbia, as well as among Serbs in Montenegro and the autonomous province of Vojvodina. As a result the leaders in both of the latter were replaced by persons inclined to Milosevic. Even Serbs who are not communists approve of what he has done so far. They point out that since he came to power, Serbs have been permitted to voice their grievances and to give expression to their aspirations.

In early 1989, Milosevic got agreement from the Kosovo leadership to amend the Serbian constitution so that Serbia would have some control over the autonomous province, which had been acting as if it were sovereign. Specifically, Serbia gained control over administration, the police, and the courts.

Most Yugoslav observers see this as a temporary solution. But is there a more lasting one? When a few years ago I asked Yugoslavia's best known dissident, Milovan Djilas, what is the solution to Kosovo, he replied: "There is none." To the suggestion from some Yugoslavs that they cede part of Kosovo to Albania, most Serbs will reply indignantly, "Never!" And will the Kosovo Albanians, who have employed every known tactic to force the Serbs out of Kosovo, be satisfied? Hardly.

Milosevic's successes and his demands that the Yugoslav constitution be amended have led to fears in some republics, notably Slovenia and Croatia, that Milosevic seeks Serbian domination and that he has ambitions to become another Tito. Just as Milosevic has exploited the Kosovo issue in Serbian areas, the Slovenian and Croatian leaders have exploited that same issue to spread fears of Serbian domination.

What does Milosevic want? He says he wants equality for Serbia. He asserts that he does not want to dominate other republics. But he also says that Yugoslavia's economic woes can't be managed without political change. He wants to do away with the constitutional provision requiring unanimity among the republics in important decisions. He doesn't like the proviso that small republics have the same representation in parliament as larger ones.

Discussion of constitutional changes are proceeding apace throughout Yugoslavia, and some decisions are expected by year's end. In the meantime, Yugoslav citizens can only wait and hope.

WHAT DOES SERBIA WANT?*

Every news story coming out of Yugoslavia that I have seen in recent months (and I read several newspapers and magazines) contains phrases such as "Serbian domination," "Serbian hegemony," "Serbian determination to rule," and on and on, ad nauseam.

No Serb or Serbian institution has authorized me to speak for them. But I have studied Serbian political history, mostly 19th and 20th centuries (as well as Yugoslav history), and have written several books based on my research. In addition, I have talked with thousands of Serbs, and I have listened to their critics. On the basis of the sum total of my knowledge, I should like to set forth what seem to be the main political goals of Serbia and the Serbs.

1. They want a democratic political system such as they had developed prior to the First World War, a functioning parliamentary constitutional order that few countries in Europe had (only France and one or two small countries).

2. If there is to be a Yugoslavia, they want it to be a federal system in which all the republics would have equal rights. Serbs insist that in Titoist Yugoslavia, the Serbs were discriminated against in several ways, particularly in drawing boundaries in such a way that 40 percent of the Serbs live outside of the republic of Serbia.

3. They want a federal system with a central government that would at a minimum have sufficient power to protect the interests of the whole. This involves primarily foreign affairs and defense. Clearly implied would be the power to raise revenue, and perhaps the power to regulate the financial institutions so as to avoid fiscal chaos. Just as it was true of the United States at the time of its founding, there no doubt would be a need to prevent tariffs on exports as well as between the republics.

4. They want a federation in which each republic would be as compact as possible, i.e., have within its borders as many of its nationals as possible. This has been an unusually aggravating sore point with the Serbs, because millions of their compatriots are scattered in all the other republics with the exception of Slovenia.

5. They want a federation in which the rights of minorities would be fully protected. They want, however, to avoid what has

---

* *American Srbobran*, April 17, 1991.

happened in one part of the Serbian republic after World War II in the region of Kosovo-Metohija. The Albanian minority that lives in Serbia is concentrated mainly in Kosovo, where they make up about 90 percent of the population. Although a part of Serbia, Kosovo was given autonomy by Communist dictator Tito. Unfortunately, the Kosovo Albanians abused their power and in a whole series of ways persecuted the Serbian minority for decades. The plight of the Serbs was ignored until 1986, when Slobodan Milosevic became head of the Serbian Communist Party. Parenthetically, it might be noted that the press in the West has done little to present the situation in its true light.

The prevailing attitude in Serbia today seems to be that if other republics find the foregoing five points unacceptable, they should be free to go their own way. If Yugoslavia breaks up, however, the Serbs will want to have as many as possible of their compatriots, now outside the boundaries of the republic of Serbia, included in a Serbian state.

I believe that I have correctly stated the aspirations and political goals of Serbia and the Serbs. If the Serbs are to be criticized, I hope that it will be for the right reasons instead of the wrong ones.

THE ONLY HOPE FOR YUGOSLAVIA*

Is there a way out of the complex Yugoslav quagmire? Perhaps, but first of all, past mistakes need to be noted.

Everyone, the Yugoslavs and outsiders who wanted to help, was at fault for undertaking simplistic measures.

The Slovenes and the Croats thought that they could secede by a simple declaration. To be sure, the preamble of the Yugoslav constitution mentions the right of secession, but legal scholars in Yugoslavia maintain that when the various ethnic groups decided to join in the formation of Yugoslavia, they had exercised the right of self-determination. Moreover, although the body of the constitution does not specify procedures for secession, it does make it clear that it cannot be done unilaterally. Accordingly, the Yugoslav Constitutional Court nullified the Slovene and Croat declarations.

In addition, the Yugoslav government, which still existed at the time and was generally supported by Serbs and others (and in which key ministries were held by Slovenes and Croats), thought that secession could be stopped by military measures, another simplistic approach.

When the 600,000 or so Serbs in Croatia declared their determination not to remain a part of the would-be state, based on fears of what happened to the Serbs in the Axis satellite of Croatia in World War II, the Serbs in Serbia believed it their duty to come to the aid of their compatriots.

Enter the European Community, pushed by Germany and Austria, with an offer of good offices to promote a peaceful settlement. Quite evidently not knowing the history of the Yugoslavs, the EC did not even wait for any results of negotiations, but declared its intention to take the simplistic step of extending diplomatic recognition to Croatia and Slovenia.

The United States was right when it foresaw that such a move would only make matters worse. Later on, however, it caved in to the EC demands. United Nations negotiator Cyrus Vance also saw the folly of the EC Actions.

Worse still, the EC and the United States jumped in to recognize Bosnia-Herzegovina, which had never been an independent

---

* *The Washington Post*, April 30, 1992. Reprinted with permission.

state, and whose problems were even more complex than those of Croatia. If would-be peacemakers had known their history, they would have known that Serbia would never willingly accept seeing 1.5 million Serbs in Bosnia-Herzegovina, who were liberated at tremendous sacrifice in the Balkan wars and in World War I, remain outside Serbia.

By all odds the greatest mistake that the EC and the United States made was to assume that if Yugoslavia was to fall apart, the internal boundaries could not be changed. This was particularly critical in the case of the Serbs. Following their victory in the civil war, the Communist in 1946 divided up the country into republics in such a way that more than one-third of the Serbs were left outside the Republic of Serbia. Earlier the Serbs had fought wars against the Ottoman Turks and the Habsburg Empire, precisely so that they could be together in one state. It should have been obvious to one and all that if Tito's handiwork were to collapse, the Serbs would not accept being divided in such a way.

Is there any way out of this clumsy effort to secede and the botched job of would-be peacemakers?

There may be. First of all, Serbs, Croats, and Slovenes and others in Yugoslavia must recognize that further bloodshed will help no one. Second, the leaders of each ethnic group should declare that they seek nothing for their people that is not rightly theirs.

Third, and most important, the EC and the United States should announce that they are proposing a peace conference to resovle the main issues in that complex situation. To that end, they should indicate the need to set up task forces, such as one on boundaries, another one on Yugoslavia's foreign debt, another one on division of common properties and others.

In a number of cases, it may be necessary to employ international arbitration tribunals.

Short of something on that order the current uneasy arrangements, including the uniting of Serbia and Montenegro to form the Third Yugoslavia, are likely to be the prelude to additional destruction and bloodshed.

THE MEDIA AND THE YUGOSLAV WAR*

Why have the media (TV, radio, press) accepted and indeed perpetuated such a simplistic and essentially erroneous view of the tragic conflict in Yugoslavia? Where has the spirit of independent critical inquiry gone? The "show me" attitude?

In its essence the war has been portrayed as a conflict between democracy and communism, the first symbolized by former Tito Communist general, Franjo Tudjman of Croatia, and the second by Serbia's president Slobodan Milosevic. The former describes himself as a democrat and the latter a socialist. Both were once Communists, and for all we know, in their heart of hearts, they may still be. Be that as it may, the one is depicted as a defender of democracy and the other a protagonist of communism.

Why has there been no questioning in the media of this "received" wisdom? Where has there been a correspondent or commentator, not only in the United States but also in the countries of Western Europe, who has said, "Wait a minute, is this simple formulation accurate?" How to explain this lack of investigative search for truth? Is it laziness? Lack of knowledge of history? Or what?

The errors of commission and omission are many; too numerous to list here. And the over-simplifications and half-truths have been legion. Let us take one example: "Serbian-dominated Yugoslav army." Over and over this phrase has been repeated ad nauseam. Sure the army's officer corps is predominantly Serbian, but why had newsmen failed to note that as of 1990, the High Command was 38% Croat, 33% Serb, 8.3% Slovene, 8.3% Macedonian, and 4.1 % Muslim (Bosnian)? And that in the regular army the officers and non-commissioned officers were as follows: Serbs 42.63%, Croats 14.21%, Yugoslavs 10%, Montenegrins 9.45%, Slovenes 6.4%, Macedonians 6.31%, Muslims (Bosnians) 5.6%, Albanians 3.15%, Hungarians 1.05%, other 1.05%? And why did no one point to the predominance of Croats in the Yugoslav navy?

---

* *The Diocesan Observer*, July 15, 1992.

Or, what about the few at the top of the Army command during the war in 1991? The Minister of Defense and Supreme Commander, General Veljko Kadijevic (son of a Serb-Croat marriage); the Deputy Commander, Admiral Stane Brovet (Slovene); Air Force Chief, Zvonko Jurjevic (Croat)? Or what about the Yugoslav national government under which the army functioned? Prime Minister Ante Markovic (Croat); Foreign Minister, Budimir Loncar (Croat)?

Moreover, in reports and analyses of the conflict, why was it rarely mentioned that the crisis and the war were precipitated by secessionist acts of Slovenia and Croatia? In the case of Croatia, some 600,000 Serb inhabitants declared that they would refuse to be part of an independent Croatian state. This attitude stemmed from the fact that hundreds of thousands of Serbs were massacred the last time Croatia was independent, a satellite of the Axis in World War II. The fears of similar events in the future were enhanced by virtue of the fact that Tudjman's regime adopted some of the trappings of the hated wartime Croatian rulers.

When Tudjman's government initiated acts of discrimination against the Serbs, such as widespread dismissal from jobs and the demanding of loyalty oaths from them, the Serbs rebelled and asserted that they wanted to remain a part of Yugoslavia. This rebellion received help from the outside, mainly from the Yugoslav Army.

The stories from Yugoslavia generally took it for granted that the Yugoslav Army was the instrument of the Serbian government in Belgrade. No proof was offered. Why?

Seemingly, the oft-repeated declarations of dictator Tito that in case of trouble, the army could ultimately be counted upon as the savior of Yugoslavia, were ignored by reporters. I have not seen any reports suggesting that the Yugoslav Army has been seeking to carry out Tito's will.

Rather the Army, as well as Serbia and the Serbs, were branded as aggressors.

Why has no one in the media suggested that under this type of logic, President Lincoln was an aggressor when he sent troops to prevent the Southern states from seceding?

And why has no one in the media compared the actions of the Serbs in Croatia to those of the citizens of Virginia who refused to secede and in 1863 formed the State of West Virginia?

And why has there been such great reluctance to admit that Communism is no more popular in Serbia than elsewhere in Yugoslavia? Or to explain why Milosevic has been able to stay in power in Serbia?

Or, if communism is the issue, why regard the republic boundaries imposed by Communist Tito as sacrosanct, when no such boundaries existed prior to Communist rule?

Why has no one challenged the charge that Milosevic wants to form a Great Serbia? Or to point out that Serbia, which struggled to regain her independence from the Turks in the last century and succeeded in establishing a democratic parliamentary system, and in this century went on to sacrifice every third male in the struggle to found the Yugoslav state, is now being asked to be satisfied with having one-third of her compatriots living outside Serbia?

And why have no reporters investigated the question of which regime faces greater public domestic opposition - Tudjman's or Milosevic's?

Why has there been such a reluctance to point out that the Serbs were our allies in two World Wars, while the Croats were in Austro-Hungarian forces during World War I, and in World War II actually declared war on the United States, Britain, and the Soviet Union and sent troops to the Eastern Front?

Finally, why has there been such an insistence on the false assertion that Yugoslavia was an artificial creation of Versailles, when in fact Serbs, Croats, and Slovenes, responding to old ideas of South Slav unity, voluntarily joined to create the state even before Versailles met?

'SENSE OF FURY' OVER
BOSNIA IS MISPLACED*

Along with former Secretary of State George Schultz, I too feel a "sense of fury" about what has been happening in Bosnia. But my fury has more to do with those who had a large part in precipitating what has been occurring in that unfortunate land.

In their haste to assist the dismantling of a sovereign country, the Western European nations made disaster almost inevitable. Acting on a seeming ignorance of Yugoslav history, they rushed to recognize the secessionist republics of Slovenia and Croatia. As a leading American expert on Yugoslavia, who has no Yugoslav ancestry, observed at a recent scholarly conference, "the Western European states went into Yugoslavia as firefighters but ended up being pyromaniacs."

Secretary of State James Baker's wise counsel did not, unfortunately, prevail. His position was that the United States preferred that the various ethnic groups stay together in one common country. If not, he said, the U.S. would respect the peoples' wishes, and if they decided to separate, the U.S. would wait until some political settlements had been made and then would take up the question of diplomatic recognition.

Moreover, Baker personally warned the Slovene and Croatian presidents that if they unilaterally embarked upon secession, there would be civil war.

After a few months, Baker caved in to the West Europeans for reasons not quite clear. The informed opinion inside the State Department is that because an Arab-Israeli peace was so important to President Bush and Secretary Baker, they yielded to Saudi Arabia's virtual insistence that the administration support independence for Bosnia-Herzegovina, "because the Muslim leaders in the latter were moderate, the type of moderate Muslims that the U.S. was counting on in the Middle East."

Be that as it may, the U.S. in April 1992 recognized Bosnia-Herzegovina along with Croatia and Slovenia. This act of the United States, and those of the West European countries, in effect aided and

---

* *Daily News-Record*, December 30, 1992. Reprinted with permission.

abetted the secessionist Yugoslav republics in violating the proviso of the Helsinki Accords against changing international boundaries by force.

At the same time, the West's message to Serbia was that it could not change boundaries except by peaceful means, which meant that the boundaries between the republics which Communist dictator Tito had instituted were now internationalized by fiat of the Western powers.

Since Tito's handiwork had left one-third of the Serbs outside the republic of Serbia, mainly in Bosnia-Herzegovina and Croatia, this was not a palatable message. Nearly three million Serbs, once liberated in the Balkan wars and World War I, were now to be left to the mercies of other masters.

During the past several months, the West has been trying to deal with the consequences of failed efforts to manage the Yugoslav crisis. And I have been puzzled by President-Elect Clinton's support of a failed Republican policy.

In no sense am I defending Serbian actions, especially the shelling of civilian areas and ethnic cleansing, of which all the participants have been guilty. And there should be tribunals to try the guilty.

But I am pointing to the basic issue in the conflict, which newsmen and pundits are unwilling to touch. By ignoring Serbian grievances and legitimate interests, the West assured the disaster that has been happening.

Until the West admits its basic mistake, openly or tacitly, and embarks on a program to remedy it, I do not see how there can be a peaceful resolution of a conflict in which there have been so many innocent victims.

BOUNDARIES BEHIND YUGOSLAV DISPUTE[*]

During the past year or two there has been so much wrong or misleading information about the former Yugoslavia carried by the media that I am moved to set forth a few facts that might help the reader:

1. The basic issue in the current strife is the matter of boundaries between the republics. Other things, such as the share of foreign debt obligations, etc., are secondary.

2. Yugoslavia's international boundaries were recognized by treaties after World War I and World War II.

3. The Helsinki Accords of 1975 stipulate that boundaries between the signatory states could not be changed except by peaceful means. The agreement said nothing about boundaries within states.

·4. The Yugoslav republics of Slovenia and Croatia were the first to violate the Helsinki agreements when they resorted to force to change Yugoslavia's borders (Slovenia fired the first shots in the Yugoslav civil war), aided and abetted by European Community members, particularly Germany and Austria, through diplomatic recognition of those two republics.

5. At the very time that EC leaders were doing this, they (later joined by the United States) declared that boundaries within Yugoslavia could not be changed except by peaceful means.

6. Boundaries between the Yugoslav republics were created right after World War II, following the seizure of power by the Communist Party, headed by Croat Tito. No such Yugoslav domestic boundaries existed earlier; the country had not been divided into republics or ethnic units.

7. Boundaries within Yugoslavia have not had and do not now have any standing in international law. Seeking to make them so by statements of Western leaders will have no standing.

8. The Tito-imposed borders were deliberately punitive as far as Serbia is concerned, leaving one-third of the Serbs outside the republic of Serbia.

---

[*] *Nashville Banner*, March 19, 1993.

9. The hasty recognition of Slovenia and Croatia, and subsequently Bosnia-Herzegovina, together with the declaration that the internal borders could not be changed except by peaceful means, was tantamount to telling Serbia that its vital interests were deliberately being denied.

10. The Serbs outside Serbia, mainly between 600,000 and 800,000 living in Croatia (where they have lived for centuries) and over 1.5 million in Bosnia-Herzegovina (who constituted over one-third of the total and occupied about 60 percent of the area) were left with no hope except to fight for their rights. Serbia had fought successfully in the Balkan wars and World War I to liberate these areas, as well as Slovene and Croat areas. The latter two in 1918 freely joined Serbia and Montenegro to form the first Yugoslavia. In 1991, Serbia was in effect told to forget its sacrifices in those wars.

11. A number of experts on Yugoslavia, including at least one former American ambassador in Belgrade, insist that if the West, when announcing the recognition of the secessionist republics, had also stated that in a final settlement Serbian grievances would also be addressed, most of the bloodshed would have been avoided.

12. There is no way of proving the validity of point 11, but there is proof that the EC and the U.S. were not evenhanded; they did nothing to assure Serbia that its grievances would receive equal attention with those of the other republics.

The foregoing does not seek to defend any actions that have been taking place in what was once Yugoslavia, especially the atrocities, committed by all sides, in that tragic civil conflict.

KOSOVO TO SEE ETHNIC CLEANSING AGAIN?*

Kosovo, news dispatches tell us, is in the process of becoming the new center of possible "ethnic cleansing" in former Yugoslavia.

If these stories prove prophetic, Kosovo may become the most notorious example of the bitter fruits of ethnic hatred.

Kosovo has experienced a traumatic history. The center of the Serbian kingdom of the Middle Ages (and even today the repository of Serbia's most sacred cultural monuments), it was conquered in the 14th century by the Turks, who brought in Albanians as their surrogates.

Over the centuries, particularly as the Albanians accepted Islam, they engaged in what today we call "ethnic cleansing." Even so, when Serbia, having regained independence in the 19th century over a limited territory, liberated Kosovo in the Balkan war of 1912, the Serbs were still in a majority.

During the much maligned First Yugoslavia (1918-1941), there was, certainly by today's standards, relative tranquillity between Serbs and Albanians in Kosovo.

In World War II, as Kosovo became a part of Great Albania, made possible by Fascist Italy, persecution of Serbs once more became the order of the day. At the end of the war, Croat Communist dictator Tito, who in effect had promised Kosovo Albanians the right to be annexed to Albania, reneged on his promise, but made of it an autonomous province in the territorially reduced republic of Serbia.

Serbs who had fled during the war, to escape Albanian and Bulgarian persecution, were officially prevented from returning.

For the next several decades, the Kosovo Albanian leaders (part and parcel of the Yugoslav Communist Party), engaged in ethnic cleansing of Serbs and their institutions on a grand scale (desecration of Serbian Orthodox churches and cemeteries, arson and theft of Serbian properties, rape and other physical violence), forcing thousands of Serbs to flee.

The ultimate result: today the Serbs make up between 10-15 percent of the population. This disproportion was also achieved

---

* *Nashville Banner*, March 30, 1993.

through the influx from Albania of several hundreds of thousands of immigrants, as well as through an exceedingly high birthrate.

The ethnic cleansing, as indicated above, took place in an area that to the Serbs is as holy as Jerusalem is to the Jews. It was also associated with the importation from Albania of more than 200 professors and countless textbooks. Correspondingly, Serbian professors were dismissed unless they agreed to learn Albanian.

Until dictator Tito died in 1980, not a word was heard of the ethnic cleansing of Serbs, and certainly no TV cameras were there to record the events. Unpublicized protests by Serbian Orthodox Church authorities and others fell on deaf ears.

In the 1980s, however, word began to leak out, and even some Yugoslav Communists began to refer publicly to the Albanian actions as genocide.

In effect, the Kosovo Albanians made the greatest contribution to the success of the Serbian Communist leader Slobodan Milosevic. He seized upon the Albanian persecution of Serbs and made it his political platform. This earned him the respect of even Serbian anti-Communists, which he exploited to stay in power. He amended the Serbian constitution to do away with Kosovo's autonomy.

Had it not been for the ethnic cleansing of Serbs in Kosovo, it may be argued, Milosevic probably would have gone the way of other Communists when Communism was collapsing in Eastern Europe.

The Kosovo Albanians responded to the revoking of their autonomy by engaging in strikes, refusing to send their children to schools, boycotting elections and pursuing other forms of disobedience. These acts have brought a large Serbian military presence in Kosovo.

There are fears that a spark may touch off a new tragedy, in which the Albanians may reap the whirlwind of their past actions against the Serbs. Such are the bitter fruits of ethnic hatreds. Given the present psychological climate in the media, the Serbs are sure to get the blame no matter who may be at fault.

TWO CIVIL WARS:
SIMILAR YET VERY DIFFERENT*

The civil war in Yugoslavia is like no other. Over the past several months I have reflected on civil wars, particularly our own and the one going on in what used to be Yugoslavia. I see some striking similarities as well as enormous differences.

Both wars produced scenes of human suffering - torn corpses, prison camps and detention centers with pictures of emaciated prisoners, lack of medical supplies, to say nothing of the destruction of buildings and other physical objects. In our Civil War, for example, more lives were lost than in all of the other wars we fought until about the middle of the Vietnam conflict.

The rebellion of the Serbs in Croatia against incorporation in a Croatian state reminds me of the rebellion of a significant number of Virginians who did not want to be incorporated in the Confederate States of America, and formed a new state - West Virginia.

While our Civil War did not seem to have an ethnic component at the outset, the question of slavery was there and it did not take long to have it come to the fore.

One immediately evident difference is to be found in the way the conflicts were reported in the media. At the time of our Civil War, there was no radio and no television, and news-gathering was in its infancy.

The striking thing about the conflict in Yugoslavia is that despite the almost unbelievable potential for news-gathering and news-dissemination, the public has been poorly served. We have seen misinformation purveyed.

Over and over, for example, we have been told that the Serbs captured 70 percent of Bosnia, but we are not told that the Serbs lived there for centuries and before the civil war held over 60 percent of the area. The brutality of the conflict is matched by the ignorance that accompanies it, despite thousands of column inches in the media.

Similarly, most of the media seem obsessed with what they call "Serbian aggression." Following that logic, our Civil War should be referred to as "The War of Northern Aggression," as Confederate newspapers called it.

---

* *Daily News-Record*, April 28, 1993. Reprinted with permission.

In seeking to explain things, media stalwarts have been going on the assumption that those who opposed the Yugoslav secessions should have accepted them without a fight. Moreover, pundits have proceeded in their commentary with assuredness and certainty, totally oblivious of the well-established maxim that in a war the first casualty is truth.

In addition, it is difficult to explain the behavior of Western leaders, generally supported by the media, in their determination to affect the outcome by recognizing the secessionist republics. And subsequently to intervene actively in the conflict on the side of the losers, perhaps motivated in part by the horrors produced by the war.

True, President Lincoln worried that some European nations, notably England, might recognize the Confederacy and utilized diplomacy to prevent it, but he was prepared for war with the British if they did so. While officially neutral, Britain did not attempt to hide its sympathies. For example, the warship "Alabama" was built in England and was permitted to sail and join the Confederate navy. Moreover, two powerful ironclads were being constructed for the Confederacy, but the project was stopped at the last moment.

The notion that the outside world should not intervene by and large prevailed. Not so in the Yugoslav civil war.

By extending recognition to Slovenia and Croatia, and subsequently Bosnia-Herzegovina, the Western nations in effect assisted in the destruction of the internationally recognized country of Yugoslavia, and thereby aided and abetted the secessionist republics in the violation of the Helsinki Accords proviso against changing international borders by force.

Underlying the West's action was the assumption that the Yugoslav republics that opposed secession should have accepted it without any consideration of their own grievances.

In the end, the West has been dealing with the consequences of its failed policy, intervening in the war on a grand scale, seeking to frame "laws of war" for a civil war in the midst of one, fashioning a compromise of doubtful value for one part of that conflict and in the process raising unreasonable hopes for a settlement.

History will have something to say about such an approach to the resolution of complicated international questions.

CLINTON SHOULD SOUND OUT THE SERBIAN SIDE OF THE WAR[*]

Increased U.N. sanctions against Yugoslavia and mounting pressure on President Clinton to "do something" in Bosnia suggest that the United States may soon take military action.

At the same time, the President in his recent press conference demonstrated that he knew a great deal more about Bosnia than his questioners, who in the past have expressed doubts about his preparation in the area of foreign affairs.

Acknowledging that Bosnia-Herzegovina was "the most difficult foreign policy problem we face," the President said that the "United States is not - is not, should not become involved as a partisan in a war." Nor can it or the United Nations "enter a war in effect to redraw the geographical lines of republics within what was Yugoslavia."

We can only speculate as to what he has learned about the mistakes of the previous administration in seeking to deal with the whole Yugoslav problem, but one can infer a great deal from the above-quoted remarks, because the West's interference has been undisguised. That he failed to point to those mistakes was perhaps less out of generosity to the Bush administration than his fear that he might be seen as backing away from tough decisions. The President has no doubt asked some important questions, but he needs to ask some others, if he has not already done so.

It is imperative that he inquire about the basic assumption that guides those who favor intervention, especially military action. That assumption is that the Serbs - even those who are native residents of Bosnia where their forebears have lived for centuries - are guilty of aggression. That assumption is entirely false. Since the civil war began in Yugoslavia, not a single soldier has gone outside Yugoslav boundaries and no military action has taken place outside those borders.

As a Southerner, the President must know that during our Civil War the Confederate press referred to it as the "War of Northern Aggression." As President of the United States he must

---

[*] *The Philadelphia Inquirer*, April 30, 1993.

have some appreciation of the situation that confronted President Lincoln.

If the international community had been strong enough and inclined to operate on the basis of the arguments of today's interventionists, the U.S. Civil War would have been declared over and Lincoln would have been told to accept the Confederate States of America as an independent country or else. We know that England wanted to recognize the Confederacy and had indeed provided some help. We also know that in that eventuality Lincoln was prepared for war with the English.

The President also needs to ask why the Bush administration, at the time that Yugoslavia was beginning to fall apart, did not talk with the central Yugoslav government, especially the Serbs in that government, about resolving basic issues without bloodshed.

Instead, the United States followed Germany's lead in the European Community and recognized the secessionist republics of Slovenia, Croatia, and Bosnia-Herzegovina, totally ignoring Serbian interests.

There are those who ask, rhetorically, why the West should have listened to the Serbs. I believe that the answer is fairly simple. Basically for the same reason that we listen to the British when we have differences.

As the only proven Balkan friend and ally of the West in two world wars, the Serbs deserved to be listened to. In addition, they were the largest ethnic group in Yugoslavia and the strongest supporters of the common state, which the West said it favored. Moreover, if one is to act as peacemaker, he needs to talk to both sides.

The Serbs' main grievance was communist dictator Tito's carving up Yugoslavia into republics, which left one-third of the Serbs living outside the Republic of Serbia, mainly in Bosnia-Herzegovina and Croatia. Serbia and Montenegro fought in the Balkan war of 1912 and World War I to liberate those regions from the Ottoman and Austro-Hungarian empires, and since 1918 the Serbs from those regions lived in a common state with the Serbs of Serbia and Montenegro.

Consequently, Serbian actions in the current war are not based on some mystical medieval dream of a Serbian Empire, but on what was achieved at the end of World War I. By ignoring these realities, the West virtually guaranteed the present tragic situation. Moreover, how can the Vance-Owen proposals be imposed on the Serbs when there was never agreement that what they proposed would be accepted as binding arbitration?

If President Clinton does not grasp the folly of past Western actions, there would seem to be no way of avoiding disaster with unknown consequences.

A REALISTIC PLAN
FOR EX-YUGOSLAVIA *

Lord Salisbury, 19th century British prime minister, at one time observed that "the commonest error in politics" is "sticking to the carcasses of dead policies." This aptly applies to the West's mismanagement of the crisis in the former Yugoslavia.

For more than a year it has been more than evident that the West's rush to play a role in the dismemberment of Yugoslavia, through the premature recognitions of Slovenia, Croatia, and Bosnia-Herzegovina, and the total failure to take into account Serbian grievances, made the civil war in Yugoslavia a certainty.

Yet Western leaders, instead of recognizing their mistakes, have in the past year sought to deal with the consequences of a failed policy by imposing sanctions on Serbia, proposing the Vance-Owen Plan, imposing a "no fly zone" and seeking to establish "safe havens" for Muslims. This is "sticking to the carcasses of dead policies."

It seems to me that the latest proposal by the Croatian and Serbian presidents for a three-way division of Bosnia-Herzegovina opens the way to a broader approach to achieve a settlement covering all of the former Yugoslavia, and thus avoid spreading the conflict - to Macedonia, Kosovo, and beyond.

To that end, the following goals should be pursued:

* Promoting a realistic division of Bosnia-Herzegovina so as to facilitate the joining of Croatian areas to Croatia and Serbian areas to Serbia, leaving a small but compact area for a Muslim state, if that's what they want. At some future date, they may want to make arrangements with Serbia and/or Croatia for a customs union.

* Promoting an agreement between Croatia and Serbia, whereby the Serbs would exchange parts of Slavonia for most of the Serbian areas (Krajina) in Croatia. The Serbs would get the areas that want to join Serbia and Croatia would get far more fertile land. Other adjustments could no doubt be made so as to give Croatia better access to the tourist-important areas of the Adriatic.

* Promoting a resolution of the Kosovo problem by a method more radical than has been suggested in the past. From the time after

---

* *The Philadelphia Inquirer*, June 26, 1993.

World War II, when communist dictator Tito prevented the return of Serbs who had been expelled or forced to flee from Kosovo and encouraged immigration of Albanians to Kosovo, the Kosovo Albanians have made it amply clear that, while declaring that they wanted the status of a separate republic, they really did not want to be citizens of Yugoslavia. To that end they persecuted the Serbs, who had become a minority, and forced thousands to abandon their properties and to flee.

Although Kosovo is as sacred to the Serbs as Jerusalem is to the Jews, the fact must be faced that today Albanians make up close to 90 percent of its population. Moreover, the Albanians not only have the highest birthrate in Europe, but have also bought land in Serbia proper, often with development money from the Yugoslav treasury.

A radical approach is needed, not only to resolve the present problem, but also to anticipate difficulties. Serbia must be willing to lose parts of Kosovo, consequently letting the Albanians join Albania. In return, once a boundary is drawn, the Albanians on the Serbian side would have to move out of Serbia.

This is easier said than done. It will be necessary to draw the boundary so as to preserve as many of the Christian holy places, churches and monasteries, for Serbia. As in the case of all geographic divisions, neither side can be completely satisfied and compromises will be needed. Exchanges of population will be painful, and property compensations will not be easy.

Nevertheless, I believe that some such approach would be in the long-term interests of both peoples, as well as contributing to peace and stability in that part of the world.

MISDIAGNOSES RESULT IN
BAD BALKAN MEDICINE*

A doctor's prescribed remedy is rarely effective unless it is based on a correct diagnosis.

Judged by this maxim, most prescriptions by columnists for dealing with the outgrowth of the Yugoslav problem suggest that they would be failures. Some of them even state that President Clinton should dump his Secretary of State, Warren Christopher, and appoint a leading Republican from the Reagan or Bush administrations. And some of them want NATO to adopt the goal of removing the present regime in Serbia. If we are to look around the globe for comparable situations, I wonder how many other regimes we would need to target?

These commentators are right, however, in suggesting that neither the Democrats nor Republicans had policy alternatives in place in case communist systems should collapse. But their views of the Yugoslav situation and how the West should have dealt with it are not only simplistic but also dead wrong.

It may very well be that in its early stages, the Yugoslav affair might have been resolved quietly by diplomacy, but the failure of Western leaders to make a proper diagnosis is at the crux of the problem.

Most of the columnists that I have read are in good company with Western leaders in knowing little or nothing about Yugoslavia. Their legalistic citations from the Charter of the United Nations rest on the contention that the conflict in Yugoslavia is one of Serbian aggression and not a civil war. That argument is difficult to sustain on several counts.

First, if we are to stick with legalisms, the secessionist republics did not adhere to the Yugoslav constitution, or to the Helsinki Accords proviso about not changing the boundaries of internationally recognized states by force. Moreover, the Western powers that recognized the secessionist republics aided and abetted them in violating those charters.

Secondly, the civil war began before the recognitions. In addition, not a single fighter has engaged in warfare outside Yugoslavia's boundaries, and not a single shot was fired outside those borders.

---

* *The Washington Times*, November 2, 1993. Reprinted with permission.

Thirdly, it needs to be asked: By what international law or usage can the world community justify cavalierly recognizing seceding parts of an internationally recognized state, in this case Yugoslavia, a charter member of the League of Nations and the United Nations?

Fourth, while some columnists cite Article 2(7) of the U.N. Charter that authorizes the United Nations to take enforcement measures in certain conflicts that are essentially within the domestic jurisdiction of a state, they fail to point out that Article 33 provides that resolution of disputes should first be sought by pacific means, including arbitration and judicial settlement. The latter were never employed by the United Nations prior to the imposition of sanctions against Yugoslavia (Serbia and Montenegro).

Finally, what about two international acts (Treaty of London, 1915 and the Versailles treaties of St. Germain and Trianon) of which Serbia is the beneficiary? The first promised Serbia and Montenegro important territorial gains, including all of Bosnia-Herzegovina, a considerable part of Dalmatia (Montenegro was to get the port of Dubrovnik and surrounding areas), and large parts of present day Croatia. The second treated the new Yugoslavia as the successor state of Serbia, to which these and other areas were conveyed. Moreover, all international agreements to which Serbia was a party were transferred to the Yugoslav state. It seems to me that such international acts simply cannot be ignored.

It cannot be too often repeated that where Western policy went off the track was in the failure to take into account the rights and grievances of the Serbs, the largest ethnic group in Yugoslavia and the strongest supporters of the common state. If Serbian leaders were assured, even as the West was recognizing the secessionist republics, that in any final settlement their interests would be honored and respected, there is reason to believe most of the bloodshed could have been avoided.

Some commentators worry about the future of our prospective entente with Russia, and are bothered by reports of Russian "volunteers" fighting with the Serbs, but they seem not at all worried about reports of a far greater number of warriors from Muslim countries fighting with the Bosnian Muslims.

As I stated at the beginning, a doctor's prescription cannot be worth much if the diagnosis is wrong.

BOSNIA: LOST CAUSE?*

The NATO leaders continue to get nowhere in their efforts to bring about a peace settlement in Bosnia. Why?

It is because despite their desire to create the appearance of having done something, the Western leaders are badly divided. The best they could do at their most recent meeting in Brussels was to reiterate last August's sterile formula - the threat of air strikes against those impeding the delivery of humanitarian supplies to Sarajevo and two other Bosnian centers.

No one at Brussels seemed to think that air strikes alone would bring an end to that tragic civil war, yet no other action was proposed. There was the clear expectation that only a political settlement could do that, but no new mediating efforts were proposed.

The Europeans wanted President Clinton to join them in endorsing the Owen-Stoltenberg plan for a three-way division of Bosnia, an idea the Russians now seem to favor. To his allies' disappointment, the most Clinton was willing to do was to praise them for their efforts at peacemaking in the Balkans. His position appeared incongruous in view of his oft-repeated assertion that Bosnia was a European problem. For one thing, the president did not like the European Union's idea of a progressive lifting of sanctions against Serbia in return for its cooperation in reaching a political settlement.

Why, it may be asked, hasn't the peace plan of the European Union and NATO led to a resolution of the conflict? The plan was accepted by the Croats and the Serbs but rejected by the Muslims. The Croats would get what they want. The Serbs, although winners in the civil war, were willing to give up nearly 30 percent of the land they hold, but not their most important gains. This would still leave them with less than they had before the fighting began. The Muslims, the clear losers in the civil war, behave as if the Serbs should give up the gains that to them are vital. And they demand that the Croats give them an outlet to the sea.

Followers of the U.S. media are puzzled by the failure of the Muslims to recognize realities. There are two basic reasons. First, the Clinton administration's negative comments concerning the

---

* *The Washington Post*, February 2, 1994. Reprinted with permission.

Owen-Stoltenberg plan raised the hope of an eventual U.S. rescue. The president dashed these hopes on January 24, when he said he did not "think that the international community has the capacity to stop people within that nation from their civil war until they decide to do it."

Second, in addition to their improved military capacity, the Muslims fight on because that is the wish of the major Muslim powers. British intelligence sources point out that Iran, Libya and other Muslim states have not only implored the Bosnian Muslims to fight on but have managed to get sizable shipments of arms into Bosnia. The Bosnian Muslim leaders have often declared that they do not need outside help, if only the embargo on arms shipments is lifted so that the Muslims can defend themselves. Lifting the embargo, the same British sources point out, would have two advantages: greater ease in getting arms shipments into Bosnia and, along with them, the dispatching of larger numbers of trained military personnel than has been possible heretofore.

The Post's Jim Hoagland [op-ed, Jan. 27] has asserted "that previous inaction and mistakes have led the United States and its allies into a dead end on Bosnia," a sentiment shared by some other writers.

In my opinion, the principal mistake of the Western leaders was their failure to recognize Serbian vital interests should Yugoslavia disintegrate. The hasty recognition of the secessionist republics in effect transformed the internal boundaries created by Josip Broz Tito's Communist government into international ones, leaving one-third of the Serbs who had lived in one state since 1918 outside the republic of Serbia. The failure of the West to recognize that if Yugoslavia fell apart the Serbs would seek to preserve the hard-won gains achieved at the end of the First World War is the main reason for its blunder and the resulting civil war.

The tragedy of the Bosnian Muslims is that twice in this century they bet on the wrong horse. The first time was in World War II, when Bosnia became part of the Nazi-fascist satellite Croatian state, which proceeded to massacre hundreds of thousands of Serbs as well as tens of thousands of Jews and Gypsies, in which massacres the Muslims also took part. The second time was when in 1992 they threw in their lot with secessionist Croats, who in 1993 turned against them, perhaps realizing that since the civil war was lost, it was imperative to reach an accord with the Serbs.

The present tragedy of the Muslims is all the greater because in 1992 they had a choice, certainly more than in 1941. The issue was debated, but the Bosnian Muslim leader who favored an accommodation with Belgrade (i.e., with the Serbs) lost out to the Islamic fundamentalist Alija Izetbegovic. The latter, contrary to propaganda efforts to convince the West that he favors a democratic multi-ethnic state, is on record in the document that he authored, "The Islamic Declaration," as stating openly: "There can be neither peace nor coexistence between the Islamic religion and non-Islamic social and political institutions."

There have been leaders in other civil wars, such as Jefferson Davis and Robert E. Lee in our Civil War, who at some point concluded that it was futile, indeed immoral, to ask their people to continue to fight and die for a lost cause. Unfortunately, Alija Izetbegovic does not seem to be such a person.

Consequently, we can be sure that so long as the Muslims refuse to accept the European peace plan, the carnage will continue.

NATO ACTIONS MAY PROLONG WAR IN BOSNIA *

Instead of helping to end the civil war in Bosnia, the recent actions of NATO, and especially those of President Clinton, will serve to prolong it.

The differences among the leaders at their meetings in Brussels were papered over with the adoption of last August's sterile formula - the threat of air strikes against the military positions of those impeding the delivery of humanitarian supplies to Sarajevo and two other Bosnian centers.

Initially aimed at the Bosnian Serbs, the new threat seems to imply that it could include Croats and Muslims. German officials, for example, said that it was getting harder to blame most of the violence on Bosnian Serbs. And one American news correspondent reported that much of the shelling at Sarajevo on January 11 was by Muslim soldiers who had "set up mortars near the main hospital and Holiday Inn." And to some United Nations monitors it appeared that bombardment of the airport was coming from Muslim army positions.

No one at Brussels seemed to think that air strikes alone would bring an end to that tragic conflict. Yet no other NATO action was proposed. Clearly, there was an expectation that only a political settlement would do that. But the meeting proposed no new mediating efforts.

President Clinton praised the Europeans for their efforts at peace-making in the Balkans but, as in the past, he refused to go along with the European request that he endorse their concrete efforts. To him, punishing the Serbs seemed more important than progress toward ending the conflict. He did not like the European Union proposal to lift sanctions against Serbia in exchange for progress toward a political agreement.

That philosophy was echoed by his United Nations Ambassador, Madeleine Albright, when she visited Croatia just before the Brussels conference. By emphasizing the importance of getting on with war crimes trials, she certainly implied that a peace agreement was secondary.

---

* *Daily News-Record*, February 8, 1994.

Once again the Clinton administration put the cart before the horse. The first priority, it seems, was not to put an end to the bloodshed, but to concentrate on who was responsible for past atrocities.

A careful reading of news stories over the past several months reveals that while all sides have been engaged in continuing the carnage, the Croats and Muslims have been killing more people than have the Serbs. And there is no indication that the fighting will stop unless there is a peace settlement.

Several months ago, European Union and United Nations negotiators put forth a peace proposal which was accepted by the Croats and the Serbs, but rejected by the Muslims. Obviously, the Muslim leadership wants to continue the fighting, but so do certain influential centers in the West, primarily the United States. This must be said openly. It does not good to "beat around the bush."

The behavior of the Muslim leadership can in large part best be explained by the actions of the Clinton administration which has said, on the one hand, that Bosnia is a European problem, but just as a settlement seemed near, it declared that the Muslims were not being offered enough. In this way, the Muslims have been encouraged to continue the bloodshed in the hope that somehow the United States was still going to get them a better deal.

In the meanwhile, not only is the shocking carnage continuing in Bosnia, but the innocent people of Serbia are suffering a genocide inflicted by the sanctions.

The approach chosen by the Clinton administration, if followed logically, would mean that the United States will be put on the side of the winners or losers in no end of conflicts within any number of countries around the world. That would be quite a platter that we would be setting before ourselves!

A DANGEROUS TURN IN BOSNIA *

Bosnia may be entering the most dangerous phase of its tragic war. Certain developments point to an explosion in the making.

The Muslims, who in the past have said that they expected the international community to produce an acceptable peace formula, are now looking down on such proposals, and have resumed fighting against the Bosnian Serbs on several fronts.

Their changed attitude stems from the fact, now revealed by the media, that they have been getting sophisticated arms from Iran and other Arab countries to such an extent that they believe they can effectively challenge the Bosnian Serbs.

The developments may snap the Serbs' patience. As the Bosnian Serbs see it, they have made a number of moves since the war began whose aim was to contribute to the creation of a favorable climate for peace. Among these are: the opening of the Sarajevo airport at the beginning of the conflict, acceptance of the stationing of potentially unfriendly forces under the United Nations' flag, agreeing to what they considered illegal patrols of Bosnian skies by NATO aircraft, and abiding by the NATO ultimatum to remove their heavy weapons from around Sarajevo.

Those moves, the Bosnian Serbs insist, were not recognized as such nor did they get public approval from the international community, and especially not the United States. On the contrary, they assert, all of their good will gestures were regularly viewed as signs of Serbian weakness, producing demands that more pressure be put on the Serbs.

The critical question that we must ask is: what if the Bosnian Serbs perceive that there is danger that they could lose their key gains? They would certainly increase their military efforts. They would probably declare that any outside interference in the civil war, notably the presence of NATO aircraft, constitutes enemy action which will be resisted.

Correspondingly, what would Yugoslavia (Serbia and Montenegro) do in such circumstances? It could very well challenge UN and NATO authority, citing international law, particularly the Helsinki Accords. The latter, signed by some 30-odd nations,

---

* *Daily News-Record*, June 13, 1994.

including European nations as well as the United States and Canada, proclaimed that the borders of internationally recognized states could not be changed by force.

Yugoslavia was such a state and its borders were changed by force by the secessionist republics, first of all Slovenia. And the recognition of those republics by the Western countries constituted aiding and abetting them in their acts.

The Western powers have maintained that these republics had achieved independence and therefore deserved to be recognized. Consequently, according to such reasoning the fighting was the result of "aggression" by Serbia.

Who is right? Is it a civil war or a war of aggression? It depends on how one interprets international law.

The Bosnian Serbs (who inhabited two-thirds of Bosnia before the fighting began), as well as those in Yugoslavia, rely on international usages at the time of the secessions in 1991 and 1992, notably the requirements for recognition that were spelled out by the Montevideo Convention of 1932. It could be said that Slovenia met these minimally, but not Croatia, and certainly not Bosnia-Herzegovina. The latter had never been an independent state and it, as well as Croatia, proclaimed independence after the Yugoslav civil war had started.

The key question is whether Western actions may have encouraged the Muslims to believe that they could win by continuing the fighting, which in turn could force the Bosnian Serbs, as well as those in Yugoslavia, to launch a massive retaliation.

We cannot ignore the fact that Serbian patience has been severely strained by what they consider unfair and humiliating sanctions, imposed solely on them.

It is time to consider the possible consequences of stoking the Muslim fires of what I believe are unreal expectations, of which the United States has been particularly guilty, much to the annoyance of the French and the British, who have indicated that they might pull their peacekeeping forces from Bosnia if there is no settlement by the end of the year.

The far greater danger is that the Bosnian powder keg could well explode beyond anything we have seen. Does the West want this on its conscience?

TAKE BACK DOOR TO BOSNIAN PEACE*

Peace in Bosnia, despite the seeming impasse between the Bosnian Serbs and the Bosnian Muslim-Croat Federation (hereafter Muslims), is possible. It will not be easy, but the cease-fire negotiated by former President Jimmy Carter is a necessary first step.

The stumbling block is the five-nation Contact Group's "take it or leave it" proposal, which was accepted by the Muslims but rejected by the Serbs. The Serbs told Carter they are prepared to accept that plan as the "basis for negotiations." The Muslims retorted that the Serbs must first accept the proposal, and only then to negotiate about matters such as exchange of territories and modification of boundaries.

The only way out of this deadlock is an agreement between the two sides to negotiate secretly behind the scenes. And when agreement is reached, the Bosnian Serbs cold announce that they accept the Contact Group's proposal, to be followed by a public announcement of the agreement reached in secret. In that way, neither side would appear victors or vanquished. Both sides would save face, as would the members of the Contact Group.

For the secret negotiations to succeed, an impartial negotiator would be needed, preferably a highly visible person such as former President Carter.

What are the basic issues? During the Carter visit, the Bosnian Serbs pointed to the major ones, and the Muslims probably would not disagree. Suffice it to say, the percentage of territory that each side would get is really not critical.

A major stumbling block has been the status of Sarajevo. The Muslims demanded complete control, while the Serbs insisted that they should be entitled to the parts of it that they now hold. The Contact Group plan would leave the divided city under United Nations supervision for at least two years.

The Serbs have now said they are willing to trade the Sarajevo districts that they hold for several minor cities in central Bosnia that

---

* *The Plain Dealer*, January 13, 1995.

the Contact Group assigns to the Muslims. For the latter this would constitute a victory, and not only a psychological one.

Another major issue involves the largely Muslim-populated cities of Zepa, Srebrenica, and Gorazde, islands in a Serbian sea. The Contact Group plan would connect these to the Muslim-held areas near Sarajevo through corridors of questionable value. This solution is not acceptable to the Serbs because, among other things, the corridors would cut off a part of Serbian Bosnian lands from others assigned to them.

The only viable solution, in my opinion, and one that the Serbs have advanced, is to exchange these for lands bordering on the Muslim-held lands near Sarajevo. The advantage for the Muslims is that the latter lands are much more valuable. The disadvantage would be the need to move sizable Muslim populations from the three cities.

The number of people to be exchanged, however, would be fewer than the number exchanged by the Greeks and Turks in the early 1920s. With proper compensations and international assistance, the task would be manageable.

Another problem is the Brcko corridor connecting the Serbs of central Bosnia with those in the eastern part. The Contact Group plan narrows the corridor to practical non-existence. Some adjustments there will be needed.

Finally, the Bosnian Serbs are demanding that they be treated at least as equally as the Bosnian Croats, who have the right to establish a confederal arrangement with Croatia. The Serbs want the right to a similar association with Serbia, which a majority of the Contact Group now support.

In the end a negotiated settlement such as envisioned above raises the question as to what kind of entity will the Muslims have in future, particularly if the Bosnian Croats and Serbs go their individual ways, a likely outcome.

They may be left with less territory than they could have had under the Owen-Stoltenberg plan, which the Croats and Serbs accepted but which they rejected. On the other hand, they must know that if fighting is resumed, they would risk being left with no territory.

Given such a prospect, there would seem to be real motivation to negotiate for the best possible outcome under the circumstances. Friends of the Bosnian Muslims should encourage them to take the road of reality.

SERBS AREN'T BLIND OR TOOTHLESS*

The Serbs, collectively, are not the toothless tiger that U.S. policy makers seem to think. The failure of the Clinton administration to grasp this elemental fact means that the international community, which it seeks to lead, is skating on the thin ice of disaster. Quite aside from the likely widening of the war, the administration's policies risk tearing the NATO alliance apart.

The administration seems to continue being guided by the assumption that somehow you can force some 10 million people to accept a resolution of the Yugoslav civil war totally against their individual and national interests.

While President Clinton has more than once called the conflict in Bosnia a civil war, the administration's actions speak louder than words, and the Serbs can see this. Severe economic sanctions have been applied only to them, and NATO military actions have been taken only against them.

Even unproved acts of violence, such as the market massacres, have been attributed to Serbs. Moreover, U.S. military advisers have been sent to help the Muslims and Croats and not so secret flights of cargo planes have delivered "something" to Muslim areas, as reported by United Nations observers, but denied by NATO sources.

In mid-March, Croatia's President Franjo Tudjman and Bosnia's Vice President Ejup Ganic were received by Clinton and others in the administration, still trying to shore up the "shotgun marriage" between the Bosnian Muslims and Croats, consummated in the State Department earlier. And Tudjman, with some $20 million being dangled in front of him, is forced to bless that marriage.

This is the same Tudjman who warned former American Ambassador Warren Zimmermann that the Bosnian Muslims "are dangerous fundamentalists" who are "using Bosnia as a beachhead to spread ideology throughout Europe and even to the United States," and that the "civilized nations should join together to repel this threat."

---

* *The Plain Dealer* (Cleveland, OH), March 25, 1995.

In addition, the upcoming war crimes tribunal at the Hague, if press accounts are to be believed, will have only Serbs in the dock, despite evidence that Croats and Muslims are also guilty of similar alleged misdeeds. Dossiers of war crimes against Serbs, systematically prepared by the war crimes commission in Belgrade, were three times delivered to those charged with preparing cases, once by diplomatic pouch and twice in person. In each case, these were conveniently lost or mislaid.

The Serbs are not blind. As they look at the actions against them, and the brushing aside of every Bosnian Serb proposal toward a resolution of the conflict, they are more than ever coming to the conclusion that they can rely only on themselves. They have looked back at history and found that it was always so. And they do not see any hope for help from their supposed friend, Russia, which historically has sold them out more than once.

The recent Moscow invitation to Bosnian President Alija Izetbegovic, Tudjman, and other Serbian enemies to help celebrate the anniversary of the end of World War II, sends shivers up the collective Serbian spine. After all, the Serbs were Russia's allies in both world wars.

Consequently, there are growing indications - we cannot yet know how strong - among the Serbs in Bosnia, Croatia, and Yugoslavia that it may be now or never to fight for Serbian rights. Those holding this view point to the fact that militarily the Serbs may never be as strong as they are at present. Before Yugoslavia's breakup, its military power was regarded as the fourth strongest in Europe.

Those in the West, and especially in the United States, ought to realize that they have backed the Serbs into a corner, that the supposed toothless tiger could strike back. They should realize that the Serbs are capable of acting irrationally. They did so when in April 1941 they said "no" to Hitler at the height of his power and at a time when they were incomparably weaker than they are today.

It would seem the better part of wisdom to heed the warning signs than to play with fire, and ultimately with American lives.

PART III

During the past several years, I submitted over 50 proposed op-ed columns to several major U.S. newspapers, usually simultaneously. The few that were published are reproduced in the preceding section. The following is a selection from among those not published, in chronological order. Understandably, the reader will find a great deal of repetition in these proposed columns.

WHY IS YUGOSLAVIA LAGGING BEHIND?
(December, 1990)

Yugoslavia was the first communist country to break with Moscow (1948), and yet today it seems in danger of falling behind the other East European states (except Albania) in the anti-communist revolutionary tide.

To be sure, 1948 was not a revolt against communism. It was a quarrel between two Communists, Moscow's Stalin and Yugoslavia's Tito - the former contending that the latter had deviated from the path of Marxism-Leninism and the latter denying it. Stalin had said to some of his cohorts in the Kremlin, "I will crook my little finger and Tito will fall."

Despite Stalin's best efforts, however, Tito did not fall. Moreover, although his communist regime was hated by the people, the only realistic alternative to his rule at that time was a pro-Soviet stooge. This is precisely what motivated Western economic and military assistance to the Tito regime, while clearly recognizing the dictatorial nature of his government.

Many Yugoslavs greeted the Stalin-Tito break with "Long Live Tito," not really wishing him longevity but hailing him as one who had kicked out the first brick from under the edifice of international communism, expecting the whole thing to come tumbling down.

For a time after the break with Moscow, Tito's Yugoslavia offered some optimism for change. There were some modest adjustments in the rigid Stalinist model, mainly in the economic and cultural spheres. In the non-agricultural sector workers' participation was inaugurated through workers' councils, out of which grew the concept of self-management, emulated by a number of third world countries. In the cultural field artists and writers could abandon the Soviet-copied guide of "socialist realism." In the political arena, however, there was not even a hint of power sharing with non-communists. Tito did open a bit of a safety value by allowing most citizens to travel abroad.

The regime's tinkering with the economy, both before and after Tito's death (1980), has been nothing short of disastrous. The current rate of inflation (over 2,000%) is higher than it has ever been. The standard of living has been going down for several years. The number of state-owned or state-controlled enterprises in bankruptcy has increased markedly. And self-management has proved to be a failure and seems on the way out, at least in some parts of the country.

Ethnic tensions have increased, especially since the recent rise to power of Slobodan Milosevic in the republic of Serbia. For the first time since the establishment of communism in Yugoslavia, the Serbs, the largest ethnic group (about 40% of the total), have been able to articulate their aspirations and to give vent to their grievances, especially about the persecution of the Serbian minority at the hands of the Albanian majority in Serbia's autonomous province of Kosovo. The complex problem of Kosovo, the cradle of the Serbian nation (where its most important cultural and religious monuments are located), has given rise to disagreements in the other republics (notably in Croatia and Slovenia) concerning the Serbian decision to limit the autonomy of the province.

The crisis in the economy has led to some mutual recriminations among the republics, a crisis resulting in large part from the policy of decentralization that fostered economic barriers between the republics and ruinous competition in search of foreign trade arrangements.

Aggravating the whole situation is the paralysis of the political system that was Tito's legacy to his successors. Not wishing to have a strong man succeed him and hoping to diminish inter-ethnic tensions, he promulgated a new constitution in 1974, which provides for an annual rotation in the office of President of Yugoslavia among the republics, and for virtual unanimity among the republics on all important matters. The outcome has been an inability to reach a consensus, or in most cases the drafting of decisions in the most abstract terms, enabling each regional leader to go back home and interpret them in whatever manner he desired.

Despite disagreements, however, the leaders in the six republics and two autonomous provinces - all at least nominally Communists - are aware that the communist system is extremely unpopular throughout the country. At the same time, they know that a popular uprising against the regime would be next to impossible to coordinate. Unlike Poland and Hungary, where ethnic and religious unity is a fact of life, Yugoslavia faces ethnic discords as well as religious tensions - Roman Catholics (primarily in Croatia and Slovenia) and Orthodox (mainly in Serbia, Macedonia, and Montenegro, but also in Bosnia-Herzegovina), together with spirited activities of Islamic fundamentalists (in Bosnia-Herzegovina and Kosovo).

Hence even the first steps in a transition from dictatorship to democracy would be fraught with peril, not only because of ethnic and religious differences but also because of political disagreements within the republics.

If we are to judge by the experience of the First Yugoslavia (1918-1941), it may be that the Croats could organize and speak with one voice, as they did in those years through the Croatian Peasant Party. This would no doubt also be true of the Albanian minority. Perhaps this might also be true of the Slovenes, although they do have a history of political party struggles.

On the other hand, divisions among the Serbs would probably be the most pronounced. In the interwar years, Serbia was beset with grave party struggles - some even joined the Croatian Peasant Party in coalition - so that the Serbs certainly were unable to speak with one voice.

In sum, a transition from a dictatorship to democracy in Yugoslavia will not be easy. The Yugoslavs did have some important experience in self-government in the interwar years, but they have been without governing experience for some 50 years.

The one positive omen in all this is that Serbia, unlike the other ethnic groups, became independent in the 19th century and rather rapidly developed democratic constitutional political institutions. Prior to the First World War, it was a functioning parliamentary democracy. But at that time it was ethnically and religiously homogeneous, far removed from the multi-national state of today.

A national party congress, due to convene in January, is charged with the task of initiating political and economic reforms. In a pre-congress announcement in December, party officials declared that the party is willing to give up its monopoly of power, that it supports guarantees of association, press, and political party pluralism. If past experience is any guide, the congress decisions are apt to be drafted in abstract and general terms so that each of the eight delegations can go back to their republics and interpret them in ways most suitable for their respective circumstances.

In the meanwhile, non-communists in all of the six republics are engaged in modest efforts at rudimentary organization of political parties or movements, suggesting the tide against communism cannot be held back in Yugoslavia.

THE OTHER YUGOSLAVIA
(August, 1991)

Yugoslavia, if we go by what we hear and read, is a conglomerate of feuding ethnic groups put together in 1945 by Yugoslav Communist leader Josip Broz Tito.

But there was a Yugoslavia before Tito. Some understanding of that Yugoslavia would help us to appreciate what is going on there now.

The First Yugoslavia, rather than being a Versailles creation as some uninformed commentators would have it, came into being on December 1, 1918, before the peacemakers met at Versailles. It was the realization of an idea long nurtured by South Slav intellectuals, mainly Croats and Serbs. Although the idea did not have deep roots among the masses, the attack on Serbia by Austria-Hungary in 1914 provided the opportunity for concrete action.

In November 1914, in the Serbian city of Nis, to which the Serbian government had withdrawn, Serbia proclaimed as one of its main war aims the unification with Serbia of all Croats, Slovenes, and Serbs.

In July 1917, the Serbian cabinet met on the Greek island of Corfu with representatives of the Yugoslav Committee, formed during the war and made up of Croats, Serbs, and Slovenes from Austria-Hungary, and concluded an agreement on the nature of the forthcoming Yugoslav state, to be known as the Kingdom of the Serbs, Croats, and Slovenes.

Pursuant to that agreement, Croat, Serb, and Slovene representatives from the Croatian city of Zagreb came to Belgrade and in a meeting on December 1, 1918 with Serbian ministers and Serbian Prince Regent Alexander Karadjordjevic, declared the coming into being of the Kingdom of the Serbs, Croats, and Slovenes.

In 1919, a Provisional Parliament was established with the primary task of drafting a constitution for the new state. After nearly two years of mainly fruitless work, the Provisional Parliament called for elections in November 1920 for delegates to a Constituent Assembly to do the constitution-making.

The latter effort got off to a bad start, mainly because the men who had represented Croatia in the Provisional Parliament were defeated by Croatian nationalist forces, known as the Croatian Republican Peasant Party, led by Stjepan Radic, who boycotted the Constituent Assembly.

The Yugoslav Constitution went into effect in June 1921. Again, the newly-elected Croatian members of parliament refused to take their seats, and it was not until 1925 that Radic and his Croatian Peasant Party (they dropped the word "Republican" from the name) deputies took their seats in parliament. Radic even became a minister in the cabinet.

With Nikola Pasic, longtime Prime Minister of Serbia and Prime Minister of the new state from 1921 to 1926, gone, parliamentary turmoil and obstructionism was the rule for the next two years, culminating in the shooting of Radic and several of his party deputies in Parliament in 1928. The Croat deputies withdrew, and efforts at several cabinet combinations seemed to get nowhere.

King Alexander sought to end the chaos by taking power into his hands on January 1, 1929. He declared all political parties dissolved, and undertook to rule through cabinets headed by persons loyal to him. He also changed the name of the state to Yugoslavia, and divided the country into nine administrative areas named after waterways (mainly rivers) as a possible way of minimizing ethnic identities. In 1931, he engineered the writing of a constitution which in effect established what after World War II came be called "guided democracies."

Alexander, while on a state visit to France in 1934, was assassinated in what was a well-planned plot, organized by extremist Croats. His assassination ushered in a new era in Yugoslav history.

Prince Paul, who became Regent after Alexander's death, began a series of talks (through his ministers) with the leader of the Croatian Peasant Party, Vladko Macek. This led to an agreement (the famous *Sporazum*) in 1939, establishing a Croatian regional unit (known as *Banovina*) that gave the Croats considerable autonomy.

The next item on the agenda was the creation of a similar Serbian unit, but with the coming of the Second World War in 1939 further Yugoslav domestic reforms were shelved.

While we shall never know, it is reasonable to say that the Yugoslavs were on the way to the resolution of their basic political problems if it had not been for the world conflict. Moreover, had it not been for the War, there would not have been a Croatian Axis puppet regime, the so-called Independent State of Croatia, in which some 750,000 Serbs (as well as some 40,000 Jews) were massacred by the agents of that regime.

Prince Paul endeavored to keep Yugoslavia out of the war through an agreement with Hitler that promised Yugoslav neutrality. Unfortunately, Yugoslav Army officers, aided and abetted by British agents, overthrew the Regency of Prince Paul. This act was aided by the populace, mainly in Serbia, whipped up by allegations that Paul had put Yugoslavia in the same boat as Hungary, Romania, and Bulgaria as Axis partners.

When the revolutionaries read the agreement, they concluded that there was nothing there that they could not accept, but it was too late. Hitler could not permit the upstarts to get away with their insult to Germany. Within days, he launched an attack, and in two weeks the First Yugoslavia came to an end.

Then came civil war, out of which Tito's Communist Partisans emerged victorious, and established the Second Yugoslavia, but that is another story.

CAN YUGOSLAVIA BE SALVAGED?
(September, 1991)

Is there something in the Yugoslav experience that might provide an answer to the present crisis? I believe that the agreement (*Sporazum*) reached on the very eve of World War II, between the leader of the Croatian Peasant Party, Vladko Macek, and the Yugoslav Prime Minister Dragisa Cvetkovic, acting for Regent Prince Paul as the representative of the crown, might provide a model for the current impasse.

That agreement established an autonomous Croatian unit, known as the Croatian Banovina (from the Croatian word for governor). The *Sporazum* was signed on August 26, 1939, and soon thereafter commissions were created for the establishment of Serbian and Slovenian banovinas. The coming of the war, however, interrupted the process.

The agreement was the beginning of constitutional reform, which in effect moved the country toward federalism, some said confederalism, a process to be subsequently completed in the writing of a new constitution.

Under the agreement, certain powers were delegated to the banovina authorities - agriculture, trade and industry, forests and mines, education, justice, social policy and health, and internal administration. All other powers were left to the central government, particularly foreign affairs, national defense, posts, telephone, telegraph, and transport. Also within the province of the central government were foreign trade, public security, commerce between the banovinas, insurance, religion, and weights and measures.

Power in the field of finance was to be shared, although a subsequent decree vested a good deal of financial power in the hands of banovina authorities.

There were some other areas of overlapping powers, and there was to be a constitutional court to decide questions of conflict between the banovina and the central government.

While we shall never know, it is possible that if the Second World War had not come, Yugoslavia might have produced a viable political system. In addition, it might have been spared the terrible consequence of the civil war and of communism.

Perhaps the present Yugoslav republics could convoke a constituent assembly whose purpose would be to write a new constitution, using the 1939 *Sporazum* as a model. The number of delegates could be proportional to the population in each republic, and the delegates could decide on the rules of procedure, the nature of the requirements for ratification, and other procedural questions.

Substantively, in addition to the division of powers, they would need to consider the question of minority rights, and perhaps authorize commissions on boundary changes.

All of the foregoing is based on the assumption that there is a desire to continue with a Yugoslav state. To this end, it is necessary to recall the reasons that brought the South Slavs into a common state - the decades' long espousal of the Yugoslav idea by outstanding South Slav writers, the work of South Slav politicians to this end, the common ethnic and linguistic roots, as well as the sharing of experiences, some good and some painful. After all, Yugoslavia was not an accidental creation, as some commentators would have it.

Finally, economic circumstances would seem to argue for the continuation of the Yugoslav state. The Slovenes, for example, need the market that the other republics offer, while Slovene industrial and commercial know-how would be of benefit to all republics. Serbia, for its part, could continue to support much of the tourist trade in Croatia and elsewhere along the Adriatic, with meats and other foodstuffs, for which Serbia might be compensated, in part at least, with the foreign currency earnings that tourism brings. There are many other examples of economic interdependence in Yugoslav society. Moreover, Slovenia and Croatia should not forget that their more advanced economies are what they are in large part because of the disproportionate investments in their regions made in both the First as well as Tito's Yugoslavia.

But is there a will to try?

YUGOSLAVIA IS NOT A SOVIET UNION
(September, 1991)

Yugoslavia is not a Soviet Union. Attempts to draw analogies between the two countries are wide of the mark. To be sure, there are some superficial resemblances. When the Yugoslav Communists consolidated their power at the end of the Second World War, under the leadership of Josip Broz Tito, they imitated the Soviet Union in several ways. They installed a party dictatorship and proceeded to construct a Communist system on the Soviet model. One part of that model was a pseudo-federal structure consisting of a national unit and regional republics with autonomous provinces.

In at least two important respects, however, great differences prevail. One concerns the ways in which the two countries were put together, and the other pertains to the relationship of the largest republic to the others.

In the case of the Soviet Union, the respective republics were brought in by force. This was particularly notable in the case of the Baltic republics of Lithuania, Latvia, and Estonia, which were independent countries when the Soviet armies took them over at the outset of World War II. The same was also true of several other republics that had been part of the Russian empire, and had enjoyed brief independence after World War I. In their cases, however, the Communist rulers in Moscow lost little time in reclaiming the tsarist patrimony in the early 1920s.

In Yugoslavia, Croatia and Slovenia, which are often erroneously compared to the Baltic republics, were not independent states when they became part of Yugoslavia. Moreover, they voluntarily joined Serbia and Montenegro in 1918 to form the Yugoslav state. While there were proponents of a South Slav state among all of the South Slavs, particularly in the 19th century and the early part of the 20th, the best known of these is Croatian Bishop Juraj Strosmajer.

Concrete plans for the formation of such a state were hammered out in 1917 by the leaders of Serbia, notably Prime Minister Nikola Pasic, and the Yugoslav Committee, under the leadership of Croat Ante Trumbic, and representing Croats, Serbs, and Slovenes from Austria-Hungary. The process was hastened by the Croats and Slovenes in 1918, when Austria-Hungary was collapsing, with the distinct prospect that they would be left under Italian and Viennese rule. Their representatives rushed from Zagreb to liberated Belgrade and pleaded with the Serbs to form a common state, which was done on December 1, 1918. The fact that they had fought in the Austro-Hungarian military units may in part have motivated them, as well as the consideration that large areas inhabited by them had been promised to Italy as a reward for entering the war on the Allied side.

Similarly, when Communist Yugoslavia was formed at the end of World War II, the Croats were once more eager to be part of the common state, in part to escape retribution for being an Axis satellite, which had declared war on the Allies, and in which hundreds of thousands of Serbs, together with some 40,000 Jews and 10,000 Gypsies, were massacred by its agents.

A second major respect in which Yugoslavia is not a Soviet Union concerns the role of the largest geographic unit. In the Soviet

Union, there has never been any doubt that the largest republic, Russia, has consistently played the dominant role in the state. The reverse is true in Yugoslavia. From the outset of Tito's regime, there was never any effort to hide the fact that Serbia's influence had been deliberately minimized, in part through the drawing of republic boundaries so that over 40 percent of the Serbs live outside Serbia, and in part through the creation within Serbia's borders of two autonomous provinces (Kosovo and Vojvodina) over which Serbia had little control until 1990. In these actions, Tito was guided less by the fact that he was a Croat than by the fact that the Serbs were hostile to Communism, as well as having a history of hostility to tyrants.

In another way, Yugoslavia is not a Soviet Union - it had far more experience with democracy than did the Soviets. This was especially true of Serbia, which prior to the First World War was a functioning parliamentary democracy in the best sense of that word.

Comparisons may be tempting, but as I have indicated, they can lead to deceptions and worse.

YUGOSLAVIA AT ITS
LAST CROSSROADS
(October, 1991)

The Yugoslav leaders may be in their eleventh hour. Now that they have apparently been given what can only be a brief reprieve, they must now tackle the really tough issues if Yugoslavia is to continue to exist as a nation.

Slovenia and Croatia have already indicated that they demand independence, a loose alliance of sovereign states, or at best a confederal state. Serbia wants a federal state, and in this it is supported by Montenegro. Macedonia and Bosnia-Herzegovina seem to want Yugoslavia to survive, and have suggested that compromises are needed.

What are the problems that need to be resolved?

First of all, is it to be a federation or a confederation? If the latter or a loose association of sovereign states, then a republic would not have powers to interfere in the domestic affairs of any other republic. In that event, the present boundaries of republics would be unacceptable, especially to Serbia, because about two and one-half million Serbs live outside Serbia (i.e., outside Serbia and her two autonomous provinces of Kosovo and Vojvodina). There are Serbs in every other republic except Slovenia, the largest concentration being in Bosnia-Herzegovina, Croatia, and of course Montenegro, nearly all of whose inhabitants are Serbs. Hence the issue of how and where to alter present republic boundaries.

The second problem, although perhaps not as important as the first or third, would be autonomy for minorities. Croatia and Slovenia, and perhaps other non-Serb republics, would insist that the Albanians, who make up nearly 90% of the population of Kosovo, be accorded republic status (not achievable in view of Kosovo's importance to the Serbs as the cradle of their civilization) or at least autonomy within Serbia. Moreover, the non-Serb republics would also demand that Vojvodina, because of its large Hungarian minority, also have autonomy within Serbia. There are other autonomy questions, e.g., Albanians in Macedonia, Serbs and Croats in Bosnia-Herzegovina, and perhaps Dalmatians in Croatia. Some of Tito's comrades argued unsuccessfully for the latter when these questions were being decided at the end of World War II.

The third major issue involved the powers of a central government, whether it be a federation or a confederation. The Serbs want a strong national government, while Croatia and Slovenia want a weak central government at best. The tasks of bridging this constitutional gap are enormous. The draft by the latter two of a confederal constitution gives the national government basically consultative powers. The draft is reminiscent of the American Articles of Confederation.

Every American high school graduate knows that after experimenting under the Articles, the U.S. concluded that we needed a stronger national government, and hence proceeded to write our present Constitution. Perhaps it is well to remind the Yugoslavs that under the Articles, Congress had the power to levy taxes but no power to collect them. The states issued their own currencies, which became so depreciated that some states as well as foreign merchants refused to accept them. Congress had no power to regulate domestic or foreign commerce, with the result that tariff walls went up between some states.

In addition, Congress could not honor its own commitments, and it could not pass laws applying directly to individual citizens. There was no national executive branch or national judiciary.

Finally, the Articles required unanimity to enact amendments. This proviso was, of course, ignored by the drafters of the Constitution in Philadelphia.

Is it any wonder that the leading political figures of the United States concluded that the system was unworkable?

Is there not a lesson here for the Yugoslavs?

Finally, the basic issue in the reform of the economy is to move from state collectivism to a market economy. Aside from the entrenched bureaucrats, there would seem to be little disagreement in principle among the republics on the need to make this transformation.

YUGOSLAVIA IN
MID-PASSAGE
(October, 1991)

Yugoslavia today finds itself in mid-passage -- toward renewal or disintegration. Some news accounts cite a CIA study that predicts Yugoslavia's breakup within 18 months and very likely civil war. Some highly placed experts in the U.S. State Department have told me that the Department has concluded that Yugoslavia cannot be held together and that the main job of the United States now and in the future is to work on how to prevent civil war. Other experienced observers, on the other hand, believe that the disparate Yugoslav nationalities will in the end realize that is in the interests of all of them to hang together.

Clearly, Yugoslavia is at a critical crossroads, facing decisions that cannot long be delayed or postponed. The tug of centrifugal and centripetal forces is very much in evidence. It may be instructive to look at these briefly, beginning with the latter.

While it is not easy to weigh the centripetal forces, one of these is the idea that brought the South Slavs together in the first place. In various contacts they discovered that they had some things in common -- language, Christian religion (even though they were of different denominations), a closely related ethnicity, and some experience of working together (mainly the Serbs and Croats in the Austro-Hungarian consultative parliament).

Another centripetal force is Serbia, the largest nationality group (about 40 percent of the population). The Serbs have been the strongest supporters of the Yugoslav state and have sacrificed the most toward that goal. Although badly stung by what they regard as the failure of the other groups to appreciate Serbian contributions (some outspoken Serbian intellectuals have questioned whether Serbs should continue their dedication to the common state), the Serbs nevertheless do not like to think in terms of failure. To them a disintegration of Yugoslavia would be tantamount to admitting defeat and that their vast sacrifices had been in vain.

Also, the fact that the South Slavs have shared a common experience, no matter how difficult and even tragic, for 70 years must also be viewed as a centripetal strength. Even when they quarrel, it is in the nature of a family spat. Of course, family quarrels, if serious, can lead to divorce or separation.

The attitudes of the international community cannot be ignored. The major European powers as well as the United States favor the continuation of Yugoslavia as one state. We do not know how strong a force this will prove, but it seems reasonable to conclude that the Yugoslav nationalities cannot take lightly the stance of the international community.

Now for the centrifugal forces.

Certainly, the vast and uniform dissatisfaction that prevails throughout the country with the existing situation, both political and economic, must be viewed as negative.

Secondly, the loss of enthusiasm among the Serbs for a common state must be looked upon as a centrifugal force. The Serbs are not only smarting from the realization that their sacrifices have not been appreciated or recognized, but also see a great indignity in being blamed for things that went wrong, and insulted by the charge that they have yen for hegemony, which they vehemently deny.

Another centrifugal force involves the Croats, the second largest nationality group (about half as numerous as the Serbs). They have never been enthusiastic about Yugoslavia, and in some respects downright hostile. The creation of the Croatian satellite state under Axis auspices in 1941, and the massacre of many Serbian inhabitants of that state, is viewed by many non-Croatian Yugoslavs as proof of the Croats' lack of dedication to the common state.

The Albanian minority, especially in the autonomous province of Kosovo where they constitute nearly 90 percent of the population, constitute a disintegrative element. The decades' long persecution of the Serbs in Kosovo, the cradle of their civilization, by the Kosovo Albanians and their desire for greater independence, some desiring annexation to Albania, constitutes one if not the most difficult problem for Yugoslav unity.

Declarations by Slovenia that it will secede if a satisfactory confederal agreement is not soon reached, is also a centrifugal force.

Another negative factor is that part of Tito's legacy that pitted one nationality group against another, so that each blamed some one else for its and the country's problems. The ultimate result was the sowing of suspicions that are difficult to eradicate.

Finally, the results of elections in 1990 have given out erroneous signals. In the Western media, the elections in Croatia and Slovenia were interpreted as victories for democracy against Communism. To a degree, the elections in Macedonia and Bosnia-Herzegovina were interpreted similarly, in that Communists were not victorious. In Serbia and Montenegro, however, the Communists (under the new name Socialist) were victorious, and in the Western media this was viewed as a victory for Communism. This is terribly misleading, because in the electoral campaigns in each of the republics the principal issues were nationalist. None of the victorious parties in all of the Yugoslav elections campaigned on a Communist platform.

Consequently, if Yugoslavia is to survive, the leaders of the respective republics will need to iron out national issues first. This is where dialogue must begin. The primary question will involve the powers of the central government as opposed to the powers of the individual republics. If agreement cannot be reached on this question, there is little hope for Yugoslavia to move toward renewal.

CIVIL WARS:
CAN THEY BE AVOIDED?
(November, 1991)

The most tragic of all wars are civil wars, brother against brother. We know this from our own experience; until about half way through the Vietnam conflict, the United States had lost more lives in our Civil War than in *all* of the other wars put together.

Could the Civil War have been avoided, and how? And could it have been stopped before all the carnage, to say nothing of material devastations?

As we ponder these questions, some of us cannot but reflect on the Yugoslav tragedy.

Should the Yugoslav federal authorities simply have let secessionist Slovenia and Croatia go their separate ways? Should Serbia have ignored the declaration of some 600,000 Serbs living in Croatia that they were determined not to live in an independent Croatia?

And could conflict have been halted after it broke out? Can it even now be brought to an end? Or must it, like our Civil War, continue until the parties are utterly exhausted and unparalleled destruction sets the people back a hundred years?

First of all, we must ask: when were the grapes of wrath sown?

While historians have a tendency to go further and further into the past for origins of certain developments, it is reasonable to say that the seeds were sown primarily by the Axis-spawned Croatian regime, whose followers (*Ustashe*) massacred some 700,000 Serbs, 50,000 Jews, and about 10,000 Gypsies during World War II.

It is today's Serbs in Croatia, numbering at least 600,000, who are determined not to risk their lives in another Croatian state. Could their attitudes have been shaped differently so as to avoid such bitter distrust?

If during the decades of Tito's Communist regime the Croats had been led to follow the example of postwar German leaders, who apologized for Nazi crimes and even paid reparations, would Serbian attitudes have been different? If as late as two years ago, when the Croats indicated their intention to secede, they had condemned the acts of the wartime Croat leaders and apologized for their acts, would the Serbs in their midst have been reassured?

When I was an American diplomat in Belgrade after World War II, an older Serbian was often my driver, and frequently made critical comments about the Tito regime. On one such occasion, I said, "But Joe, the Tito dictatorship has at least prevented Serbian revenge against the Croats, and thus avoided much bloodshed." To this he replied, "Ah, Mr. Dragnich, that time is yet to come."

While I saw the brutality of Communist rule, I often reflected on Joe's statement, and hoped that after a generation or two, the urge to retaliate would decline and even pass away.

When Tito's onetime Communist general, Franjo Tudjman, became president of Croatia, he opened Pandora's box. Not only did he and his associates not follow the example of postwar German leaders in condemning and apologizing for the misdeeds of the wartime Croat state, but, on the contrary, they sought to deny or minimize them, and even adopted some of the trappings of that state. Moreover, they engaged in widespread acts of discrimination against their Serbian citizens.

Even when the latter took up arms after the Croat announcement of secession in June 1991, was there not a way to prevent all-out civil war?

The Croats (and Slovenes) suggested a loose confederal union, but when Serbia saw that the proposed draft of a new constitution left the national government with only consultative powers, and hence no power to protect Serbian minorities in other republics, the proposed draft could not be accepted.

In the circumstances, the Serbs in Croatia asked for political autonomy or annexation to Serbia, which the Croats were determined to prevent. These Serbs saw themselves somewhat as those Virginians at the time of the Civil War who wanted to remain in the Union, and in 1863 were formally admitted as the state of West Virginia.

Even after hostilities had broken out, Serbia's Slobodan Milosevic and Croatia's Franjo Tudjman met more than once. It would be interesting to know *what* they proposed to each other. We do know that Milosevic emphasized the need for some type of boundary changes, arguing that the Tito-imposed boundaries were artificial, but we do not know if Tudjman made any counter-proposals.

If there is to be secession with peace anytime soon, the problem of boundary rectifications must be resolved. Otherwise, the Serbs and Croats (and perhaps others in Yugoslavia) may be condemned to repeat the grim tragedy of a prolonged civil war, much as we in the United States had to endure.

Even at this late date, is there not another way? Seeking to punish one or more of the Yugoslav republics, or all of them, through embargoes, recognitions or non-recognitions, certainly will not do it.

SERBIA IS NO RIDDLE
(December, 1991)

Many readers who know some Balkan history have been puzzled by what they have read in the course of the past year about Yugoslavia, and especially about its largest republic, Serbia.

These readers know that Serbia and the Serbs were U.S. allies in two world wars. They are aware that the Serbs have historically been committed to struggling for freedom and independence. Moreover, they know that when Serbia regained its independence from the Ottoman empire in the nineteenth century, it proceeded to develop a model parliamentary democracy, far ahead of nearly all European countries. In this process, Serbia was guided by leaders who were educated in Western Europe and/or were influenced by it.

Yet media stories and commentaries have increasingly been conveying the impression that the Serbs are backward Balkan types whose Orthodox Christianity somehow keeps them in unenlightened darkness, that they support Communism, and that they are intent on lording it over the other peoples of Yugoslavia.

These contentions give an entirely false picture.

It is true that the Serbs fought for what was theirs, often against overwhelming odds and at great sacrifice. As the English historian, Harold Temperely, wrote in 1919: "There is no race which has shown a more heroic desire for freedom than the Serbs, and achieved it with less aid from others - or at more sacrifice to itself." At the same time, the Serbs have never sought what was not rightfully theirs.

It is true that the Serbs took the lead in the creation of the First Yugoslavia in 1918, in large part because they were told by Croats and Slovenes that they wanted to unite with Serbia. The Second Yugoslavia was imposed at the end of the Second World War by Croat dictator Josip Broz Tito and his Serbian, Croatian, and Slovene Communist comrades, and without consulting any Yugoslav ethnic group, least of all the Serbs. Serbia's guerrilla leader, Drazha Mihailovic, lost out to the Communists in large part because of Allied aid to Tito, who in 1946 engineered a show trial and then executed Mihailovic.

It is also true that Serbia played a leading role in the First Yugoslavia, not because it was hegemonistic, but because the Croats at first even refused to engage in constitution-making and later resorted to obstructionist tactics in parliament. But it is also true that in 1939 the Serbs and Croats agreed to the creation of an autonomous Croatian unit, which gained powers in most spheres of governmental activities, except foreign affairs, defense, posts, foreign trade, and commerce between the several geographic units.

If the Serbs had wanted a Great Serbia, they could have had it when it was offered to them on the proverbial silver platter by Britain, France, and Russia, after they had concluded the secret Treaty of London in 1915, by which they promised to Italy large areas of the northern Adriatic (populated mainly by Croats and Slovenes) in return for Rome's joining the war on the Allied side. Serbia was offered Bosnia-Herzegovina, parts of Dalmatia, and other areas populated by Serbs (among those in present day Croatia), but Serbia refused to take the bait, preferring to remain faithful to its announced war aim of liberating and unifying all Serbs, Croats, and Slovenes.

The Serbs do not want to force any group, against its will, to live with them in a common state, provided there is an orderly settling of accounts, including adjustments in boundaries that were imposed by dictator Tito.

The Serbs do not hate Croats (or any other ethnic or religious group), but they are understandably fearful of what could happen to 600,000 to 800,000 Serbs in a future independent Croatia, in view of the fact that approximately that number of Serbs, as well as a smaller number of Jews and Gypsies, were massacred in the Nazi-quisling Croatian state during World War II. This is especially true in view of the fact that the present so-called democratic regime in Croatia has re-instituted many symbols and policies of the hated quisling state.

The Serbs have finally come to realize just how costly the Yugoslav experiment has been to them. Economically, Serbia sacrificed, in both the First and Second Yugoslavias, in order that the industrialization of Croatia and Slovenia could be advanced, and in order that poorer regions of the country could be uplifted.

Serbia also paid dearly through tremendous losses in war, including the massacres referred to above, and the depopulation of the cradle of the Serbian nation, Kosovo, through the actions of Kosovo Albanians, who forced the Serbs to leave their homes, and through the influx of Albanians from Albania, which was aided and abetted by Tito, intent on punishing the Serbs.

The years of Communism, when Serbia was relegated to a position of inferiority, were terribly costly to the Serbs.

It is also true that the Serbs responded favorably to Slobodan Milosevic in the past years, not because of his Communism, but because for the first time since the World War II years, during which the Serbs were brutalized in Kosovo, a government leader came along who listened to their cries and gave voice to their grievances. Because solutions to key problems have escaped Milosevic, he has lost much of the support he once had among the Serbian masses and intellectuals.

As the Serbs (as well as other Yugoslavs) face a difficult and uncertain future, is it too much to ask that writers and commentators, who aspire to inform the public, familiarize themselves with the basic aspects of Yugoslav history, so that they will not fall prey to misinformation and questionable generalizations?

YUGOSLAVIA: ANOTHER VIEW
(March, 1992)

For some time I have been troubled by what I have read in the press and heard over the radio and TV about the fighting in Yugoslavia, which leads me to make a few observations that I hope will help those whose minds are not already closed.

First of all, as one who has spent most of his professional lifetime researching and writing about Yugoslav history and politics,

I am simply aghast and appalled by the extent of biased reporting in this country about the Yugoslav tragedy. It seems as if there is a calculated and planned onslaught against the Serbs and Serbia.

Secondly, it seems hopeless to try for a balanced and fair presentation. A few observations, such as those of former American Ambassador John Scanlan, who has pointed out that the Serbs did nothing until Slovenian secessionists began establishing frontier posts around their republic, remain voices in the wilderness. Other unilateral acts by Slovenia and Croatia, calculated to destroy the unity of the country, could not be ignored. This was, after all, a voluntary union. When one party decides that a marriage should be dissolved, there are procedures that must be followed.

A civil war is a terrible thing; we know from our own experience. We should also remember that no small number of Virginians did not want to secede from the Union, and in 1863 they formally became the state of West Virginia.

Thirdly, when it comes to the 600,000 or so Serbs living in Croatia when the fighting began, they demonstrated their desire to remain a part of Yugoslavia. About a year ago, when the Croats were talking about seceding, a plebiscite in the most concentrated Serbian area indicated near unanimous agreement that in case of secession, they did not want to remain part of Croatia. And any informed soul knows why those Serbs feel that way; but for the un-informed let me point out that it is because of the massacre of hundreds of thousands of Serbs by the pro-Nazi regime in Croatia during World War II, which has been the source of Serb fears.

Fourth, I am firmly convinced that there will be no peace unless there is a revision of some boundaries, so that fewer Serbs would be left in an independent Croatia. After all, the post-World War II internal boundaries were drawn by Communist Croat Tito, who for a variety of reasons was determined to punish the Serbs. Prior to that time Yugoslavia was not divided into ethnic units. If the Croats want independence, the Serbs will agree, but only if there is a change in the boundaries. Anyone who proceeds on other assumptions is in for a rude awakening.

Fifth, all the talk about a Serbian-dominated army is wide of the mark. It is a Yugoslav Army, in which Serbs predominate, and it may serve some of Serbia's goals, but in the Army's command structure, the Serbs are a minority. There is no credible evidence that I am aware of that Serbian authorities can control the Army. It is still Tito's Communist-controlled army that he always emphasized would be the ultimate protector of Yugoslavia.

Finally, I believe that it is important for United States policy makers to keep in mind who have been our friends in the past. In two world wars, the Serbs were our strong allies while the Croats fought on the other side, and in December 1941 even declared war on the U.S., Britain, and the USSR, and even sent troops to the Russian front. And unlike the postwar German leaders, the Croatians have made no apologies or expressed any remorse. None of these considerations can excuse recent atrocities by Serbs or Croats, and there have been such on both sides. And we should keep in mind that the Communist system was imposed on Serbs, Croats, and Slovenes alike, and that that system has not been popular in any part of Yugoslavia. None of the republics is completely free of it, but one day they will be.

THE DRIVING FORCE BEHIND SERBIAN ACTIONS
(June, 1992)

It is understandable that most observers should condemn the violence that has been taking place in what was once Yugoslavia, and I count myself among them. The increasingly hysterical responses in the press do not, however, contribute to an understanding of why some of these things have been going on.

What bothers me about these emotion-laden outbursts in the press is the absence of even a mention of the basic issue that has led to so much bloodshed.

When it was evident that Yugoslavia was breaking up, EC and the U.S. indicated that they would respect the wishes of the peoples of Yugoslavia. As it turned out, this meant respecting the interests and wishes of the secessionist republics, while completely ignoring the interests of the largest ethnic group, the Serbs, who had been the strongest supporters of the common state.

The clear indication of this were statements that boundaries between the republics could not be changed. These were the work of Communist dictator Tito, who was intent upon punishing the Serbs, leaving over one-third of them outside the republic of Serbia, with the largest number in Croatia and Bosnia-Herzegovina. It is ironic that those in the west who applauded the downfall of Communism now seem bent on fighting to the death in defense of one of Tito's major injustices to the Serbs.

The failure of the EC and the U.S. to indicate that Serbian interests would be considered along with the others enabled Milosevic to pose as the only defender of Serbian interests, with the effect that the Serbian people, who hate the Communist system, have been driven into his arms unwillingly.

On the basis of information at my disposal, the vast majority of the Serbian people do not defend Milosevic's actions or methods.

At the same time, the Serbs may be forgiven if they are paranoid, for it was Britain and America that helped the Tito Communists to seize power and impose Communism upon them.

Moreover, the Serbs remember that Serbia and Montenegro fought the Ottoman Turks in the Balkan wars in 1912 and the Austro-Hungarians in 1914 to liberate Serbian territories (Bosnia-Herzegovina among them), as well as Slovene and Croatian areas, and at indescribably enormous costs.

Yet in 1991, the latter two were told by the EC and the U.S. that they could retain their territorial gains, and that Serbia and Montenegro, despite their past sacrifices and their contributions as allies in two world wars, should be satisfied to have one-third of their *once-liberated* compatriots revert to being ruled by others.

No independent observer has suggested that the Serbian grievances justify Milosevic's actions or those of the remnants of Tito's Yugoslav Army. Some knowledgeable and disinterested commentators have, however, noted that if EC and the United States had publicly recognized Serbian interests by, for example, proclaiming that in any final settlement, there should be plebiscites in contested areas, such as those in Croatia and Bosnia-Herzegovina to determine the wishes of the inhabitants, most of the bloodshed might have been avoided.

Be that as it may, it still may not be too late for EC and the U.S. to admit that they acted precipitously, and that all of the Yugoslav peoples should be brought together in a peace conference, where the rights of each ethnic group would be respected, with specific mention of plebiscites and the possible use of arbitration tribunals.

It seems, however, that admitting mistakes comes hard to the Western leaders. It is easier to concentrate on the consequences of those mistakes.

THE NEXT CIVIL WAR IN YUGOSLAVIA
(June, 1992)

Civil war, which is once again erupting in Yugoslavia, this time in the republic of Bosnia-Herzegovina, threatens to be worse than the earlier one in Croatia. As this new tragedy unfolds, one would hope that Western media reporting would be better than in the earlier one. The reporting from Croatia almost totally emphasized the struggle for self-determination of the secessionist Croats. Rarely was there any mention of self-determination for the Serbs, the largest ethnic group in the country.

Friends of mine who were recently in Yugoslavia report that the Serbs are bitter, that they cannot fathom why the Western media have been hostile to them and to Serbia. They recount that Serbia always struggled for democracy, that it was an ally of the West in the two World Wars, that the Serbs had sacrificed the most for the Yugoslav state, and they point out that after World War II, Communism was imposed on them, and that Communist dictator Tito punished Serbia by creating republics and autonomous provinces so that one-third of the Serbs live outside the Serbian republic. All that Serbia is doing, they say, is trying to protect its legitimate rights.

While I cannot pretend to explain the frequent Serb-bashing in the media, I am inclined to believe that it results mainly from the lack of historical knowledge by reporters and commentators, or the acceptance of perverted views of the past. It has seemed to me that the media have been enamored by the actions of the break-away republics, and have uncritically accepted their charges that the Serbs were responsible for all of their troubles.

In the interest of more objective reporting, as well as in the hope of promoting a better understanding of events in that complex nation, it seems desirable to present a thumbnail sketch of Serbia's history and the West's reaction to the Serbian past.

When after centuries of Turkish occupation, the Serbs early in the nineteenth century led a successful revolt against the Ottoman

Turks and resurrected the Serbian state, Western Europe reacted with fulsome praise. Even greater praise came when the Serbs fought for democracy by overthrowing their domestic despots and established a constitutional parliamentary system.

And when Western Europe saw little democratic Serbia lead its Balkan allies in throwing the Ottomans out of Europe in the Balkan war of 1912, there was more applause and acclaim. And when in 1914, Serbia stood up to the attack by the Austro-Hungarian empire, the West seemed in awe, and welcomed Serbia as the Allies' brave partner.

Serbia, which had listened to the pleas for help from the Croats, Slovenes, and Serbs who were still part of Austria-Hungary, declared as its major war aim the liberation and unification of all Serbs, Croats, and Slovenes.

In 1915 this Serbian aim came into conflict with the policies of the Western Allies - Britain, France, and Russia - who had promised Austro-Hungarian territories in the northern Adriatic (populated mainly by Croats and Slovenes) to Italy as the price for weaning it away from the Triple Alliance and joining the Allies.

As a way of resolving this problem, the Allies offered to compensate Serbia with a promise that Serbia could annex Bosnia-Herzegovina and Slavic areas of the Dalmatian coast, which would have resulted in a Great Serbia. But this compromise would have left most Slovenes and Croats (and some Serbs) under foreign rule. Serbia, to her horrible misfortune as it turned out, refused the Allied offer and remained loyal to the commitment of liberating and uniting all Croats, Serbs, and Slovenes.

Serbia's war aim was realized with the creation of the Yugoslav state on December 1, 1918. It would be impossible in this piece to survey the next two decades. Suffice it to say that Hitler's and Mussolini's forces destroyed this first Yugoslavia in 1941. Once again the Allies praised the valiant resistance, mainly Serb.

Two major consequences ensued. A Croatian fascist state was created, whose regime massacred close to three-quarters of a million Serbs and a lesser number of Jews and Gypsies. Secondly, at the end of World War II, a second Yugoslavia was created by the Communist-led Partisans, who defeated the Serbian-led resistance under Colonel Mihailovic. When the latter raised the flag of the first guerrilla movement in Europe, the Serbs were again glorified in the

West. Subsequently, in 1943, when it suited their policies, the Allies resolved the clash between the two guerrilla movements in favor of the Partisans, led by Communist Josip Broz Tito.

The failure of Yugoslav Communism and the attendant consequences of the breakup of Yugoslavia are history.

Serbian friends who recently visited relatives in Belgrade were asked why it was that in the West there were so few expressions concerning the rights of the Serbs. What is so sacred about the Tito-imposed boundaries, they asked. And why is it, they beg in disbelief, that after everything that Serbia achieved in the Balkan wars and World War I, the West expects Serbia to be satisfied to return to its pre-1912 boundaries?

Anyone who knows Serbian history also knows that the Serbs are not likely to accept such an outcome.

It is an elementary dictum of politics as the art of the possible that a stable solution cannot be based on the disregard of the interests of the major player.

DEALING WITH THE CONSEQUENCES OF FAILED POLICY
(June, 1992)

The recently voted UN sanctions against Serbia are very much like treating the symptoms of a disease. They are an attempt to deal with the consequences of failed policies. Unless there is a willingness to seek the cause of the consequences, the prospects for a desired outcome are slim indeed.

The largest contributing factor to the violence in what was Yugoslavia were the actions of the European Community (EC), initially opposed by the United States but subsequently joined in with a vengeance.

The offer by the EC of its good offices in the hope of a peaceful resolution of differences was a positive step, but one soon negated by the premature diplomatic recognition of two of the Yugoslav republics - Slovenia and Croatia. Before EC negotiator, Lord Carrington, could proceed very far in his efforts, EC, under pressure from Germany and Austria, declared that they planned to recognize the two republics. This was enough for the Croatian and

Slovenian leaders to go ahead with their announced intentions. Armed conflict soon followed.

It is interesting that the German and Austrian actions were contrary to the recommendations of their ambassadors in Belgrade, who opposed the action. To compound the error, Carrington made an initial mistake by presenting to the Yugoslav parties a document that declared the existing Yugoslav state at an end, and proposed that negotiations begin on the creation of a new one. This action was viewed unfavorably by the Serbs, who did not want a breakup of the country, but played into the hands of the Slovenes and Croats, who did.

Moreover, the EC leaders declared that the internal republic boundaries could not be changed except by peaceful means, which was what the secessionist republics wanted to hear, but which to the Serbs was further proof that they were not being treated evenhandedly.

The EC leaders seemed to have known little Yugoslav history. For example, they took no account of the fact that prior to the Communists' seizure of power, Yugoslavia was not divided into republics or other ethnic units. Secondly, they should have known that Tito, a Croat, carved up the territory in such a way as to punish the Serbs, whom he blamed for all the ills of the First Yugoslavia and signified his resentment that his wartime resistance movement had almost no support in Serbia. The result - over one-third of the Serbs were left outside the republic of Serbia.

The EC and the United States had indicated that they would respect the wishes of the peoples of Yugoslavia. If there was to be a divorce, many questions would arise. For the Croats and Slovenes, their first wish was to be free of Yugoslavia. For the Serbs, however, their first priority was to bring into the fold as many as possible of the Serbs that Tito's handiwork had scattered.

Slovenia was not a problem since few Serbs lived there. In Croatia, however, between 600,000 and 800,000 Serbs decisively declared that they would not live in an independent Croatia, painfully remembering that some 700,000 of their compatriots were massacred by the minions of the fascist Croat Axis regime in World War II. Following the declaration of secession, the Serbs took up arms and were aided by Serbs in Serbia. Similarly when subsequently the Muslims and Croats in Bosnia-Herzegovina announced that they were going to seek recognition from EC, the Serbs, who numbered about one-third of the population, avowed that they wanted to remain in Yugoslavia and announced the formation of a Serb republic of Bosnia. Again violence erupted.

In the reports of correspondents and the statements of political leaders in the West there was a seeming haste to brand Serbs and Serbia as aggressors. No mention was made of the fact that Serbs have been in these areas for hundred of years, that Serbia had fought in the Balkan War of 1912 and in World War I to liberate Serbian areas, including those in Croatia and Bosnia-Herzegovina. And no one reminded the reader that it was Communist Tito who had excluded these areas from the republic of Serbia.

It is easy to condemn violence, of which all sides have been guilty, but unless there is a willingness to face its basic cause, and to proceed to peace negotiations where the rights of *every* ethnic group would be respected equally, the outlook for putting an end to bloodshed is not promising.

COULD YUGOSLAV BLOODSHED HAVE BEEN AVOIDED?
(July, 1992)

Are the Yugoslavs such bloodthirsty barbarians that nothing could have prevented what has happened? Is there a centuries-old history of ethnic violence? A heritage of blood feuds? An accumulation of unsettled scores? Seeking answers is a tall order, yet it deserves a try.

There is no simple answer, or perhaps several qualified "yeses" and "noes," plus some questions.

One essential fact needs to be noted at the outset: ethnic violence among the Yugoslavs is primarily the product of this century, first when Slovenes and Croats fought in Austro-Hungarian uniforms against Serbs and the Allies in World War I, and when the Croats fought as allies of Germany and Italy in the Second World War.

What we do not know is the extent to which the Serbs might seek revenge for the massacre of some 700,000 Serbs by the Croatian Nazi puppet state, mainly in 1941 and 1942.

We also do not know to what extent the Serbs would seek revenge against Muslims, particularly the "ethnic cleansing" to which they had been subjected during Tito's rule of some 35 years by the Albanian Muslims in Serbia's Kosovo province.

Another question: we do not know to what degree the Serbs would have been satisfied (consequently avoiding violence) if, at the time that Yugoslavia was breaking apart, they had been told by the West that in any final settlement, their grievances would also be addressed.

As a matter of fact, they were essentially told the opposite, the West declaring that the boundaries between republics could not be changed except by peaceful means. This, in spite of the fact that Slovenia had already used force to change Yugoslavia's international boundaries, an act in which it was aided and abetted by the European Community.

Be it noted that Croat Tito's carving up of Yugoslavia into republics, contrary to the earlier organization of the country, left one-third of the Serbs outside the republic of Serbia, mainly in Croatia and Bosnia-Herzegovina. Be it also noted that Serbia and Montenegro fought against the Ottoman Turks in the Balkan wars (1912-1913) and against Austria-Hungary in the First World War to liberate these territories.

And we do not know how much Tito's creation of a religious ethnic category - Muslim - played in the tragedy in Bosnia-Herzegovina, particularly the assertion of the Muslim leader, Izetbegovic, that there "can be neither peace nor coexistence between Islamic faith and non-Islamic social and political institutions."

Another question: what did U.S. Secretary of State James Baker know that his haughty counterparts in Western Europe did not know when he told the leaders of Slovenia and Croatia, in the spring of 1991, that if they went ahead unilaterally with their announced plans to secede, there would be civil war?

He was no doubt thinking of the Yugoslav National Army, to which the late dictator Tito often referred in public speeches as the ultimate savior of Yugoslavia. How far would this army have gone? We know that it pulled back rather quickly after the Slovenes fired the first shots in what was to become the civil war. We also know that it was far more determined when Croatia and Bosnia-

Herzegovina sought to secede. But we do not know the role of the ethnic components of that army.

Baker had the only sensible and realistic approach when he told the Yugoslavs that if they insisted on going their separate ways, we would respect their wishes, and that when they reached a political settlement, the U.S. would take up the question of recognition. We do not know what made him cave in to the European Community's position.

As one looks at the various questions and considerations, one is left with a tentative conclusion: much, although not all, of the bloodshed might have been avoided if the European Community had listened to James Baker, and avoided the lack of evenhandedness which every would-be peacemaker must possess if there is to be any hope for success.

ETHNIC CLEANSING
IN YUGOSLAVIA
(August, 1992)

Rational human beings are horrified by the reports of "ethnic cleansing" in what was Yugoslavia. It is not pretty and it is to be condemned. Many outsiders are angry and frustrated, because they feel helpless and because they are at a loss to explain why it is happening. This often leads to false or misleading statements in news stories, editorials, and letters to the editor.

Although primary blame is being heaped upon the Serbs, there is ample evidence that the Croats and Muslims are also guilty. It is time that all be blamed.

We know what "ethnic cleansing" meant in Hitler's Germany, and we had hoped that it would never be repeated.

To understand the Yugoslav situation, a bit of history is a must. Most of the ethnic violence among the Yugoslavs is not ancient, but a product of this century, beginning with the First World War, but mainly related to the Second World War.

Much of what we are condemning in Yugoslavia, sad to say, is irrational revenge for happenings in World War II and in the years of the Tito regime. During the Second World war, as a Yugoslav historian has written, "the Serbs were on everyone's hit list" (Hitler's and Mussolini's, but also Bulgaria's, Albania's, and Hungary's, as well as Yugoslavia's Croats and Muslims).

The Serbs did not invent "ethnic cleansing"; it was practiced on them on a grand scale by Hitler's imitator, the Nazi puppet regime in satellite Croatia. Some 700,000 Serbs, as well as some 60,000 Jews and 20,000 Gypsies, were massacred by the minions of that regime.

What is more, many of those brutalities were more odious than any we have been witnessing recently, but TV cameras were not there to bring them into our living rooms.

Serbian communities were not simply shelled. Serbian men, women and children were herded into Serbian churches and then the structures were set on fire. Moreover, in one part of the Croatian puppet state (Herzegovina), Serbs were brutally murdered and thrown into deep crevasses, some still alive. Elsewhere there were death camps, where the inmates met the same fate as the Jews in Germany.

The Serbs were also the subjects of ethnic cleansing after the war in Serbia's Kosovo province (the cradle of the Serbian nation and the location of its historic cultural monuments). For some 35 years, Muslim Albanians persecuted the Serbs, so that their percentage of the population in Kosovo was reduced from nearly 50 percent to about 12 percent. The persecutions - murder, rape, beatings, desecration of churches and monasteries, setting barns and haystacks on fire, theft of livestock and timber, etc. - were calculated to force the Serbs to leave Kosovo, and they did in large numbers.

Ironically, Tito's Communist comrades aided and abetted the persecutions. Pleas for help fell on deaf ears.

Only when Slobodan Milosevic became head of the Serbian Communist Party in 1986, and came to the defense of the Serbs in Kosovo, did the world come to realize that the Serbs had been victims of ethnic cleansing for some 35 years! But we seem not to remember today!

Why cannot the world see that the grapes of racial wrath were stored in Croat Tito's Communist vintage? He told the world that his regime had brought "Brotherhood and Unity" to the peoples of Yugoslavia, but we can now see what a tragic farce that turned out to be.

Under Tito, no effort was made to make amends to the Serbs for the misdeeds of Hitler's imitators in Axis Croatia. And all the while his regime was tolerating the ethnic cleansing of Serbs in Kosovo, perpetrated by his Muslim Albanian comrades.

Granted, Yugoslavia is a complex and complicated problem, but that should not give the media license to spread biased and often vicious information. Just one example: the Serbs did not drop into Bosnia from Mars or from Serbia, for that matter. They have been there for centuries. Before any fighting broke out, the Serbs inhabited about 60 percent of the territory.

Another example, Serbia did not sneak guns into Bosnia. After his break with Moscow in 1948, Tito moved most of the country's armaments industry to Bosnia, so that the Bosnian Serbs already had guns and ammunition.

And why, many may ask, does the media concentrate on the acts of Serbs and ignores those of Croats and Muslims, even though the commander of the UN mission in Sarajevo, General MacKenzie, has provided ample information? One example: for more than a month, Croatian army forces have been shelling the city of Trebinje in Bosnia-Herzegovina, and yet not a word about those horrors from either the media or the State Department!

Once upon a time we boasted that we were the best informed people in the world. Sad to say, that boast has come to haunt us today.

OPEN LETTER TO THE U.S. MEDIA
(October, 1992)

For well over a year, as Yugoslavia moved from disintegration to civil war, I tried to keep abreast of the reporting and commentary on that tragedy. I have been struck by a colorless and largely meaningless sameness in all of the media, with no effort to analyze except to suggest that Serbia's president, Slobodan Milosevic, wanted to create a Great Serbia. Moreover, in most of the reporting there seemed to be an unexamined assumption that the conflict was a struggle between the forces of democracy (the republics that wanted to secede from Yugoslavia) and the forces of communism (mainly Serbia) that wanted to keep the country intact.

I have been puzzled why such a simplistic and misleading view has not been challenged by any prominent reporter or commentator. Or why have leading Democrats endorsed rather than challenged a failed Republican policy? In my 60 years of observing political events, if memory serves, there was always someone endowed with the spirit of critical inquiry - the "show me" attitude - to challenge "received" wisdom. I recall, for example, that in the 1930s a number of our leading pundits defended what Hitler was doing in Europe on the grounds that he was rejecting the supposedly punitive Versailles Treaty.

In the case of Yugoslavia, we cannot avoid asking why our major media outlets have become so homogenized that they treat events there in a way that reminds one of the output of propaganda ministries in dictatorships?

It is interesting that in a number of leading British newspapers, at least recently, one can find significantly varied commentaries and analyses of the issues in the Yugoslav civil war that is lacking in the American media.

How can one explain the lack of investigative search for the truth in American publications? Is it laziness? Lack of knowledge of history? Something else?

The errors of commission and omission are many, and the over-simplifications and half-truths have been legion. Let me be specific.

1. Why has not the assertion that Yugoslavia was "Serb-dominated" been questioned, when much evidence exists to support the contrary position?

2. Why have not newsmen questioned the contention that the Yugoslav Army was the instrument of Serbia? Why has not Tito's ideological mission for the Army been pointed to as the motivating force for what that Army has done?

3. Why has no one in the media pointed out that those who wanted to save the Yugoslav nation acted similarly to Lincoln when he sent troops to the Southern states to prevent secession?

4. Why has no one in media compared the actions of the Serbs in Croatia to those of the citizens of Virginia who refused to secede and in 1863 formed the State of West Virginia?

5. Why has there been such reluctance to admit that Communism is no more popular in Serbia than in other parts of

Yugoslavia? Or if Communism is the issue, why regard the boundaries imposed by Communist Tito as sacrosanct, when no such boundaries existed prior to Communist rule?

6. Why has no one in the media challenged the justice of the West's asking Serbia to be satisfied to have one-third of her compatriots living outside Serbia, when Serbia in more than one war sacrificed enormously to liberate the Serbs of Bosnia and elsewhere?

7. Why have the media repeatedly asserted that the Serbs seized or captured two-thirds of Bosnia, but never told their audiences that *before* any fighting took place, the Serbs inhabited over 60% of it, that they had lived there for centuries, etc.?

8. Why have newsmen not asked about how much the West contributed to the bloodshed by the hasty recognition of the secessionist republics and thereby sought to internationalize internal Yugoslav domestic borders, opening the floodgates of ethnic hatreds?

9. Why did not reporters ask Western leaders, when they were expressing sympathies for the grievances of the secessionist republics through the recognitions, did they give their *only* ally in the Balkans in two world wars, Serbia, any assurance that in any final settlement, its grievances would also be addressed?

10. When reporting on "ethnic cleansing," why have the media concentrated on Serbs' actions exclusively and not even a paragraph on the equally brutal atrocities committed against the Serbs by the Muslims and Croats?

11. Why have the media been so reluctant to acknowledge that some of the most odious atrocities in Sarajevo that were blamed on the Serbs subsequently turned out to have been the work of Muslims?

12. And when trouble erupts in Kosovo, as it is likely, will the media totally ignore the "ethnic cleansing" of Serbs by the Kosovo Albanians during 35 years of Tito's rule?

The questions could go on. President Bush asserted recently that in Bosnia there was a "flagrant disregard for human life." When, in a civil war, has there been a regard for human life? And when it comes to war prisons, what about Andersonville in our Civil War?

Looking back on the reporting on Yugoslavia in the U.S. media, can anyone really say that we are the best informed people in the world? What does the media have to say for themselves?

YUGOSLAV EXPERTS
DISCUSS YUGOSLAVIA
(December, 1992)

Yugoslavia received prominent attention from scholars at the recently held annual convention of the American Association for the Advancement of Slavic Studies in Phoenix (November 19-22). I sat in on three sessions, titled as follows: "Bridging Ethnic Cleavages: Soviet and Yugoslav Lessons"; "Political Events in the Yugoslav Republics, 1991-92"; "The Sources of Serbian Discontent with Yugoslavia."

Among the panel of scholars were: Professors Robin Remington (political science, University of Missouri); Robert Hayden (anthropology, University of Pittsburgh); John Treadway (history, University of Richmond); and Dennison Rusinow (history-political science, University of Pittsburgh). There were others, but I single these out because (1) none of them is of Yugoslav ancestry, and (2) all have devoted years in following Yugoslav events, have spent time there, and know the primary language.

While none of the sessions were closed, I do not want to attribute exact quotes to any one panelist, or to others who participated, but rather to report on general conclusions.

First, there seemed to be general agreement that the West had mismanaged the Yugoslav crisis, particularly by the hasty recognition of secessionist republics. No panel member defended the West's policies and none supported military intervention. Some panel members bitterly criticized Germany's role. One panel member asserted that the "West went into Yugoslavia as firefighters but ended up being pyromaniacs."

Some commentators observed that none of the basic problems were tackled prior to the secession declarations, e.g., agreement on boundaries and the arsenals of the Yugoslav National Army, which were located in each of the republics. One commentator pointed out that many projects had been financed from federal funds (e.g., dams and factories) or were built by the Yugoslav National Army (e.g., highways and the Olympic Village in Sarajevo). Some agreement on these and similar matters, he said, should have been sought if secessions were to avoid armed conflict.

Second, there was substantial agreement that the West should have distinguished between the Serbs' legitimate interests and the methods that Serbs have used in efforts to achieve them. Moreover, the West should have distinguished between the Serbian people and the Communist rulers that were part of the Titoist system which the West had supported, and who were not freely chosen by the people.

While not defending Serbian use of force, some commentators insisted that the lack of evenhandedness by the West in its approach toward the Serbs left the latter little choice. For example, the West recognized the right of self-determination for the Slovenes and Croats but not the Serbs. A particularly sore point for the Serbs was Communist Tito's division of the country so that one-third of the Serbs (mainly in Croatia and Bosnia-Herzegovina) were left outside the Republic of Serbia.

A primary stumbling block to peace is the seeming inability of the countries of the West to face the consequences of a contradiction that they created, i.e., that it was okay for the Slovenes and Croats to change borders by force while denying the same right to the Serbs.

Third, there was basic agreement that in Bosnia-Herzegovina all parties (Serbs, Croats, and Muslims) were guilty of "ethnic cleansing" and the accompanying atrocities, but that numerically the Serbs committed a larger number.

As to the future, one of the panelists observed that the West's latest plan for Bosnia-Herzegovina (dividing it into seven or eight units, but not along ethnic lines) would not work. He gave two reasons: (1) at present Bosnia-Herzegovina does not exist; it is a legal fiction, and (2) the proposed constitution looks like the Yugoslav Constitution of 1974, which Serbs, Croats, and Slovenes did not accept, but worked on nationalist agendas. Consequently, there was no reason to believe that the three Bosnian groups would accept its counterpart.

In all, there was a great deal of pessimism, and some audience participants did engage in ethnic recriminations. But no one seemed to have a solution.

NEW COURSE IN SEEKING
PEACE IN YUGOSLAVIA
(March, 1993)

Given the past policies of the West, the prospects for a resolution of the Yugoslav civil war are almost nil. Therefore two realistic alternatives present themselves: (1) adopt a hands-off policy or (2) adopt a new course. There is little else that merits consideration. Responsible leaders must face up to this position.

In view of the alarm that has been built up concerning the nature of the civil war, public opinion may find the first alternative unacceptable. But if responsible leaders find for such a course, they must sell it to the public. And in view of so many seemingly intractable foreign policy problems around the world, I am confident that a hands-off policy can be defended.

On the other hand, adopting a hands-off policy would be tantamount to an admission of defeat for leaders in the West, who might find it difficult to abandon their efforts.

If the second alternative is chosen, a demonstration of impartiality is the first prerequisite, which until now has been lacking. To this end, the United States will need to take the lead, because in the view of the largest ethnic group - the Serbs - it was not the U.S. that initiated the failed Yugoslav policy, but the West Europeans. Moreover, historically the U.S. has been seen by all the Yugoslav ethnic groups as impartial and fair. It is the only power, in my opinion, that has the possibility of reclaiming the high ground so as to promote a fair settlement. Of course, it will need the advice and support of its allies.

First, the United States must declare its willingness to undertake the task, and to ask all Yugoslav participants to cooperate in reaching a fair settlement.

Second, it must state that Western efforts to find a solution through the recognition of the secessionist republics was a mistake, because the legitimate grievances of the ethnic groups that did not want to secede were thereby ignored.

Third, it must assert that the legacy of Tito's arbitrary drawing of Yugoslavia's internal borders is not sacrosanct, and that a lasting settlement will aim at re-drawing borders so as to follow ethnic lines in as practicable a way as possible. Moreover, it should say that plebiscites and arbitration tribunals would be employed when appropriate.

Fourth, the U.S. must operate from the framework of the three areas that initially constituted Yugoslavia - Slovenia, Croatia, and Serbia (the latter now allied with Montenegro to form the Third Yugoslavia).

Fifth, if the Serbs and Croats of Bosnia-Herzegovina should opt to join Serbia and Croatia respectively, which seems very likely, the heretofore projected multi-ethnic Bosnian state must be abandoned. At the same time, the Muslims that would find themselves in Croatia or Serbia must be guaranteed autonomous units with broad powers, comparable to those given Croatia in the August 1939 agreement (*Sporazum*).

Sixth, Kosovo must be given broad powers of autonomy comparable to that given the Muslims. If such an arrangement should prove impossible, Serbian and Kosovo authorities would be advised to seek a division of Kosovo so as to separate Serbs and Albanians permanently, understandably with provision for exchange of populations and compensation for properties.

Finally, Macedonia would have to be considered for a United Nations trusteeship, pending the working out of relations between Yugoslavia and the peoples of Macedonia to the end that Macedonia would be an autonomous unit within Yugoslavia. This will prove difficult, because of Albanian, Serbian, and Bulgarian minorities, which may raise questions similar to those in Bosnia-Herzegovina, i.e., just how many people would be left that considered themselves Macedonians.

It is only by making a fresh start, free from preconceived value judgments and notions, that the U.S. may contribute to a just lasting solution in the Yugoslav quagmire. This fresh beginning demands a thorough re-examination of the historical, ethnic, cultural, religious, legal, and moral origins of the present conflict. The diagnosis on which a failed policy was based must be discarded in favor of a new diagnosis, one that can provide the basis for a policy that has a chance of achieving a fair settlement.

PRESIDENT CLINTON'S LESSON IN BOSNIA
(April, 1993)

At his recent press conference, President Clinton demonstrated that he knew a great deal more about Bosnia than his questioners, who in the past have expressed doubts about his preparation in the area of foreign affairs.

Acknowledging that Bosnia-Herzegovina was "the most difficult foreign policy problem we face," the President said that the "United States is not - is not, should not become involved as a partisan in a war." Nor can it or the United Nations "enter a war in effect to redraw ... the geographical lines of republics within what was Yugoslavia."

We can only speculate as what he has learned about the mistakes of the previous administration in seeking to deal with the whole Yugoslav problem, but one can infer a great deal from the above-quoted remarks, because the West's interference has been undisguised. That he failed to point to those mistakes was perhaps less out of generosity to the Bush Administration than to his fear that he might be seen as backing away from tough decisions.

The President has no doubt asked some important questions, but he needs to ask some others, if he has not already done so.

It is imperative that he inquire about the basic assumption that guides those who favor intervention, especially military actions. That assumption is that the Serbs - even those who are native residents of Bosnia where their forebears have lived for centuries - are guilty of aggression. That assumption is entirely false. Since the civil war began in Yugoslavia, not a single soldier has gone outside Yugoslav boundaries and no military action has taken place outside those borders.

As a Southerner, the President must know that during our Civil War, the Confederate press referred to it as the "War of Northern Aggression." As President of the United States, he must have some appreciation of the situation that confronted President Lincoln. If the international community had been strong enough and inclined to operate on the basis of the arguments of today's interventionists, the Civil War would have been declared over and Lincoln would have been told to accept the Confederate States of America as an independent country or else. We know that England wanted to recognize the Confederacy, and had indeed provided some help. We also know that in that eventuality Lincoln was prepared for war with the English.

The President also needs to ask why the Bush Administration, at the time that Yugoslavia was beginning to fall apart, did not talk with the central Yugoslav government, especially the Serbs in that government, about resolving basic issues without bloodshed. Instead, the U.S. followed Germany's lead in the European Community and recognized the secessionist republics of Slovenia, Croatia, and Bosnia-Herzegovina, totally ignoring Serbian interests.

There are those who ask, rhetorically, why the West should have listened to the Serbs. I believe that the answer is fairly simple. Basically for the same reason that we listen to the British when we have differences. As the only proven Balkan friend and ally of the West in two world wars, the Serbs deserve to be listened to. In addition, they are the largest ethnic group in Yugoslavia and were the strongest supporters of the common state, which the West said it favored. Moreover, if one is to act as peacemaker, he needs to talk to both sides.

The Serbs' main grievance was Communist dictator Tito's carving up Yugoslavia into republics, which left one-third of the Serbs living outside the Republic of Serbia, mainly in Bosnia-Herzegovina and Croatia. Serbia and Montenegro had fought in the Balkan war of 1912 and the First World War to liberate those regions from the Ottoman and Austro-Hungarian empires, and since 1918 the Serbs from those regions lived in a common state with the Serbs of Serbia and Montenegro.

Consequently, Serbian actions in the present civil war are not based on some mystical medieval dream of a Serbian Empire, but on what was achieved at the end of World War I.

By ignoring these realities, the West virtually guaranteed the present tragic situation. Moreover, how can the Vance-Owen proposals be imposed on the Serbs when there was never agreement that what they proposed would be accepted as binding arbitration?

If President Clinton does not grasp the folly of past Western actions, there would seem to be no way of avoiding a disaster with unknown consequences.

WAS BOSNIAN INTERVENTION IDEA BASED ON SHIFTING SAND?
(May, 1993)

President Clinton's search for a military option in Bosnia, and the failed attempt to sell it to the Allies, no doubt gave him time to wonder if perhaps he had a more serious problem. On the basis of the available evidence, he seems initially to have acted on a fundamental misunderstanding of the Yugoslav situation and particularly that in Bosnia-Herzegovina.

His statement on May 6, 1993, that "The Serbs' actions over the past year violate the principle that internationally recognized borders must not be violated or altered by aggression from without," seems to have given way to a recognition that it is after all, a civil war.

Instead of leading him to high ground, his advisers had ill-served him by leading him into a political swamp. They failed to point out that instead of a war of aggression, this was a civil war. Not a single shot has been fired or a single soldier killed outside the boundaries of what was the Yugoslav state. Moreover, the fighting in Bosnia has been by persons - Serbs, Croats, Muslims - who are residents of the area. In most cases, their ancestors had lived there for hundreds of years.

Of equal importance is the fact that prior to the outbreak of the civil war, the only internationally recognized borders were those of Yugoslavia. It was Slovenia and Croatia that first violated those borders, followed by Bosnia-Herzegovina. The West, by recognizing them and thereby seeking by the stroke of a diplomatic pen to create new international boundaries even where none had existed historically, aided and abetted them in the violation of the Helsinki Accords proviso against changing internationally recognized borders by force. It is important to note that the fighting began before the Western leaders could "create" these new boundaries. They, in effect, sought to determine, in its early stages, the outcome of at least one part of the Yugoslav civil war so as to favor some contenders at the expense of others.

Secondly, the President's foreign policy advisers misled him into proceeding on the assumption that the losers in the civil war, i.e., the Muslims, should somehow be rescued. Instead of encouraging them to lay down their arms and seek an armistice and eventually a peaceful settlement, the West held out the hope that help was coming, and thereby contributed to prolonging the carnage.

Correspondingly, Mr. Clinton's advisers proceeded on the assumption that the Serbs should be made to accept a loser's peace. Even the peacemakers - Cyrus Vance and Lord Owen - who generally tried to be neutral, wound up proposing a solution for Bosnia that was detrimental to the Serbs.

Instead of the 70 percent of the area that the Serbs now hold, they would get only 43 percent under the Vance-Owen Plan, even though they inhabited over 60 percent before the fighting began. Moreover, the Plan proposed geographical lines unfavorable to the Serbs, while rewarding the Croats and Muslims with industrial regions as well as those with natural resources.

The question arises as to why the President has been so ill-served by his advisers. One answer is that his top national security team simply knows very little about Yugoslavia. Secretary of State Warren Christopher demonstrated some appreciation of the Yugoslav problem, but both he and the President have been under great pressure by members of Congress, the most vocal of whom have exhibited very little knowledge of what the Yugoslav civil war is all about. And some young professional foreign service officers have argued with Christopher, contributing to a basically false view of what has been going on in Yugoslavia. Their motivation is far from clear.

The President has also been ill-served by the media, both print and electronic, which seem determined to make U.S. foreign policy. Only recently have one or two pundits begun to admit that the public has been given an erroneous view of the civil war in what was Yugoslavia.

The President would seem to be on firmer ground with this suggestion of sending peace-keepers to monitor Macedonia's borders and those between Serbia and Bosnia, but in that case there should be monitors on the Croat-Bosnian border as well. It is to be hoped that the faulty analysis undergirding the idea of military intervention in Bosnia has been discarded in favor of a more realistic appraisal of what lies behind that tragic civil war.

It is too early to predict how the newest idea, i.e., creating several "safe havens" in Bosnia, principally for the Muslims, will work out. It was rejected by Bosnian President Izetbegovic the day after it was announced in Washington. The Serbs, however, viewed it favorably as a step leading to the division of Bosnia into three parts - Serb, Croat, and Muslim.

It should be noted that the newest idea is but a further attempt to deal with the consequences of an initially failed Western policy.

SERBIA: WHY DID THE WEST MISCALCULATE?
(August, 1993)

Serbia and its president, Slobodan Milosevic, may stand condemned in the eyes of the international community for their part in the Yugoslav civil war. Whatever one's view of Serbia's actions, several questions need an answer. First of all, did anyone in the West make an assessment of Serbia's capabilities and intentions? If so, why were the Western leaders' estimates of Serbia's national interest so faulty? Again, assuming that Western leaders did make an effort to assess Serbia's possible actions, why was their judgment so wide of the mark?

These questions inevitably lead to others, which may give us a better picture of considerations that Western policy-makers should have been aware.

Did the West forget that in 1911-12, Serbia organized the Balkan states (Bulgaria, Greece, Montenegro, Romania, Serbia) for the conflict that drove the Turks from Europe? In that Balkan war, Serbia regained the cradle of the Serbian nation, Kosovo, which the Ottoman Turks took over in 1389, as they destroyed the Serbian state.

Did the West forget that in 1914, the Serbs stood up to the mighty Austro-Hungarian Empire, and that in that war the Serbs of Montenegro and Serbia lost 40 percent of all mobilized men, losses that were three times those of Great Britain and France? That in that war Serbian lands in Bosnia-Herzegovina and Croatia were liberated, and that Slovenes and Croats implored Serbia to form a common union - a Yugoslav state - which was done?

Did the West also forget that in 1941 the Serbs said "No" to Nazi Germany at the height of Hitler's power, and that in the resulting war and civil war Serbian losses exceeded one million lives?

Did anyone take into account this historic persistence, determination, yes, even stubbornness, of the Serbs in defense of their national interests? Did the West believe that the Serbs would sit idly by and see their achievements, won with so many sacrifices, go down the drain?

Did Western policy-makers consider the long term implications for the West in the Balkans, given the fact that Serbs had been allied with the West in two world wars, and would probably play a pivotal role in that part of the world in the future?

Did Western leaders contemplate the impact of their aiding in the demise of Yugoslavia, a charter member of the League of Nations and of the United Nations, on the Serbs, the strongest supporter of the common state?

Did the United States weigh the possible consequences of suggesting to the Bosnian Muslim leaders that the European Community brokered agreement of dividing Bosnia-Herzegovina along ethnic lines, which they signed with the Serbs and Croats in March 1992 (before the fighting broke out), was a bad agreement? We know that the Muslims reneged on the agreement soon after they signed it.

Did responsible leaders in the West make an assessment of the depth of determination of the Serbs in Croatia and Bosnia not to live in a Croatian or Muslim-dominated state?

It would not seem reasonable to conclude that Western leaders were not aware of the foregoing considerations, although there is little doubt that they underestimated them. In any case, it is necessary to ask what factors led the West to conclude that the Serbs would do nothing as they saw their hard-won achievements begin to disappear?

First of all, the civil war during World War II and in the early years of Tito's Communist dictatorship, the cream of Serbia's potential nationalist leadership was wiped out, imprisoned, or fled abroad.

Secondly, and a corollary of the above, the Serbs in the Yugoslav Communist party were supine collaborators in Croat Tito's anti-Serb policies. Hence there was little or no expectation that Serb Communists would defend Serbia's traditional national interests.

Thirdly, it had been generally recognized that the Serbian cadre in the Yugoslav Communist party was weak, and Serb Communists who were suspect of the slightest independence were purged. In the post-Tito period, 1980 and after, the Serb cadre was still looked upon as weak, and initially Slobodan Milosevic seemed to be no exception. After all, he came out of the same party structure.

Fourth, for years the Serbs in the national leadership did nothing about the persecution of their fellow Serbs at the hands of the Albanians in Kosovo. Desperate pleas of Kosovo Serbs fell on deaf ears, even in the 1980s after Tito's death. Even after the Kosovo Albanian demonstrations in 1981, which were clearly anti-Yugoslav, the responsible Communist leaders in Kosovo (Albanians and even Serbs) did not lose their positions. From time to time, the Yugoslav Communist party leadership issued declarations critical of separatist Albanian actions, and insisted that party policies must be adhered to, but nothing really changed.

It is true that after Milosevic became head of the Serbian party, he did in 1986 and 1987 take stands in defense of the Kosovo Serbs, but even then doubts remained as to his real commitment. Urgent and repeated pleas from the Serbian Bar Association for the rectification of specific injustices were more or less ignored. And most of the Kosovo bureaucrats continued in their positions.

Fifth, another reason for the West's miscalculation concerns the Yugoslav National Army, which in Tito's frequent public statements, had been depicted as the ultimate guardian of Yugoslavia. When it failed to stop the secession of Slovenia, the West may have viewed Tito's assurances as empty boasts. We now know that while the Yugoslav National Army's officer corps was falling into disarray along nationality lines, it was far from impotent, as experience was to demonstrate.

Finally, the key positions in the Yugoslav national government, at the time of the Slovene and Croat secessions in June 1991, were in the hands of non-Serbs except for the minister of defense and supreme commander, who was the product of a Serb-Croat marriage. While that cabinet acted promptly and forcefully, it was generally viewed as weak.

Others may be able to add to my analysis, but whatever the reasons, there is no escaping the fact that the West miscalculated badly and with tragic consequences.

BOSNIA: IN DEFENSE OF CLINTON
(October, 1993)

President Clinton has been getting a bad rap with respect to his actions or inactions in Bosnia-Herzegovina, and he has been getting it from all sides. The most vocal have been the hawks, most of whom were doves in the Gulf and Vietnam wars. But those who feared a quagmire in what was Yugoslavia have also made themselves heard.

In point of fact, Clinton faced an impossible task, made particularly difficult by his own careless comments during last year's presidential campaign. He, in effect, adopted a failed Republican policy and became stuck with it. So instead of tackling the problems that brought about the civil war, he and his advisers have been battling the consequences of a failed policy.

President Bush and his Secretary of State, James Baker, were on the right track initially, when they indicated that the U.S. would wait until the Yugoslav groups had reached political settlements before taking up the question of diplomatic recognition. But at some point they were sold a bill of goods by the West Europeans, who had acted mainly on German initiative, orchestrated by Bonn's foreign minister, Hans Dietrich Genscher, who subsequently resigned because he realized that his policy of hasty recognitions had failed.

Bush and Baker had followed the general policy of the West of supporting an integral Yugoslav state, a founding member of the League of Nations and of the United Nations, and a defector from the Soviet Union's international Communist movement.

When in early 1991 the signs of Yugoslavia's possible disintegration were fairly clear, Secretary Baker indicated to the Yugoslavs that the U.S. would prefer that the various ethnic groups stay together, but if they should split up, the question of diplomatic recognition, as indicated above, would be deferred until political settlements were reached. Moreover, he warned the leaders of Slovenia and Croatia, the two republics that seemed determined to secede, that if they seceded unilaterally there would be civil war.

The West Europeans exercised no such caution, proceeding in January 1992 with the recognition of Slovenia and Croatia, totally ignoring possible actions by Serbia in defense of its national interests. Regrettably, for still not completely clear reasons, the U.S. changed its policy and in April told the Europeans that if they recognized Bosnia-Herzegovina, the U.S. would recognize the three secessionist republics. That was done.

Governor Clinton did not know the Yugoslav problem, but Senator Gore did, or thought he did, and he is primarily the one who misled Clinton.

Gore's knowledge of Yugoslavia - misinformation is a better word - came from his foreign policy adviser, a retired American foreign service officer who had served in Zagreb, Croatia, and who had become pro-Croatian, anti-Serb, and anti-Yugoslav.

To compound President Clinton's lack of balance concerning the Yugoslav question is the fact that he was badly served by his foreign policy team, either because of a lack of expertise or for other reasons.

In addition, the State Department professionals were also lacking in expertise, or their voices never reached the all-important policy-making level. The former seems more likely, because State Department officials who resigned in protest of Clinton's and Christopher's Bosnia policy had never served in Yugoslavia. My own experience and association with U.S. foreign service professionals, who were heads of the Yugoslav desk, indicates that they were appointed to that position only after having served in Yugoslavia.

We may never know why there was a seeming shortage of Yugoslav experts at the working level in the State Department at this critical time.

In any event, it needs to be noted that in every conflict, especially a civil war, there are at least two sides to be heard from. For some unknown reasons, neither the Bush nor Clinton administrations, judged on the basis of their actions, ever heard the Serbian side in that tragic conflict.

To be sure, many of the Serbian actions in that civil war led to condemning the Serbs and Serbia, but there is something suspicious in the way that the anti-Serb campaign has been orchestrated, to the almost exclusive neglect of the acts of the Muslims and Croats.

Moreover, the President's vacillation as demonstrated by assertions that the U.S. "should not become involved as a partisan in a war," that the United Nations should not "enter a war in effect to redraw the geographic lines of republics within what was Yugoslavia," and his statements that encouraged the Muslims to believe that the U.S. would rescue them by military intervention, would seem to need explanation.

Taken together, all of the above-mentioned factors must be weighed in any fair assessment of the Clinton administration's actions concerning the Yugoslav tragedy.

BEHIND THE YUGOSLAV CIVIL WAR
(October, 1993)

Nearly all non-specialists with whom I have discussed Yugoslav events of the past two years are confused and puzzled. They repeatedly ask: what are the issues in that conflict?

Yugoslavia, admittedly a complex and complicated subject, has been made all the more so by the ineptitude of the Western great powers, and made almost incomprehensible by the failure of the media to present an understandable story.

At the risk of over-simplification, it can be said that two major factors contributed to the break-up of Yugoslavia and the consequent civil war.

The first is the failure of the Communist system to deal effectively with the country's economic and political problems. As in the case of other Communist-ruled states, the economy was "run into the ground." The resultant bickering among the ethnic groups making up the country as to who was at fault led to the division of the country's ruling Communist party into individual Communist parties based on ethnic or nationality lines. Moreover, as Communism was failing, the various dissident elements were never able to agree on a national alternative to the failed system.

Contributing to the difficulties was the "Communist solution" to the nationality problem. Communist dictator Josip Broz Tito (of Croat-Slovene parentage) divided the country into republics, something that was not true of interwar Yugoslavia (1918-1941). That in itself might not have been bad if it had not been for Tito's determination to punish Serbia, where the wartime Communist movement was not successful. He did that by drawing the republic lines so that one-third of the Serbs were left outside the Republic of Serbia, mostly in a republic not based on nationality, Bosnia-

Herzegovina, but also in Croatia. His anti-Serb action was to constitute a time-bomb when Yugoslavia began to disintegrate.

Adding insult to injury, Tito created two autonomous provinces inside the republic of Serbia - Kosovo, the cradle of the Serbian nation, but by 1946 having a small Albanian majority (to which Tito's policies significantly contributed) and Vojvodina, with a large Hungarian minority.

Moreover, Tito proclaimed the nationality problem solved, and brutally punished anyone who would dare to disagree. Hence, grievances could not be addressed, and no dialogue could take place, with the result that ethnic hatreds seethed below the surface. To a large degree, this explains the eruption of unusually bitter ethnic violence when Communism was in the process of disintegrating.

The second factor that led to the break-up of Yugoslavia was the West's mismanagement of the Yugoslav crisis. When in 1991, Slovenia and Croatia declared that they were seceding from Yugoslavia, they not only violated the country's constitution, but also the Helsinki Accords proviso against changing internationally recognized borders by force (Slovenes fired the first shots in the civil war).

The European Community's hasty recognition of the Slovene and Croat secessions (subsequently also Bosnia-Herzegovina's) thus aided and abetted the secessionist republic's violation of the Helsinki Accords, of which Yugoslavia and the EC countries were signatories. That in itself may not have led to civil war, if the EC had been even-handed toward Serbia. On the contrary, EC had decided that while self-determination was okay for the secessionist republics it should not apply to the Serbs, some 600,000 in Croatia and 1.5 million in Bosnia-Herzegovina. That policy was a formula for disaster, as the revolt of these Serbs demonstrated.

Parenthetically, it should be noted that the West's lack of evenhandedness enables Serbia's Communist president, Slobodan Milosevic, to pose as the sole defender of Serbian interests, with untoward troubles. For their part, the Western leaders, instead of admitting their mistakes and seeking to correct them, concentrated on attempting to find ways of dealing with the consequences of a failed policy.

The Serbs in Croatia feared being part of that state because of the massive massacre of Serbs during the existence of the quisling

Croat state that was allied with Germany and Italy during World War II. And the Serbs in Bosnia-Herzegovina feared an Islamic state, as promised by the republic's president, Alija Izetbegovic, in his book *The Islamic Declaration*, first published in 1970 and reissued in 1990. That work, among other things, states that "there can be neither peace nor coexistence between the Islamic religion and non-Islamic social and political institutions." In addition, "the press, radio, television and film should be in the hands of people whose Islamic moral and intellectual authority is indisputable."

For tactical reasons, the Muslims have avoided publicizing these aims, but they have never renounced them. Also for the same reasons, they forged an alliance with the Croats to fight against the Serbs. For their part, the Croats should also have feared an Islamic state. In any case, the alliance fell apart in the summer of 1993, and the two began to war on each other.

Tragically, the media rarely shed any light on the essential factors discussed above. On the contrary, the main stories were about the actual fighting - the shelling of cities, atrocities, and other acts of war, of which Serbs, Croats, and Muslims were all guilty, if not in the same measure. And nary a reference to the basic causes of the conflict. Much was said about "Serbian aggression," with no attempt to define who is the aggressor in a civil war. Our own Civil War comes to mind. Was it the "War of Northern Aggression," as Confederate newspaper depicted it?

Moreover, there were no references to Serbian grievances, or the fact that Serbs had lived in Bosnia-Herzegovina for centuries, that before the civil war began they held over 60 percent of the area, and that two international acts supported the Serbs.

The first of these was the Treaty of London (1915) which promised to Serbia all of Bosnia-Herzegovina, some of present-day Croatia, and much of Dalmatia, while some of the latter, including the city of Dubrovnik, was promised to Montenegro. At that time, these areas were part of the Austro-Hungarian empire.

The second international act consisted of the Versailles treaties of St. Germain and Trianon, which ceded the above and other areas to the newly formed state of Yugoslavia (then known as the Kingdom of the Serbs, Croats, and Slovenes). This new state was regarded as the successor to Serbia, and all international acts to which Serbia was a party were transferred to it.

Quite aside from these acts, it should be noted that Serbia fought to liberate Serbian areas, at tremendous sacrifices, in the Balkan wars and the First World War.

Finally, no one seemed to question the right of great powers to provide international standing, with the stroke of a pen, to areas (e.g., Bosnia-Herzegovina) that had never existed as independent states. Or, with that same pen, convert a civil war into a war of aggression. And no one seems to have remembered that a portion of Virginia that did not want to join the Confederate States in seceding but wanted to remain a part of the Union, formed a new state - West Virginia.

None of this, however, is any comfort to the inhabitants of what was Yugoslavia.

NATO ACTION IN BOSNIA LEADING TO CATASTROPHE?
(March, 1994)

Before NATO leaders engage in too much self-congratulation with respect to their "achievements" in the Sarajevo operation, and are tempted to use a similar approach elsewhere in Bosnia, they need to reflect on what they accomplished and what precedent they may have set.

Secretary of State Warren Christopher pointed to the most important result - the creation of an opportunity for a peace settlement. If the Muslims can be persuaded to accept something close to the Owen-Stoltenberg Plan, accepted by the Croats and Serbs some months ago, then the Sarajevo operation will be judged a success. If not, great dangers will confront the NATO leaders.

All of us need to be reminded that NATO leaders, with the main initiative coming from President Clinton, violated a basic principle once enunciated by former Secretary of State, Cyrus Vance. He said that anyone seeking to be a peacemaker must not only be neutral, but must also be seen as neutral by all sides in a conflict.

The President and his NATO allies, before they proceed further down that road, should ponder the words of Cyrus Vance, as well as those of the former United Nations commander in Sarajevo, General Phillipe Morillon, who observed that recent history teaches us that "military intervention in a civil war to the benefit of one of the parties invariably leads to catastrophe."

It is one thing to seek to mediate between the parties in a civil war, but it is quite another thing to seek to reverse the result.

Clinton's lack of evenhandedness is once again illustrated by the news that his emissary, Ambassador Redman, has been meeting Croats and Muslims in an effort to patch up their former alliance against the Serbs. It should be noted that is was that alliance in 1992 that really set off the civil war in Bosnia-Herzegovina.

If the President is aware that this may get him deeper and deeper into a civil war, he will do his utmost to promote the much-needed peace settlement without delay. Surely, he cannot believe that the winners of that civil war, the Serbs, can be forced, step by step, to give up their victories.

Moreover, it does not seem realistic that Mr. Clinton and his advisers could completely ignore the warnings of United Nations commanders, e.g., General Morillon, that the Muslim president, Alija Izetbegovic, has been "basing his policy on a plan for international military intervention." Moreover, UNPROFOR reports have indicated that most often cease-fires were first violated by the Muslims.

It is imperative to be reminded of how Western leaders botched foreign policy making so crudely earlier in the conflict. Simply put, the hasty recognition of the secessionist republics was as if a divorce judge granted a decree to the party that first filed, without ever stopping to hear the other party. Worse than that, the other party (Serbia) was in effect told that it might as well forget about those other Serbs (areas and people) who had lived in a common state since 1918.

And anyone with even a smattering of Yugoslav history would have known that if Communist Tito's organization of that state were to disintegrate, the ethnic group with the greatest grievances would be the Serbs.

What is really puzzling is why no known American political leader, in or out of Congress, has seen through what to me seems fairly fundamental, and consequently proceeded to ask some pertinent questions.

Even more puzzling, why has no well-known media outlet, or known pundit or correspondent, raised any embarrassing questions? Why have they failed to inform the public of the basic issues in that civil war? Where is the traditional attitude of the inquiring reporter - the "show me" trademark? There have been a few scarce exceptions, but rarely if ever in a major publication or television broadcast.

In private conversations, many of my acquaintances have expressed puzzlement, and have asked me to explain the demonization of the Serbs to the exclusion of the other parties in that conflict. Sad to say, I am as puzzled as they.

More critical of all those in Bosnia as well as for the rest us: Will General Morillon's warning go unheeded - that military intervention in a civil war on behalf of one of the parties "invariably leads to catastrophe?"

There may still be time to avoid it if the United States can exert strong pressure on the Muslims to accept a peace proposal. Otherwise, the efforts to relieve Sarajevo may be for naught.

Finally, it is not too early to ask two critical questions: (1) what kind of precedent are NATO and the UN setting for intervention in other civil wars?, and (2) has the West now paved the way for Russian dominance in the Balkans, something that historically it had feared?

FORCE NOT THE WAY TO BOSNIAN PEACE
(April, 1994)

President Clinton has finally done it. He has led the West to drop all pretense of being evenhanded in Bosnia. He has several times referred to the conflict as a civil war - which it is - one in which we would not take sides. Moreover, he also said that the United States would send peace-keeping troops there only when the three sides in the conflict had freely reached a settlement. At the same time, he criticized the internationally-sponsored peace plan - accepted by the Serbs and Croats - as being unfair to the Muslims.

With the NATO air strikes, the mask of pretense to even-handedness has been dropped. In point of fact, however, for two years now the West has not been evenhanded. The pretense was only that, and not well-disguised.

The United States, it seems, is not immune to the tendency of all Great Powers to expect that other nation-states will do as they are told. Alas, all nation-states seem to believe that they should be treated as equals. The Russians have told us not to pressure them. The Chinese have said that they don't want us to lecture them. The North Koreans have in effect told us to butt out. Even the lowly Somalis and some others have told us where we can go.

And lo and behold! Even the Serbs have asked to be treated as equals, at least as equal as the Croats and Muslims, the other combatants in the civil war in Bosnia.

But we seem unable to learn. We pose as would-be peace makers, yet fail to adhere to the time-worn principle that an honest broker must not only be impartial, but also must be *seen* as impartial by all sides in a conflict.

From the beginning of the civil war in what was Yugoslavia, the United States, as well as the other Western powers, have operated on the assumption that only force can influence the Serbs.

In the latest foray by the Clinton Administration to clarify our policy in Bosnia, the President's National Security Adviser, Anthony Lake, indicated in a speech at Johns Hopkins University that we are still relying on threats of force as a way of getting Serb cooperation in the peace process. We must make it clear to the Serbs, he said, that "the costs of continued intransigence are high."

We ought not forget that two despicable actions in Sarajevo - the "breadline massacre" of May 1992 and the open market explosion of February 1994 - both unfairly attributed to the Serbs, were used as reasons for action against the Serbs. The first was the imposition of UN sanctions against the Serbs, and the second was the threat of air strikes unless the Bosnian Serbs withdrew their heavy weapons from around Sarajevo.

Consequently, we need to ask ourselves how would we expect someone to react who is being punished for things he has not done.

We are told that a wise old philosopher once observed that those who do not know history are doomed to repeat it. Now that we have pushed NATO to use air strikes, we seem determined to prove how *not* to achieve foreign policy objectives. By our actions we have also endangered another one of our proclaimed objectives, i.e., the survival of Yeltsin in Russia. And we will be no nearer to peace in Bosnia.

Serbs can be stubborn and not given to compromise, especially if convinced that they are right, and particularly if they are being pressured or threatened. We need to be reminded that in 1941 they said "No" to Hitler at the height of his power. As it turned out, it was a tragic mistake on the part of the Serbs, our allies in two world wars, but that is another story.

GREAT POWERS CONTINUE TO BUNGLE IN BOSNIA
(May, 1994)

As one who has followed the evolving tragedy in what was Yugoslavia, and particularly the Great Powers' efforts to deal with the conflict in Bosnia-Herzegovina, I am reminded of a farm hand friend of mine with whom I once worked at harvest time. He was trying to repair a piece of machinery, and I could see that he was going about it wrong. Just as I was about to say something, the foreman came along and tried to tell him. But my friend was bull-headed and continued his effort, determined that his way would prove to be right. In the end he had to admit that he was in error. As a result, we lost important time, but otherwise there were no serious consequences.

In Bosnia more than two years have passed since the Great Powers got involved, and they continue to bungle, determined that their way is right. The West's failure or refusal to recognize realities - first the failure to agree that the conflict was a civil war and secondly an unwillingness to acknowledge that the Bosnian Serbs had won it - prolonged the bloodshed. The West Europeans did suggest in February 1992 a three-way division, and in March such an agreement was signed by the leaders of the three groups, but the Muslim leader reneged after a conference with American Ambassador Warren Zimmermann. Moreover, the West Europeans, more realistic than the United States, subsequently proposed other solutions, first the Vance-Owen Plan, and later the Owen-Stoltenberg formula. The Bosnian Serbs and Croats accepted the latter, while the Muslims, encouraged by ill-advised statements from the Clinton Administration, rejected it and continued the war.

Had the U.S. backed the Europeans in support of the Owen-Stoltenberg Plan, the civil war could have ended a year ago. Although the area that the Serbs would get under that plan would have been about the same as the latest proposal, they were willing to accept it mainly because it allowed them to become a part of Serbia within a relatively short period of time. The plan was also attractive to the Bosnian Croats for precisely the same reason, i.e., that they could join Croatia.

The contact group's take-it-or-leave-it proposal does not afford the Serbs that choice, but it does allow the United States-sponsored Bosnian Muslim-Croat federation the right to establish a confederate relationship with Croatia. Paradoxically, the contact group, instead of building upon the earlier plans, produced a scheme that seemed designed to win the acceptance of the so-called Bosnian federation and almost certain rejection by the Bosnian Serbs. Did the contact group really believe that the Serbs might accept less than previous plans had offered them? Moreover, do the Great Powers believe that attempting to create a multi-ethnic Bosnia will succeed and that stability, their avowed goal, will result? Dream on, dear leaders!

The Bosnian Serbs, who inhabited nearly two-thirds of the area *before* the fighting began and now control approximately 70 percent, were willing to see their territory reduced to 50 percent, but clearly this was secondary to the right of joining Serbia.

We cannot, it seems to me, avoid the question of whether the costs of seeking to reverse what is viewed as an undesirable outcome of a civil war are justified in terms of the additional carnage of Bosnian Croats, Muslims, and Serbs.

Many will find this a troublesome, and indeed an unpalatable question, but I do not see how it can be avoided. Moreover, we cannot at this time be sure that citizens of the Great Powers will not also need to be sacrificed. Who can guarantee that a wrong approach, step by step, will not lead to the spilling of American blood in the Bosnian morass?

If our leaders are convinced that they are on the right path, they ought to tell the American people what may face them, so that all of us can proceed with eyes open. Anything less should not be acceptable.

DANGERS OF A WORLD WAR
(June, 1994)

The possibility of another world war is unthinkable to most of us, yet a cloud is on the horizon that may portend one. That cloud, no bigger than a man's fist, is the picture emerging from news stories that tell of the arrival in Bosnia of hundreds of Revolutionary Guards from Iran. Their avowed purpose is to radicalize the Bosnian Muslims, and no doubt eventually to set up a terrorist network in several European countries.

The arrival in Bosnia of Islamic fundamentalists from Arab countries is not new; we have been hearing of their presence for a number of months, as well as the dispatch of millions of dollars worth of arms and other aid from Saudi Arabia to the Bosnian Muslims. These activities are supposedly forbidden by the United Nations embargo.

What makes the present situation particularly dangerous is the attitude of the Bosnian Muslims. Heretofore, they have been saying that they desired to sign a peace settlement, while always finding some reason not to accept the solutions proposed by international negotiators Owen and Stoltenberg. Their recent actions and statements demonstrate that they want to continue the fighting, believing that they can now successfully challenge the Serbs.

Should the Bosnian Serbs conclude that there is danger of their losing key gains, there is little doubt that they would counterattack in force. Moreover, they would no doubt challenge the legality of the "no fly zone" edict of the UN and NATO's right to enforce it.

Under such circumstances there would be no way of keeping Yugoslavia (Serbia and Montenegro) out of the conflict, which would no doubt challenge UN and NATO authority, citing international law, particularly the Helsinki Accords, signed by thirty-odd European nations as well as by the United States and Canada. That agreement proclaimed that the borders of internationally recognized states could not be changed by force.

Yugoslavia was such a state and its borders were changed by force by the secessionist republics, first of all Slovenia. And the recognition of those republics by Western countries constituted aiding and abetting them in those acts.

The Western powers have maintained that those countries had achieved independence and therefore deserved to be recognized. Consequently, according to such reasoning, the fighting was the result of "aggression" by Serbia.

Who is right? Is it a civil war or a war of aggression? It depends on how one interprets international law. The Bosnian Serbs (who inhabited two-thirds of Bosnia before the fighting began), as well as those in Yugoslavia, rely on international usages at the time of the secessions in 1991 and 1992, notably the requirements for recognition that were spelled out by the Montevideo Convention in 1932. Perhaps it could be said that Slovenia met those minimally, but not Croatia, and certainly not Bosnia-Herzegovina. The latter had never been an independent state and it proclaimed independence *after* the Yugoslav civil war had started. Moreover, not before and not after recognition did the Muslims control as much as 30 percent of the territory of Bosnia-Herzegovina.

It would seem to this student of international law that the Serbs have the better of the argument. In addition, we need to note that earlier international acts recognized Serbia's legitimate interests in Bosnia as well as in Croatian areas.

These considerations, however, are not as important as the fact that the Bosnian Muslims have been led, mostly by the United States, to believe that they could get back some of the lands lost in the civil war. If the present Muslim attitude is indicative of their intentions, then the danger of provoking the Serbs in Yugoslavia is very real. This, together with the fact that Serbian patience has been severely strained by what they consider unfair and humiliating sanctions that were imposed solely on them, should cause all of us to pause.

We know that the British and the French have not been happy with the United States' stoking of Muslim fires, to say nothing of the attitude of the Russians. The latter certainly would not sit idly by if there was the possibility of a Serbian defeat.

There are those who say that the Serbs would never challenge the power of NATO, but persons holding such opinions should reflect on the fact that the Serbs in 1941 said "No" to Hitler at the height of his power. There is one enduring characteristic of the Serbs, which has not always served them well, and that is that when they are convinced that they are right, they don't ask about the odds.

It is often said that the assassination in 1914 of the Austrian archduke in Sarajevo by a Serb (at that time an Austrian citizen) brought on the First World War. The first United Nations commander in Sarajevo, General Lewis MacKenzie, warned as early as 1992 that the Bosnian Muslims counted on Western military intervention to assist them. Their "spear carriers" in the U.S., Senators Biden and Dole, used the Congressional recess (no doubt at taxpayers' expense) to go to Sarajevo to encourage them. Are they and the Clinton Administration aware that by encouraging the Bosnian Muslims, the result could be a world conflict that nobody, except perhaps the Muslims, wants?

A WAY OUT OF
BOSNIAN HELL HOLE?
(June, 1994)

President Clinton and his NATO partners, as well as the Russians, all say that the only way out of the Bosnian morass is a negotiated settlement. Clinton has several times asserted that the purpose of threatening the Bosnian Serbs and actually hitting them with air strikes was to bring them back to the negotiating table. But the Bosnian Serbs have been at that table often, and they agreed to the most recent international proposal - the Owen-Stoltenberg Plan - so what do we really want from them?

Perhaps to surrender? But that can't be (or can it?) because the President has also said that we would agree to send Americans to keep the peace only if all three parties to the conflict voluntarily agreed to a settlement. This means that the Bosnian Serbs would not be pressured any more than the Muslims or Croats. What is the way out?

In seeking to bring peace to a civil war, a prerequisite is to recognize realities. The first reality is that all the talk about not taking sides in the Yugoslav civil war is insincere. For two years now, the West has taken the side of the Serbs' enemies. And Serbia is the only unit of former Yugoslavia against whom UN sanctions were imposed.

The second reality is that for all intents and purposes, the Bosnian Serbs have actually achieved their goals in the civil war. The West Europeans, somewhat tardily, realized this when they backed the European-Community brokered plan - the so-called Owen-Stoltenberg proposals. These were accepted by the Serbs and Croats, but the Muslims held back, hoping that international military intervention would save them. The Clinton Administration, by not supporting the Europeans, in effect killed the proposed solution, and encouraged the Bosnian government to reject subsequent proposals to end the bloodshed.

The third reality is that the Bosnian Serbs, who before the war began, numbered a third of the population of Bosnia-Herzegovina but inhabited two-thirds of its territory, now control about 70 percent. They have indicated that they are willing to give up about 20 percent, which means that they would have less territory than they had before the conflict.

Unfortunately, President Clinton and Western European leaders have been ignoring the warnings of those most involved in Bosnia. Former U.S. Secretary of State Cyrus Vance, a previous United Nations mediator for former Yugoslavia, more than once reiterated the time-worn principle that anyone seeking to be a peacemaker must not only *be* neutral, but must also be *seen* as neutral by all parties in the conflict. And former United Nations commander in Sarajevo, the French General Phillipe Morillon, warned that recent history teaches us that "military intervention in a civil war on behalf of one of the parties invariably leads to catastrophe."

Many European observers believe that the United States, instead of seeking to determine the kind of settlement that the Muslims would accept, should have been talking with the Serbs to ascertain what might be the best deal that one might obtain for the Muslims.

Paradoxically, the U.S. threatened the Serbs, and ultimately persuaded NATO to use air strikes against them, while at the same time telling them that America was not taking sides. If you are shooting at some one, can you really expect him to believe such statements?

If there is a way out, it is to go to the Serbs, and to say to them that, for our sake and theirs, we must find an honorable settlement, that we are not anti-Serb as the long history of cordial American-Serb relations has proved. It is a fact that the only great power that the Serbs really trusted over the decades was the United States.

Hopefully, some of that good will remains in the reservoir on both sides, and if so, we can begin acting as an honest broker.

We might begin with the offer of gradually lifting the sanctions against Yugoslavia (i.e., Serbia and Montenegro), and at the same time offering some of the same promises of reconstruction aid, etc., that we offered to the Croats as a way of getting their agreement to the formation of the Muslim-Croat federation in the parts of Bosnia that they controlled.

While we might criticize the Bosnian Serbs for resorting to military actions, we need to recognize that the civil war might have been avoided if in the early months of the Yugoslav crisis, the West had demonstrated an awareness of Serbian grievances, and had acted on them.

That, of course, is water under the bridge. Now the question is: will the West turn to impartiality or will it proceed blindly as in the past, getting more involved in a bottomless quagmire? More threats and military action against the Serbs will not lead to peace.

There are indications that the Bosnian Serbs, in contra-distinction to the Bosnian government, are eager to see an end to the fighting, and that they are ready for a compromise settlement, perhaps such as that proposed by Owen-Stoltenberg, but the West cannot expect them to sit around indefinitely while the Bosnian government, being supplied surreptitiously with an increasing supply of weapons, attempts to wrest more territory from the Serbs.

The leaders in the international community concerned with Bosnia must keep two things in mind: (1) the Serbs inhabited roughly two-thirds of Bosnia before the conflict began, and (2) they have won the civil war.

SACRIFICE OF AN ALLY
(October, 1994)

History will record that the last decade of the twentieth century witnessed one of the most perfidious examples of the sacrifice of an ally. That ally of the West in two world wars was Serbia. But history will also show that in the anti-Serb hysteria, widely fanned by the media in Europe and in the United States, no responsible person in the West stepped forward to ask who else might be liable for the carnage taking place in what once was Yugoslavia.

Moreover, no responsible person bothered to ask to what extent the West contributed to the tragedy. Causes were not important; condemning Serbia and the Serbs was the order of the day.

Understandably, no rational person could condone wanton destruction and the killing of innocent civilians. But once Serbia and the Serbs were targeted as the bad guys in that civil war, no one referred to equally dastardly acts by the other participants if these could be blamed on the Serbs. Yet history has demonstrated that civil wars are the most tragic of all wars, with tales of unimaginable atrocities.

In the Yugoslav case, it was easy to focus on the president of Serbia, Slobodan Milosevic, and to blame him for everything.

Who is Milosevic? He is the product of the Communist system imposed upon all Yugoslavs by Croat dictator Tito at the end of World War II, with considerable help from the West.

This was particularly painful for the Serbs, whose guerrilla leader was Colonel Draza Mihailovic, and who sought to prevent the victory of the Communists. The West, which initially glorified and supported him, abandoned him in 1943 and assisted Communist Tito.

But why would the West want to impose Communism on the Yugoslavs? Mainly because British leader Winston Churchill fell victim to Communist disinformation, cleverly purveyed by agents within British intelligence, to the effect that the Tito-led Partisans were doing the bulk of the fighting in Yugoslavia against the Germans, even accusing Mihailovic of collaborating with the enemy.

For the Serbs this was a double whammy. Mihailovic was defeated and subsequently executed by Tito. The latter not only imposed the hated Communist system, but also punished Serbia by carving up Yugoslavia into six republics and two autonomous provinces, so that one-third of the Serbs were left outside the boundaries of the Republic of Serbia, mainly in Croatia and Bosnia-Herzegovina, but also in Macedonia.

When Yugoslavia began to fall apart in 1991, another double whammy hit the Serbs. While it was acceptable for the Slovenes and Croats to violate the Helsinki Accords proviso against changing international boundaries by force, the Serbs were told that they could not alter the Tito-imposed internal borders (the West sought to make them international by unilateral declarations). Moreover, the Serbs were mercilessly pilloried because they could not get rid of Milosevic, the product of the system which the West was considerably responsible for imposing on the Yugoslavs.

The Croat and Slovene acts of secession were viewed as legitimate exercises in self-determination. But, ironically, self-determination for the million and one half Serbs in Bosnia-Herzegovina and the three quarters of a million in Croatia was not legitimate! There was not even a hint from the West that in any final resolution of the Yugoslav question, Serbian grievances should also be addressed. This lack of evenhandedness contributed in no small degree to the civil war.

As the Serbs look back, the past three-quarters of a century have been one long nightmare, but unfortunately all too real.

Serbia entered the twentieth century as a vigorous young democracy, having won the struggle for a functioning parliamentary political system, something that practically all other continental states could only dream about. In addition, progress was being made on many fronts, including balanced budgets and a currency convertible to gold.

In the Balkan wars of 1912-13, Serbia and the other Serb state, Montenegro, in alliance with other Balkan states, drove the Ottoman Turks from Europe, opening new vistas for South Slavs (Serbs, Croats, and Slovenes) still under foreign rule.

In 1914, the Austro-Hungarian empire, supported by Germany, launched an attack upon Serbia. The Serbs resisted with considerable success for over a year, but with the arrival of heavily armed German troops were forced to retreat. In the winter of 1915-16, remnants of the Serbian army and the government were compelled to flee over the Albanian mountains, ending up on the Greek island of Corfu, leaving Serbia and Montenegro occupied by the enemy.

This setback was followed by the return of the surviving Serb forces to their homeland in 1917-18, the victory of Serbia's allies, and the achievement of Serbia's major war aim - the liberation and unification of all Serbs, Croats, and Slovenes - and the consequent establishment on December 1, 1918, of the Kingdom of the Serbs, Croats, and Slovenes.

Serbia's and Montenegro's armed forces' losses in the war were enormous - two and one half times as high as the French, three times as high as those of Great Britain and Italy. An even greater number of deaths occurred among the civilian population, and the material losses were staggering.

Yet for the Serbs, who had played the greatest role in the creation of the new state, the future seemed to offer untold promises. In fact, it was the beginning of a long and painful tragedy.

During the First Yugoslavia (1918-1941), the Serbs exerted great efforts to build a new nation made up of peoples many of whom had never lived in one state. While there were many setbacks and the odds were against them, they nevertheless persevered.

There were failures and successes, and while it is not easy to draw a balance sheet, history will note that before Hitler destroyed the First Yugoslavia, a promising step had been taken in August 1939, combining two administrative areas to give the Croats a considerable amount of autonomy. This was the first step in the reorganization of the country, but further steps were foreclosed by the outbreak of the Second World War in September.

The government of Yugoslavia attempted to stay out of the war, but in March 1941, Serbian army officers, believing that too much had been conceded to Hitler, overthrew the regime. This brought Nazi vengeance in April and Yugoslavia was destroyed. Germany and Italy annexed parts, while other areas were "occupied." An enlarged Croatia was made an Axis satellite. The minions of that Croat fascist state massacred, by most brutal means, some 700,000 Serb inhabitants of that state, along with some 40,000 Jews and 20,000 Gypsies.

It is no wonder that in 1991 the 600,000 to 800,000 Serbs living in Croatia did not want to be a part of the new Croat state, especially when it adopted anti-Serb policies and took on some of the symbols of the hated wartime fascist state.

As if the massacres weren't enough, the clash of two underground movements - the Serbian-led guerrillas of Mihailovic and the Tito-led Communist Partisans - resulted in the loss of untold Serbian (as well as other) lives and properties. Tito's victory, referred to above, imposed a Communist dictatorship on Yugoslavia and punished the Serbs by carving up the country in such a way that one-third of them were left outside the Republic of Serbia.

When in 1991 the Second Yugoslavia began to fall apart, the Serbs, hitherto the strongest supporters of the common state, were willing to see the other republics go their separate ways, but believed that in that case as many Serbs as possible should be together. They were most concerned, as indicated above, with the Serbs in Croatia and those in Bosnia-Herzegovina. When the Serbs of those two republics sought self-determination for themselves, the Serbs of Serbia and Montenegro were willing to offer some assistance.

So a new civil war for the Serbs, for which the West blamed them alone!

That brought endless amounts of disinformation. For example, the media constantly referred to Serbs "capturing," "seizing,," "over-running" two-thirds or seventy percent of Bosnia, whereas they have lived there for centuries and *prior* to any fighting they occupied about sixty percent of it. Another example: the media often reported that some republics were seceding because they did not want to live in "Serb-dominated Yugoslavia." This is a canard, because at no time during Communist-ruled Yugoslavia were the Serbs dominant. In terms of material welfare, the Serbs were considerably behind others. In 1991, the average per capita income in Slovenia was $12,618, in Croatia $7,179, and in Serbia, the supposed exploiter, only $4,870.

Moreover, it was often said that the Yugoslav Army was Serb-dominated. The Serbs may have had a disproportionate number of the officers, but in the high command they were underrepresented. Moreover, when fighting broke out in 1991, the key civil and military positions in the Yugoslav government were in the hands of Croats and Slovenes. In addition, it should be noted that Tito sought to have a united national army without ethnic concerns. He demonstrated his pride in that army when he often said publicly that in any time of trouble, the army could be counted on to save Yugoslavia. There is reason to believe that in the course of the civil war, at least in its early stages, army officers may have been motivated by their interpretation of Tito's testament.

So, while history will condemn the brutalities of all the participants in the Yugoslav civil war - Serb, Croat, Muslim, and others - it will also record that Serbia, faithful ally in two world wars, and before Communism was imposed upon it dedicated to liberal-democratic values, was sacrificed on the altar of expediency by the West while it searched for an answer to the consequences of its failure in seeking to manage the Yugoslav crisis.

PRESIDENT CARTER AND BOSNIA
(January, 1995)

It is too early to judge what Jimmy Carter did or did not do in Bosnia. He did, however, utter one truth that could not be delayed forever - the media have been giving us a picture that is biased against the Bosnian Serbs. But for the future that is less important than the resolution of that tragic civil conflict.

Outsiders can only hope that the agreed upon cease-fire will lead to a settlement. The actions of all sides must be monitored. We are used to being told about Serbian violations of cease-fires, but each one of the United Nations commanders in Sarajevo has said that in most cases it was the Muslims who violated them first.

The stakes are enormous. The warning of the Bosnian Serb president, Karadzic, that either there will be a peaceful settlement or "we will settle it militarily" should not be taken lightly if we want to avoid a massive carnage. As a footnote, I should add that some months ago a Bosnian Serb official told me that they had not used the really sophisticated weapons in their arsenal, adding that in the future "we will not fight with one hand tied behind our backs."

We should also note that the supposed disagreements between the Clinton Administration and Britain and France are more apparent than real. Clinton is anxious to get Bosnia off his foreign policy agenda. He has cooled toward the Muslims. One indication was his recent assertion that the military option was being rejected in favor of diplomacy. A person with connections inside the administration, who recently traveled to Bosnia, told me that one reason behind the administration's coolness was that the "Muslims have lied to the administration." And while the President has offered to evacuate the peacekeepers, mainly French and British, if that became necessary, he does not want to be blamed for the mass starvation that would likely follow. Hence he has a huge stake in a peaceful settlement. The Muslims must know this.

Concretely, the issue is not what percentage of the Bosnian territory should go to the Serbs. They inhabited over 60 percent of it before the fighting began. They now control over 70 percent. But they have said that they would be willing to give up close to 20 percent of it. The Contact Group proposal would give them 49 percent, but Karadzic has said that as winners in the civil war there is no way that they could accept less than half of it.

Karadzic has also said that the real issue is particular territories. For example, under the Contact Group proposal one relatively narrow corridor linking Serbian areas is narrowed to practical nonexistence, and another is eliminated. Currently, the Bosnian Serbs hold more than adequate corridors.

Another point of disagreement concerns the Contact Group's assignment to the Muslims and Croats of most of the industrial areas, mines, hydroelectric plants, as well as communications facilities.

In some ways, the most difficult problem involves the preponderantly Muslim cities of Srebrenica, Zepa, and Gorazde, which are islands in a Serbian sea. Since the Carter visit, Karadzic has been specific as to what areas could be exchanged. Significantly, he has given up his claim to part of Sarajevo, and is willing to trade its Serbian districts for other areas. Some of the exchanges would involve exchanges of populations. But the Serbs point out that as painful as such exchanges would be, the number of people to be moved would be less than was the case of the Turkish and Greek exchanges in the 1920s.

Finally, the Bosnian Serbs assert, and they are supported in this by France and Britain, that constitutionally they must be given the same rights conferred on the Bosnian Croats (the right to a confederal arrangement with Croatia) - that is, a right to a similar association with Serbia.

It now remains to be seen if the parties will be serious in the pursuit of a solution. Ironically, the Muslims may get less than they could have had under the Owen-Stoltenberg proposal which they rejected a little more than a year ago, and which the Bosnian Serbs and Croats had accepted. The outcome will also be influenced by the Bosnian Croats, now in an uneasy alliance with the Muslims, but who have always wanted to be part of Croatia.